D0494591

THE TOP THIRTY

Here's a complete list of the thirty rock legends profiled in *Where Have They Gone? Rock 'N' Roll Stars!*

Brenda Lee
Archie Bell
Bobby Rydell
Del Shannon
Gene Chandler
Johnny Tillotson
Tommy James
Gary "U.S." Bonds
Johnny Maestro
Tommy Sands
Dion
Mark ("Teen Angel") Dinning
Bill Medley
Paul Petersen
Tony (Platters) Williams
Bobby Vee

Dave Clark
Sheb Wooley
Steve Alaimo
Dolores (Crystals) Kenniebrew
Freddy Cannon
Bill (Drifters) Pinckney
Gary Lewis
Tom (Happenings) Guiliano
Sam "The Sham" Samudio
Lou Christie
Peter (Herman) Noone
Bobby Lewis
Jackie Wilson
Billy Joe Royal

On the cover: (clockwise from upper right) Brenda Lee, Tommy Sands, Jackie Wilson, Peter Noone, Bobby Rydell

WHERE HAVE THEY GONE?

ROCK 'N' ROLL STARS

by Bruce McColm & Doug Payne

tempo
books
GROSSET & DUNLAP
A Filmways Company
Publishers • New York

To Lucille and Millie

Cover photos by United Press International

Where Have They Gone? Rock 'N' Roll Stars
Copyright © 1979 by Bruce McColm and Doug Payne
All Rights Reserved
ISBN: 0-448-17025-6
A Tempo Books Original
Tempo Books is registered in the U.S. Patent Office
Published simultaneously in Canada
Printed in the United States of America

Acknowledgments

The authors would like to acknowledge John Apostal, Dr. Winston Boogie, Dan Bourgoise, Mike Branch, Les Cauchi, Sal Dali, Skipper Lee Frazier, Harold Fuller, Bill Jeffros, Ken Kragin, Brandon Ledger, Mamie, Our Neighbors, Janet Oseroff, Connie Pappas, Renée, Ray Reneri, Zoot Horn Rollo, Marvin Shnayer, Feldspar Shiss, our editor Mark Becker, and especially Paul Wolfe for his rock 'n' roll mind and invaluable assistance on the Jackie Wilson story, about which he will answer all inquiries addressed to Friends of Jackie Wilson, P.O. Box 262, Carteret, New Jersey 07708.

Contents

Michael Ray.

8/1/80

Introduction

"Even now a rocket ship goes to Mars," LBJ reminded us in 1968. Things had certainly changed since Ike told us that today is even more like yesterday. Do you remember beehive hairdos, clam-diggers, ID bracelets, bobbie socks, hula hoops, fallout shelters, the islands Quemoy and Matsu, bunny hops, 3-D movies, head cheese, mooning, cruising, drag racing, Chinese fire drills, stuffing phone booths, Curtis LeMay, Edsels and cars that looked like planes, Sid Caesar and Imogene Coca, Uncle Miltie, Sputnik, monkeys in space, Jayne Mansfield, hot water bottles, Estes Kefauver, Khrushchev out at Idlewild, Floyd Patterson knocking out Pete Rademacher, and the song, "Jesus Is God's Atomic Bomb"? Social critics have since called the time heralded by the birth of rock and roll as an "extraordinarily senseless and unnatural time," "an amusing waste of life," and "one of the worst decades in the history of man." America was daydreaming about leisure, universal luxury, and happy hunting grounds when the kids put out the smoke signals for everyone to wise up and get outfront. Rock and roll woke the whole joint up and took the culture for an extended detour that later became a refuge when the urban sprawl took to riot and the rice paddies became an American graveyard.

In April 1955, *Life* zeroed in on the hubbub caused by the "frenzied teenage music craze.... Some American parents, without quite knowing what it is their kids are up to, are worried that it's something they shouldn't be." While adults were busy roasting chestnuts of their own at the McCarthy hearings, the kids were listening to the highest of fi on record players the size of Kleenex boxes in preparation for the big blowout at the local record hop, the social happening where you could hear the sound properly shot through a PA. The older folks tapped out their own musical code, a souped-up version of Morse, straight-jacketing any emotion remotely moving or raw. The kids needed their Green Hornet decoder rings to figure out that Rosemary Clooney wasn't talking about spreading diabetes when she sang, "I'm gonna give you candy." They didn't need anything to understand Elvis, Chuck Berry, Bill Haley, Little Richard, and Jerry Lee Lewis.

The war vets and their brides thought they'd program the kids into a world without genitals, hunger, blacks, and wars. School and lots and lots of wholesome spare time was the order of the day. Boys wore crewcuts and hoped to make varsity. The girls could grow old quickly by wrapping their bodies in casings of spandex and assuming mother's mature airs as the snare to nab Mr. Right who would work for the corporation and bring home TVs, cars, barcaloungers, and power-mowers to keep the crowd happy. The poolroom, the street corner, and the boardwalk were exits for the degradation ramp. The model teen was concerned about his or her rep, avoided JDs, plotted the future with grave certainty, never plunged into sexual swamps, and hung out at the malt shop with Richie and the gang. But according to one survey done in the fifties, what kids wanted most of all was to vanish. And they did, right into the music.

The older folks with a lot of practice at head-hunting could smell subversives a mile away. Rock and roll was a plot for the mass submission of kids to the Mafia, drugs, the African jungle beat, and left-wingers. The disc jockey or platter spinner was most definitely a crazed hophead who seduced the innocent into meetings with black people and Reds. As Elvis said, "Ah just act the way Ah feel." And this was alarming. He was a menace. Music had crept out of various ethnic closets and captured the mass media with the closest that America has ever come to a national sound. Rock and roll was here to stay and people better get used to it. Many didn't. Record hops were outlawed in

New Haven, Connecticut. Cops stormed Presley concerts with injunctions against his bringing his filthy act into town. Disc jockeys were fired for raving up the new sound. Religious groups were formed to deprogram the wayward youth.

While Sherman Adams collected vicuna coats, Alger Hiss allegedly dropped code books off at the nearest pumpkin, Richard Nixon pedalled some tall tale about a dog named Checkers, and later Bobby Baker was caught with his hand in the till, public enemy number one was Dick Clark. Or so Oren Harris, the chairman of the House's payola committee, thought. The twist, stroll, hully-gully, watusi, duck, cool jerk, walk, frug, mashed potato, hitchhike, limbo, Freddie, and the bristol stomp were bizarre rituals to be placed under close surveillance. At least, Dick cleaned up the rock act. Looking the part of a young ad executive, he let a gaggle of neatly dressed white kids harmlessly romp around the American Bandstand set. Soon whole families tuned in. "It has a good beat and you can dance to it" became the familiar war cry.

The moguls could hear those cash registers ringing. For the first time in business history, the youngsters had their own wallets and purses. They had money to burn and the entertainment industry immediately danced to that tune. If the kids had oodles of time to muse over the ramifications of dating and flipping the Ramblers' front seat down on Saturday night, they also had time to spend. Fast foods, clothes, cars, fads. Let's stuff it all down their throats. Megabucks became the name of that tune. Accentuate the "now" and jettison everything else.

They needed performers or more accurately voices. With lip-synching, you didn't need a slick entertainer. All you needed was a warm body. They collected them from the stoops, settlement houses, and street corners of the Italian ghettos in the Northeast; from the dust bowls, scrublands, truck farms, and oil fields of the South; and the black circuit of the Apollo, Regal, and Howard theaters. When TV conquered all, they took media babies, gave them some teen-oriented sheet music, and let them warble. Even if it was a one-shot deal for the performer, the record companies would clean up. Bang the disc loud and long and you made gold.

But, most of the performers frozen in the image of the teen idol were seasoned entertainers by the time they were called on to pedal the goods. The product counted; the performer didn't. Thousands of regional record labels went boom or bust until giants emerged who could send out thousands of new singles a week from their assembly line of writers, arrangers, and background singers. The managers, agents, and producers knew how to play rough and ready. The artist did not. The performers thought it was their image and sound that sold the record; the companies thought otherwise. The rock and rollers were carted out to the record hops. Thousands of kids got their ya-yas out at the high school gym by throwing a happening of throbbing proportions. The performer did three or four of these a night, lip-synching from town to town to town for little or no money while the companies sold their platters and tipped the beaming disc jockeys.

Soon the raw, innocent, yet suggestive sounds of early rock 'n' roll lost touch with the chaos cutting loose across the land. It was time for a change and the British provided it, sending us half their Gross National Product in the form of the Beatles, Animals, Hollies, Who, Stones, Hermits, and Kinks. American music proceeded to splinter into heavy metal, protest, acid rock, folk, bubble gum, jazz noodlings, plastic soul, and various canned funk. Moonshot technology landed in the studio and resulted in thirty-two track productions, wah-wah pedals, fuzz boxes, guitars with more electronic pickups than a singles bar stud, and finally the synthesizer. Satellite hookups, laser light shows, hydraulic stages, wall-to-wall and ceiling-to-floor amplifier stacks, and pyrotechnic goings-on became the order of the day.

But the stars of less complicated days haven't rolled over and played dead. Some migrated abroad where they carry on in the limelight. Others have applied decades of stage and studio experience to the fields of production, promotion, and management. And still others are cutting new vinyl with unabated ambition and visions of rebirth. The truth of the matter is that these are the veterans of a revolution in music that has had profound cultural consequences. Even though they're not as visible as they once were, they've seen it all and have plenty to tell.

Brenda Lee

Connie Francis sang about breaking boys' hearts, the telling lipstick on the collar, dreamboats, and the hidden secrets of her pillow. She was the tease, an appendage to the teen scene, a young pro with designs on cornering all markets, young and old. Under her father's protective gaze, Connie slipped into the mainstream, her songs soon conjuring up the romance of the Mediterranean soul. Shelley Fabares revealed that even if her television family just sat around munching cornflakes in the blinding white of a spanking new kitchen, she could secretly closet herself away in a bedroom filled with pom-poms and stuffed animals, and pine about Johnny Angel and wonder when Ronnie would have a chance to call about the things they did last summer. Lesley Gore, the high school girl from Tenafly, New Jersey, pouted about crying at her party, snidely suggested the other girl's a fool, and maybe it was Judy's turn to cry for a change. What more could a girl hope for? If the white female singers were the images of the daylight teen world, the black girl groups were liquid night, the smooth silk of cool cats and kitties alone and probing the voodoo that happens when two bodies slide together and the world disappears into sighs.

Brenda Lee conveyed none of these images of teen womanhood. She was a pint-sized truthteller, putting you on notice that human emotion wasn't something to play around with, that everybody came from someplace and don't you forget it. Life takes work. She took the feelings in the country songs of broken homes, divorces, hard-driving men burning themselves out, and sexual games played out of boredom, abstracted them and poured every ounce of the distillate soul into her phrasing and explosive stage presence. She overwhelmed her audience with the ability to combine an inner gutsiness with a fragility that kept you mesmerized. When Brenda revved her engines into high torque and power overdrive, the audience was transported into the song itself, felt every syllable resonate against the spine. The lady projected, projected, and projected until she disappeared and the fans were caught up in a world where the eternal female spoke her mind about all those sweet nothings, wanting to be wanted, having your heart in your hand, and breaking the bad news gently. Then, Brenda reemerged, slowing to a still, holding the mike loosely in her hand, and bowing slightly to acknowledge the fans' applause. You were left wondering where the hell did she come from.

Brenda Lee was born Brenda Mae Tarpley on December 11, 1944. "We were very, very, very poor. I was born in the charity ward of Emory University Hospital in Atlanta, Georgia. My dad was a carpenter. He never knew how to drive and made very little money. He was killed on the job in 1952. I have a brother and an older sister. My mom remarried about four years later. She only stayed married a couple of years. That's where my little sister comes from. We came from a very poor background. That was the story of my life until I got a record. It was mostly through the goodness of people's hearts. I used to have a girl friend who lived up the street from me. We were so poor that I used to wait until lunchtime and I would go up on the pretense of a visit so I could eat. Of course, they knew. They knew. Later on in years, I figured out that they knew. But it was no embarrassment. I had a lot of people like that who helped me through the years.

"Everybody asks, 'Who did you listen to?' Well, I didn't listen to anyone because I didn't have a radio, television, or a record player. The first record I received was a Mahalia Jackson record and I had to go over to a friend's house and play it. The reason I received that was because the only type of music I sang for four years before that was gospel."

Brenda started singing at the age of four. "My aunt enget a little in yearly installments, not in one lump sum."

Brenda's loot was locked away under Tennessee's version of the Jackie Coogan law, which stipulated that 100 percent of a minor's earnings had to be turned over to the courts. "I didn't get any of mine until I was twenty-six. When I bought my mom a home in '62, I had to go to the judge and he had to look at the property and house to make sure it was a good investment. My mom got an allowance, a certain amount of money each week. I had the number one record in the nation and I was living in a two-room trailer with an outdoor toilet. So I've been there. I kinda liked it. It was cosy.

"I was big in Europe before I was ever big over here." In 1959, the music critic for *Le Figaro*, the prominent French newspaper, caught her act at a three-week run at the Olympia Theatre in Paris. Brenda wasn't just another cute little girl; the French considered her a major artist. "Not since Judy Garland has this city seen an opening night like that of the dynamic young American artist, Miss Brenda Lee," the newsclip read. "That's great; I don't know how they meant that. I guess the strong voice and the emotion. I met Judy Garland. She was a marvelous person. Of course, she left us a great legacy. I watched her because she had such great movements and great emotions in her hands, arms, and her whole body." For her thirty-fourth birthday, Brenda bid at the auction of Garland memorabilia and bought a bronze box inscribed "Judy Garland, London Palladium, 1951." It had been presented to Judy by King George VI and the Queen Mother to commemorate Garland's first London appearance.

tered me in a talent show. The prize was an audition for a local television show in Atlanta called the 'TV Ranch' on WAGA. I won and then became a regular every weekend. I had my own kiddie show and then we moved to Augusta, Georgia. I was about eight or nine. I was discovered there by Red Foley who came down to do a show. I used to travel every weekend on a bus from Augusta to Springfield, Missouri, to do the television show. We used to leave after school every Friday, stay on the bus all night

A young Brenda with Elvis in 1957. *Elmer Williams photo*

and half the day Saturday. We'd do the show and get back on the bus and stay on it until I got back Monday. Then I'd go to school. We did that for six to eight months. I finally moved to Springfield for six months. Then to Nashville in 1956 and I've been here ever since."

It's 1956. Ike swamps Adlai once again and tells us "The future lies ahead." It's also the turning point in Brenda's career. She drops the Tarp in Tarpley and becomes Brenda Lee. Her "Jambalaya" becomes a national hit and is followed by "One Step at a Time" and "Dynamite." Her nickname in the trade becomes "Little Miss Dynamite." At the age of twelve, she signs the first of two long-term contracts with Decca, the second signed in 1962 calls for twenty years of recording. About a year ago, Brenda managed to obtain her release from its obligations. "That was the thing to do then. It was a way to protect your money and save it without paying so much to the government. You'd

On her style: "I've never listened to anybody to get any

kind of style. I already had my own style. Or thought I did. I listened to a lot of Edith Piaf, Bessie Smith, and Billie Holiday. I learned a lot about phrasing from Frank Sinatra. I watched Tommy Dorsey for circular breathing. Those are the things I did instead of emulating or copying. I wanted to learn techniques and how to do a phrase without breaking the thread. At that young age, it wasn't enough to sing good. There were so many people. I was competing with grown-ups. Even though I was honest in what I was singing, you had to make people believe. I still think you have to do that. They have to believe it. If you don't believe, they're certainly not going to.

"I think it's not as tough now for a woman. It's still tough. You have to remember that ten years ago when I was singing about eighty percent of the record buyers were female. It was hard for a girl to do any good. Part of my success was because I wasn't a threat. I wasn't built up. I wasn't a beauty queen. I wasn't going to steal their boyfriends. If their boyfriends liked me, it was because I was like their little sister or the girl next door that they'd come over to and say, 'Now, how do I tell Jane I love her?' It was that kind of thing. Mothers liked me and daddies liked me; Grannies liked me and girls liked me. I had hundreds of fan clubs and only two or three were run by boys. They were all run by girls."

1960 was pure gold for Brenda with "I'm Sorry," "That's All You Gotta Do," "I Want to Be Wanted," and "Rockin' Around the Christmas Tree" rolling off Decca's assembly line. That spring, Brenda fired up the already-simmering Brazilian mobs when she landed in Rio. The population had never seen anything quite like her. They lost their cosmopolitan cool and pulled a scene which could have been scored with mariachi music. Brenda and her entourage had to hide behind the national police who stood guard, waiting to thump the adoring, yet unruly crowds. "They're crazy in Brazil. I don't mean that detrimentally. They're so emotional. When they like you, they like you. They just got a little carried away. So they had to have some protection for me." The President of Brazil bit his tongue and scored some brownie points by declaring her, "The Best Goodwill Ambassador that America Has." It happened wherever she went. She had the knack of unlocking people's strongest emotions and sending the citizenry into crazed behavior. In Santos, Chile, she was trapped in a hotel for several hours until the Governor sent mounted troops to clear the way.

"I used to play Europe every year until 1966. Then I started going to the Far East every year. I'm the number one female vocalist in Japan. I also won the NME, or New Musical Express award, five times in a row, longer than any girl ever won it. My national fan club is run from there. I haven't been over there in four years. You have to go and sing. But you can't do both Europe and Japan and do here, especially when you're married and have children."

Throughout the sixties, Brenda's records roosted in the eaves of the Top Ten. "Emotions" was followed by "I'm Learning About Love," followed by "You Can Depend on Me," followed by "Dum Dum," followed by "Fool #1," followed by "Break It to Me Gently," "Everybody Loves Me But You," "All Alone Am I," and "Losing You." And that's only two years of chart busters. From 1957 to 1967, Brenda Lee averaged eight Top Ten singles a year. The hits tapered off in 1970, but the record sales never did. To date Brenda has sold eighty-five million records, which means a lot of greenbacks to paper the wall with.

She limped through one Dick Clark run around the country. "I only did one Dick Clark tour and I flew. Not because I'm too good for a bus but I was the only girl on the tour. So they didn't want to throw me in with all the boys. There was Jimmy Clanton, Freddie Cannon, Bill Black, Chubby Checker, Fabian. Just a whole bunch of them. It was forty days and was the only tour I did. Every night a different city. It cured me of tours. I said, 'No more.'"

In 1963, she married Ronnie Shacklett. "What does he do? You have about three days? He owns one of the largest mills and lumber companies in the state. He's into the supermarket, liquor store, and real estate business. He makes the steady money and I make the funny money. He turns my funny money into stuff that will remain steady." They have two girls, Jolie, who is ten, and Julie, who is fifteen. "She was born on April Fool's Day. It was foolish. She was due at the end of May. So it fooled us all."

Brenda still performs as a club and television entertainer. "We've been doing concerts, private parties, and conventions. I'm trying to get into another audience, the record-buying audience. In clubs people are not recognized. It's good money and it's nice because you're in one place longer than two or three days. Since we play the same places, those people remember what you do and what you wear. They remember everything. So you have to keep on your toes. They put you where you are and you've got to give them everything you've got.

"I did Dick Clark's 'Back to Basics' with Seals and Croft and Glen Campbell. I like those TV things when they're not so congested and have different ways to show off your talent, instead of being on for three minutes and getting shoved off. Glen and I sang together; I did a medley and sang with Seals and Croft. It was really neat.

"I don't work but five and a half to six months spread out. I have a lady who's here every day. She's like one of the family. She's been with me for ten years. I have a Japanese girl who watches the children and their daddy's here. We've worked it out pretty good.

"We've been here now for seven years. It's a seventy-five-year-old home which was a complete shell. My husband took six months to remodel the whole thing. It's yellow clapboard with a wood shingle roof and bay windows. It looks like a little Cape Cod house. I'd lived on Franklin Road all my life until we moved to this house. We just bought five acres next door to Tammy Wynette who lives on Franklin. Tammy, Loretta Lynn, and Barbara Mandrell are my closest show biz friends. I've lived in three houses on Franklin Road. My old two-story house is four doors down from the one I'm going to build. We got the plans drawn up but we're kinda attached to this little old frame house. It's on the wrong side of town and we kinda like it.

"My husband says if I hang one more thing, the walls are going to cave in. I'm a pack rat. I collect everything in the world. I collect art. I collect antique books. I have over 4,000 volumes. History and poetry mostly. I have Shakespeare, Tennyson, Schiller, Oscar Wilde, Ogden Nash, F. Scott Fitzgerald, Hemingway. Oh, there are so many; I've got everybody. I hunt them up at flea markets and yard sales. I have a dealer in Florida and Missouri. I found all the works of Mark Twain in one book which is hard to find."

When Brenda started touring, she began searching out the local spots for turtles of all materials and sizes. It was an activity to fill in the void during the day before show-time. "I originally started collecting frogs when I was about eleven. But they were hard to find. So I just started collecting turtles. Not all my turtles are ceramic. Some of them are solid gold. Some of them are amethyst. Some of them are tamarine. They interested me for the way they take life, for their slowness. Nothing seems to bother them. That's my vision of what their attitude on life is."

Archie Bell

Around 1949, a five-year-old Archie Lee Bell sat in the back of the Philport Baptist Church in Houston, Texas, listening to his mother singing in the choir. "There must have been thirty or forty people up there, but her voice was so strong it sounded like she was doing a solo. That's where my inspiration came from. And then I sang in the choir too. I got my basic music roots from the church."

But Archie's ma isn't the only one in the family to sing up a song. Every second Sunday in August, the entire Bell clan, featuring relatives, distant relatives, and friends, gather in Long Branch, Texas, about 185 miles northeast of Houston for a giant reunion. "When I was younger and before everybody got so spread out, we'd have maybe six thousand show up. We'd take over the whole county for three days, everybody coming home. I was born in Henderson myself, right next door to Long Branch. That whole area up there, that's where all my people come from. And when we get together there's plenty of food, plenty of singing and revival and different preachers coming in from all over. And we're still doing it every year."

While Archie was singing in the church in Houston, where his family moved when he was just a few months old, he was picking up on the rock 'n' roll and rhythm 'n' blues that were being played in the fifties. "That sound really got to me. After that, church was just Sunday. I wanted to be an entertainer, travel all over the world, and play for people."

By the time he was thirteen, Archie already had a reputation for singing, in church, in school, glee clubs, or just anywhere he might improvise something. At that time, "A band of real young guys called Little Pop and the Fireballs were playing at a place down the street from my house called Club 44. They asked me to get up and sing with them one night and after that other bands who had heard were asking me to get up with them at places like Club DeLisa and the Double Bar Ranch. I did that kind of thing for awhile and then decided to get organized. I was singing with some guys in the glee club who were into the same sounds I was, like the Drifters, the Clovers, the Coasters, the Peacocks, and especially the Impressions. I started a group with James Wise, Julius Watson, Cornelius Fuller, and L.C. Watson. I called it the Drells because I just wanted something that rhymed with Bell. When people ask me what a Drell is I tell them it's a very talented young man. When people started identifying me as the leader we became Archie Bell and the Drells."

The group played all the clubs in Houston and built up a large following. After they'd won about a dozen local talent shows, they were discovered by Skipper Lee Frazier who is their manager to this day. They cut a single, "She's My Woman, She's My Girl." The flip side was "a little dance thing we invented called 'The Yankee Dance.'" The single was a regional hit in Texas, Oklahoma, and Louisiana. So even though Archie and the boys weren't even out of high school, they were already on the way and already in the habit of inventing "little dance things."

The next little dance thing was to become a smash national hit, but the circumstances, especially for Archie, were a little curious. "After high school I ended up in the Army. I mean I was drafted. At that time I wouldn't have joined the little Brownies. And then on a weekend leave from basic training, we had an idea to do a thing called 'Tighten Up.' We cut it that weekend, early in 1967, and then I was sent to Vietnam with the 101 Airborne and forgot all about it. When you're doing search-and-destroy missions over there you tend to keep your mind on only what's going down right then and there. Dodging those bullets, I mean, that's when I was really doing the 'Tighten Up.'"

Meanwhile, back in the States, "Tighten Up" was rocketing up the charts. Archie didn't have the faintest idea.

After six months in combat and one too many bullets to dodge, he was wounded and airlifted out to Korea where doctors spent four months working to save his leg. By the time he reached the Seventh General Hospital in Worms, Germany, "Tighten Up" had hit the top of the charts and he still didn't know. "So there I am rolling around the wards in my wheelchair, and all these guys are saying 'Hey, man, I really dig that sound,' and I didn't know what they were talking about, so I just said thanks and figured that the war made people crazy. Then Skipper Lee finally reached me on the phone and let me in on what my song was doing."

Eventually, Archie recovered completely from the wound. "I almost lost the leg; it was pretty bad there for awhile, but it's fine now. I'm still doing the 'Tighten Up,' right?" But he was still in Germany and the Army was in no great rush to discharge him yet. One of the greatest rewards for a performer is to go on the road with a hit but there wasn't anything he could do. "You could say I've had a very funny career. At that time I was making $126 a month and losing fifty thousand dollars a week. Finally Skipper Lee worked it out so I could get a thirty-day leave. We toured around the States but by that time it was really too late. I met up with the guy who had helped me arrange 'Tighten Up.' I wrote it and produced it myself. We were talking about dudes that have one big hit and end up doing nothing else. So I really had that on my mind. I was thinking about what to do next when by coincidence we were playing a place called Loretta's High Hat in Lawnside, New Jersey. At that time Kenny Gamble and Leon Huff were just getting their thing together and they saw us at the club and said they'd like to produce us. But by the time Skipper Lee got the whole thing worked out, I was supposed to be back in Germany again. So what we did was this, every time I could get a weekend leave, I'd fly to New York on a Friday, work straight through with the Drells and Gamble and Huff cutting a single, be on a plane Sunday and back in Germany in time for reveille Monday morning." Hopping back and forth across the Atlantic,

Archie Bell (second from the right) with the Drells.

Archie managed to cut some successful singles like "There's Gonna Be a Showdown" and "My Balloon's Going Up," but none that soared like "Tighten Up." "I really don't know what it feels like to have a hit. I still don't know what it's like to have a record in the top ten and be right there with it."

By the time Archie was finally discharged on April 19, 1969, "I'll never forget that day," at least a dozen bands were running around the country calling themselves Archie Bell and the Drells, even an all-white band out of Memphis. So Archie and the boys went on the road to clear the air of phony Bells and Drells. "Once we got to playing around, people got to know us and that kind of thing was cut down, but even now people come up to me saying, 'You're not him; I saw him and he's 6'3" and has a process and you're not him.'"

For the last nine years, Archie and the Drells (presently

James Wise, the only other original member, Lucius Larkin, and Archie's brother, Lee Bell) have been on the road at least 320 days of the year, all over the U.S. and throughout the world. "When I finally got out of the Army things slowed down for us. We had record company problems, promotion and all that, and we couldn't get another hit out. If it weren't for North and South Carolina, things might have been really rough. You see, they got a thing there called Beach Music. All up and down that coast, just in those two states, there are hundreds of clubs and Holiday Inn lounges, and all these groups are playing there, Maurice and the Zodiacs, Bill Dill and the Rondells, the Drifters, the Embers, the Occasions. I couldn't name them all. But everybody really gets down to it and they call the whole scene Beach Music. That really helped us out and we still go back every year. It's the only place I know where it exists."

Archie and the group have toured the world, including "some places they didn't have names for." On Saudi Arabia: "Hot and dry, hardly anybody spoke English, but music is an international language and we got on with everybody, played all their cities; it was great." On Rio de Janeiro: "Best place I ever played, and do those people know a few things about percussion." On Ghana and Senegal: "It was beautiful, just like going home, all the rhythms, all the flavors." Not to mention Australia, the Phillipines and the Far East, the Carribean, Hawaii, and all over Europe. "We still go on those tours too. I wouldn't trade it for anything. I've learned more on these trips than I would doing anything else. The music, the people, the life-styles. In Africa they turned me on to a thing called the 'talking drum.' It's shaped like a girl. You hold it under your arm and while you're playing it you squeeze it around the middle. It talks back to you. When I'm on the road, I'm not just working, I look at everything. It's like I'm going to the University of the World."

In the meantime, Archie feels that people don't really know what he and the Drells are up to now. "Some say we're disco, some say dance music, some say jazz. We've

The group today. Archie is first on left.

done lots of jazz festivals. I guess we do all that. But I don't care how we're classified as long as people get off on what we're doing." With that in mind, Archie and the Drells have a new album due out on the Philly International label, once again produced by Gamble and Huff. He's also thinking about releasing a disco version of "Tighten Up," a song now heralded by many as the Father of Disco, a song that's sold forty-six million records worldwide according to Archie, and is still selling.

We tracked Archie down in North Carolina where he was preparing for an upcoming Southern tour. He hoped to hit Tampa, Florida, before the football season ended to check out his brother, Ricky Bell, former All-American at the University of Southern California who now dodges would-be tacklers for the Tampa Bay Buccaneers of the National Football League. Archie actually has six brothers all together, "no sisters, just seven hardheads." But his family is really much larger and includes all the people he and the Drells play for. "My first objective is always to please the people, get the music and the people together. The people and the music, that's what it's all about."

Bobby Rydell

Bobby Rydell was one of the first authentic teen idols. He readily admitted taking lessons in singing, drumming, and talking to fulfill the part, but that didn't diminish his personal appeal. He seemed honest and upfront when Dick Clark interviewed him in his family's home in South Philly. But the album cover of *Bobby Sings* on Cameo Records showed a thin Rydell in a finger-snapping pose, dressed in a dark suit with a white tie, shades of a scrawny Sinatra suggesting something brooding beneath the smiling image. The good-natured way the teen idols participated in the various Beech-Nut Gum contests on Bandstand, submitted their prefab dates to close scrutiny, and revealed their private lives made them suspect. Their whole act suggested some subliminal code like the outlawed Coca-Cola ads flashing in microseconds on your screen and driving you to the fridge. They seemed to say this is the way you're supposed to act in public with these silly suits, white patent leather shoes, and ties. But we all know what happens offstage. They promised something other than what they delivered on camera. When you came from the tough part of the city, you had to be more street-wise than the teen idols let on. Rydell, Fabian, and Avalon were definitely suspect. Paul Anka was obviously going on to become a lounge act and do some acting. But he didn't count. After all he was a Canuck, not a denizen of South Philly.

South Philly was the lower-middle-class white ghetto of the city, a place marked by two-story brick row houses crunched together on streets designed as if an urban planner had doddled on the blueprint. It was the catch basin of the ethnic groups who dribbled in a regular intervals, first the Irish, then the Italians, Poles, Jews, and blacks. In the forties and fifties, it produced Mario Lanza, Eddie Fisher, Al Martino, and Buddy Greco. But as Bobby admits, "Let's face it. It really is strange that out of a ten-block area came myself, Avalon, Fabian, Chubby Checker, James Darren, the Dovelles, the Orlans, and Dee Dee Sharp."

When the Philadelphia Sound blasting forth from the powerhouses of Cameo/Parkway Records, Chancellor, and Swann came to dominate the American musical scene, the U.S. House Subcommittee chaired by Rep. Oren Harris of Arkansas also thought it strange, actually downright preposterous, that so many no-talent nothings were snatched off the streets and promised lucrative recording careers if they would only look like young Apollos on television. The Representatives thought the house bands, arrangers, middle-aged backup singers must have been in a conspiracy with the recording engineer to turn out million-selling products. The Committee's rather orthodox musical tastes prevented them from understanding the value of doo-wops and shoo-be-doos. They could never fathom how a Rydell could be a smash the minute he walked onstage without even opening his mouth. He exuded something that the teen audience hooked into. Besides, Rydell was a good singer with a youthful baritone voice and an adequate drumming ability. Unlike their favorite target, Fabian, who was said to be discovered on a stoop, Bobby didn't appear out of thin air. He had been working a nightclub act since the age of six.

Robert Lewis Ridarelli was born in South Philly on April 26, 1942. He grew up in a very, very Italian family with his mother, his maternal grandparents, and his father who worked as a foreman at the Electro-Nite Carbon Company which made brushes for motors and generators. His father had played violin in his teens, but the musical talent came from his grandfather, Tony, who had played vaudeville in Italy before coming over to the States.

But it was his dad who was quick to spot Bobby's talent and help develop it. Until 1960, when Bobby got him out of work, he was his son's road manager. At four years old, Bobby began mimicking such television personalities as Louis Prima, Milton Berle, and Johnnie Ray. "My dad was the first to pick that up, saying things like, 'Look at the kid, Jennie.' And she would say, 'Oh, just leave the kid alone. He's just fooling around.' " Then Bobby saw Gene Krupa with Benny Goodman's band at Philadelphia's Earl Theater, which in the days of the swinging, big bands was like Chicago's Aragon Ballroom and New York's Paramount. He was hooked. He had to be a drummer.

His father, convinced of his son's talent, knew all the club owners at places like the CR Club and Colombo's in Philly. A local piano player took a fancy to Bobby and worked up a few arrangements off Johnnie Ray records. "At six years old, I practically had a nightclub act, with three songs that Johnnie Ray did. Back in the early forties, Johnnie Ray was big. I had 'Walking My Baby Back Home,' 'Broken Hearted,' and 'The Little White Cloud That Cried.' My dad would go up to the club owner and say, 'Would you mind if my son got up and sang a few songs and did some impersonations.' There was never any 'No, we couldn't do that.' At that age, when I was onstage, whether I was good, bad, or indifferent, the applause was always there. That always stuck in my heart. Gee, I can do this and people do that. That's great. What a feeling it is."

At the age of nine, Bobby went on Paul Whiteman's "TV Teen Club" and dis some comedy and impersonations. He subsequently became a regular on the show for two and a half to three years. The teen magazines claimed that Whiteman couldn't pronounce Ridarelli and just shortened it. In fact, Bobby's shrewd father thought Rydell up. When the show was cancelled, Bobby was eleven and concentrated on his first love, drumming. He worked in nameless small groups playing dances, weddings, bar-mitzvahs, and Elk clubs for five bucks a performance.

A half a block away lived Fabian, who Bobby didn't know as a friend, but they went to the South Philadelphia Boys Club together. "I just knew him to wave at. He was always athletic and played a lot of basketball while I was

downstairs shooting pool."

When Bobby started going to Bishop Newman High School in Philly, he was gigging around for fun with a group called the Strollers, then with Tony Carangi and the Skylarks. "At that time, with the Skylarks, we did things by Chuck Berry. We did our big song called 'Witchcraft' recorded by a group called the Spiders. It was basically a twelve-bar blues with the old rock and roll bass line "Boom-Doo-Doo, Boom-Doo-Doo.' That's how the melody went. It went with the bass line. I sang that behind the drums."

At Bishop Newman, Bobby was the sergeant of the drums for the high school marching band, in the dance band, and the concert orchestra. At this time, 1957, Bobby and Frankie Avalon became friends. Frankie played trumpet in Rocco and the Saints, a name that sounds more like an Italian street gang than a band. The group needed a drummer and Frankie corralled Bobby. Bobby remained with the group for a year and a half, while Frankie split to do two flops, "Cupid" and "Teacher's Pet."

Bobby was playing a joint in Somers Point, New Jersey. "I met my first manager, a man by the name of Frankie Day, who was playing bass with a group called Billy Duke and the Dukes. He saw something in me that dad had seen back when I was young. He talked about management. I didn't know what the hell he was talking about. So I said, 'Talk to my father.' And he did. We more or less had a handshake. I went with Frankie until 1966." They formed a company called Veko Records and promptly issued a bomb. Bobby signed with Cameo in 1957 but released five or six records that all died.

"I was ready to forget about it because that was going nowhere. I wasn't having any fun. I really thought about going back and playing drums. Then Bernie Lowe, Cal Mann, and David Appel (of the Appeljacks), who later wrote everything for everybody on Cameo, came up with a song called 'Kissin' Time.' That's how it all happened."

In the summer of 1959, Bobby Rydell had his first hit with "Kissin' Time," which sold 700,000 copies. "Kissin' Time" and later "We Got Love" seemed to sum up everything which was important to the white teenage girl, who wanted to be encased in the cotton candy world of high school with its throbbing but muted dreams and fears. For Bobby they were something else. "I remember when 'Kissin' Time' was a big hit and 'We Got Love' was a big hit. It's something you can't really describe. At that time I was still in high school. Every day, I was going to the office after school. I can remember seeing the sales reports coming in—Chicago 100,000, Philadelphia 250,000, LA and Pittsburgh 300,000. It was mindboggling. I said, 'Jesus Christ, this is happening to me.' It was a great feeling." Bobby felt the sensation a few more times with his three golds, "Wild One," "Forget Him," and "Volare," his mother's favorite. The others that Cameo machine-gunned out at a blistering pace were adolescent-oriented, "I Dig Girls," "Little Bitty Girl," "Ding-A-Ling," and the classic statement of the high school consciousness at the turn of the decade,

"Swingin' School."

> Yay, yay, yay, I go a swingin' school
> Where the chicks are hip and the cats are cool.
> Well, we dance the greatest and we dress the latest
> Whoa, Whoa, Whoa I go to a swingin' school.

Bobby became red-hot appearing on every television show which meant anything like the Sullivans, the Comos, and the Red Skelton Show. He did Skelton twelve times in four years with the Seagulls, Gertrude and Heathcliff. "Instrumentally, Skelton was the guy for network television. My rapport and association with him to this day has been absolutely tremendous. I don't know what it was; he took to me like a son. Right after the first show we were taping, he said, 'Bobby, you're going to be on my first special.' I said, 'Thank you, Mr. Skelton.' I never called him Red. He used to get bugged by that. So he called me, 'Mr. Rydell.' It became a bit between the two of us. After I don't know how many years, I finally called him Red. I was just seventeen or eighteen years old, but son-of-a-gun, about a year later, Red had his first special. The guests were George Raft, Frank Sinatra, and myself, which was pretty damn good company. That's the way it went for years."

Anytime Dick Clark needed a fill-in, the Philly crowd of Avalon, Fabian, and Rydell were on fifteen-minute notice for an appearance on Bandstand. Likewise, when one of them cut a record, a spot on Dick Clark was almost automatic. "Whenever a new record came out, boom, we're on. Back then, I would classify Dick as far as my career was concerned, as a grand-slammer, a Greg Luzinski. Before Dick jumped on a record, to save face in case it bombed, he would say to Bernie Lowe, 'Put the record out and let's see if you get any sales reports.' Then we'd go to Dick and say, 'Look, Dick, the record is moving. There's action on the record. Can you help us?' Then he would get on the record. In other words, you get the first three men on base, and Dick would step to the plate and knock the ball over the wall. It was every day five times a week. It would be played coast to coast. Complete saturation. So if the record had anything in it, it was going to make it.

"The Philadelphia Sound came from Cameo/Parkway because back then Cameo was the Motown of Philadelphia. Anything that they turned out was an immediate hit. They had a definite sound which the label produced. I think basically my tunes were all upbeat. They were all happy. Lyrically, there wasn't too much to think about; the music content was very, very good. The three girls who were on my records who never had a name, (they were on all my records singing 'Woo-Woos, Yeah-Yeahs, Go-Go, Bobby, everything's cool') were definitely an associated sound with me. They were three black grandmothers living in Philadelphia who Bernie Lowe found. They came in and read music and had a definite sound."

The publicity sheets on Rydell quoted Bobby as wanting to have a career as a nightclub singer. Twenty years later, that's where Bobby is, working on the road ten months a year at such places as the whole Playboy circuit, the Hyatt-Regency chain of hotels, and the Vegas-type clubs around Australia where the people down under still go crazy for him. While other teen idols were doing the record hops, the raggedy bus tours, and DJ promo appearances, Bobby was working up a cabaret act for the Copacabana.

"I was locked into the image of the boy next door, which was a good way to go. But as far back as I can remember, which goes back to five when my father brought me to these clubs in Philadelphia, all I always wanted to do was be a cabaret and saloon singer. At that time [1960] I remember spending close to $50,000 putting a nightclub act together.

"Noel Sherman wrote all the special lyrics and Lou Spencer produced and staged the act. We worked for close to a year before we brought the act into the Copacabana. We did tunes like 'Lots of Living' from Bye-Bye-Birdie, 'Old Man River.' We did a special piece of material that went 12½ minutes long called, 'They Don't Write Them Like That Anymore' which incorporated my hit records. I couldn't sing songs like 'What's New' or any of the saloon-type of songs because where the hell have I been at seventeen? Who's going to believe a seventeen-year-old kid singing 'What's New'? I stayed within the confines of what was written for me to the point that the 'Good Nights' and 'Good Evenings' were practically written for me. It didn't come out that way. We wanted it to sound as if it wasn't a written piece of material. But from opening downbeat to closing downbeat, it was words coming out of someone else's mind that I was projecting onstage, it sounds like a tape-recording.

"Working the Copa at eighteen was the epitome of the nightclub world. It was a tremendous club with the Copa girls with the fruits and bananas piled on their heads. Everybody looked like Carmen Miranda up onstage. It was an intimate, small club which held 500 people who were on top of you. It was a tremendous feeling onstage. The prestige of working the club alone was enough. Everyone from Sinatra on down had worked the club." And Bobby concluded a smashing stay there in 1961.

From late 1960 on, Bobby released "Sway," "Good Time Baby," the perennial favorite, "That Old Black Magic," "The Fish," "I Wanna Thank You," "I've Got Bonnie," "I'll Never Dance Again," and "The Cha-Cha-Cha."

In 1963, Bobby swung a screen test with Ann-Margaret for a film version of the Broadway hit Bye-Bye-Birdie about a rock and roll idol and his adoring fans who become traumatized when he enters the service. Under the direction of George Sydney, Bobby played Hugo Peabody to the antics of Dick Van Dyke, Paul Lynde, Janet Leigh, Ann-Margaret, and Ed Sullivan.

What might have appeared to be a natural film career, especially with the mass of beach party flicks, didn't materialize. "Back at that time I looked like a pair of pliers with a Bandaid. I was about ninety-four pounds and I looked like the 'before' in the ads you used to see in the comic books with the guy getting sand kicked in his face. So I didn't think I was the beach-picture type.

"I really didn't dig California. I didn't feel like moving out there like Frankie did. Frankie kept telling me, 'What are you doing in Philadelphia? There's nothing happening in Philly.' I said, 'I just can't make it out there, Frank. I don't dig it. I like coming home, the family thing, and I dig going to Eagles football games. It's a release for me. I need it.' I can't stand the life out there, going around, talking to a director, and lying out in the sun and waiting for the phone to ring."

Bobby's recording career tapered off with "Wildwood Days," "Forget Him," "Make Me Forget," and his last Cameo record, "A World Without Love" in late 1963 and early 1964. The early television exposure and his nightclub work kept his name popular. By that time he had acquired the rep of being a class act, "Mr. Personality," who, unlike other teen idols, could project to an audience.

In the next two years, he had the frustrating experience of watching as "The Loving Thing," "The River Is Wide," and "It's Getting Better" were shelved by his record company. Later, the first two became monster hits for the Grassroots, and the latter a number one hit for Mama Cass. His "Diana," by all rights a hit, sold 15,000 in Chicago and another 15,000 in Philadelphia the first week of release only to be buried under his label's promotion of Wayne Newton's, "Red Roses for a Blue Lady." A few years ago, he rerecorded for Pip Records his 1961 hit, "Sway," to a disco beat. Without any hype it sold 200,000, reached 26 in *Billboard* on the Easy Listening list, and became number one in Canada for a while.

For the past sixteen years, he has lived with his wife Camille, his parents, daughter Jennifer, and son Robert in Penn Valley, a suburb of Philadelphia and twenty minutes away from the old neighborhood. "It's good because that's the way I was brought up, living with my grandparents and mother and father. It's a great family feeling."

Ironically, Bobby's madness for the hard-checking Philadelphia Flyers led to a meeting with a local sports personality at the Spectrum which has resulted in a partnership destined to put Bobby back on vinyl. A middle-aged man named Tony Luisi is cranking out new material for Bobby to sing in the half dozen different styles he's perfected over the years. Even though he's been on the road with his

drummer most of every year since the beginning, Bobby manages to find time to be the city's campaign chairman for the March of Dimes and works on Philly's great annual zany tradition of the Mummer's Parade. After all, he says, "This is my city."

"It's the greatest business to be in. Even today, I truly love to be onstage. I get total enjoyment out of doing it for an hour or so. And when it's over, you can't wait for the second show or the next night to happen. It's not a job to me. When it becomes a job to me, that's when I will forget about it and hang up the shoes. If I ever got to that point, I'd feel that I would be just taking up space. You're up there doing what you really like to do. You're trying to make people forget the problems they've had over that day or week. If you can just ease their minds, make them laugh a bit, cry a little bit, sing some songs, clap their hands, and have a good time, that's what makes me feel good.

"Nothing has really knocked me out or overly impressed me to the point where it turned me around. There are unfortunately a lot of people in the business for whom it didn't happen like that. I'm basically a very down-to-earth guy. Nothing has really affected me all that heavily. I think that comes from my early management and my family and the saying, 'You meet the same people on the ladder on the way down as you do on the way up.' There's no sense in being a bad guy while you're up there because if you're on the way down, they'll give you a shove to get down quicker. They always say, 'Nice guys finish last.' That's OK with me. If that's the way the ballgame has to go, I'd rather go out that way, than the other. When I'm home, I'm home. When it's over, it's over. My mother hollers at me the same way any other mother hollers at her kid."

Del Shannon

In the spring of 1961, Del Shannon's "Runaway," that burning declaration of teen heartache featuring Del's rocketing falsetto, was the number one single in the country for a solid month. Almost eighteen years later, after doing a series of rock shows, he says about rock 'n' roll, "It never seems to die. It just goes on insane."

Del Shannon, performer, songwriter, record producer, band manager, and music publisher, and never necessarily in that order, has been around through the British invasion, psychedelia, heavy metal, the country and western surge, and the disco blizzard, and still, "All I am is just a basic rock 'n' roller."

Born Charles Westover on December 30, 1939, in little Coopersville, Michigan, outside of Grand Rapids, Del was given a ukelele when he was about thirteen. His mother taught him how to play a little ditty called "Doodly Doo." Then he was getting into country music, especially artists like Hank Williams and Webb Pierce. Tough stuff to play on a uke. "But I heard some guy five miles away was selling a guitar for five bucks. I peddled down on my bicycle and bought it. It was kind of whipped. The neck was bowed and the strings were way up in the air. I tried to straighten it out with baling wire, but my hands still bled every time I played it. I figured out a few chords myself, but in this small town nobody played guitar, not like they do today. And I didn't want to take lessons, notes and all that, boring. So on Saturday nights I'd get into these country western dance halls, watch the guitar players in the bands, watch their hands. The people in those places were always fighting, not the bands but the people. They'd go there just to fight. No grass going around, just people drinking and kicking ass. I grew up with all that. Good for my background I guess. Brought something out in me, in the songs I write, the rebel I guess. Man, when I was a kid I'd see guys get the hell beat out of them, blood, heads smashed against telephone poles, broken bottles, flying bottles."

Meanwhile, Del was going to high school. "Somehow I ended up on the football team. And I found out you could get great echo in the shower room. I took my guitar in there and it was unbelievable. So I discovered echo in the damn shower. And the principal of the school was good to me. I don't know why. But he let me go down there and play during study hall. I guess he knew I wasn't going to study anyway."

Down in that tiled sound booth with shower heads for mikes, he worked on his singing and started learning songs. He also started picking up on the falsetto technique from listening to the Ink Spots. "I started doing assemblies before football games. I'd get out early, go up and sing and play for the kids; then all the cheerleaders and the pompoms would come running out with we got to win this game and all that. I was on the team too but all I wanted to do was play music for the guys. I could play after a game if we won but not if we lost. The rules. Pretty weird. But that's all I wanted to do, sing and play. I'd hide my helmet, do anything to get out of football. My father wanted me to be a big football star. He never liked my guitar playing. Always kicked me out of the house—'Go on out in the backyard and play that damn thing!' He liked to play the spoons."

When Del was about seventeen, he got enough dough together to send away for his first axe. "It was a Silvertone. Seemed like I waited ten years for that thing. It finally came in on the train, the Coopersville Special, and I plugged it right in. I would work my way into the dance hall bands for a number or two, but that's all they'd let me do. It used to piss me off, but they were probably right because I was just getting up there and banging out the three or so chords I knew."

After high school, Uncle Sam insisted on treating Del to an extended stay in Germany. He managed to join up with the Get Up And Go Show, an all-soldier entertainment group that would travel around the west side of the Wall playing for the troops. "I ended up playing guitar for this Mexican dancer. He said I never played fast enough for him, but hell, I couldn't play that kind of music anyway. So I faked it, just strummed as hard and fast as I could and somehow he was dancing to it.

"That lasted for about four months, touring around on buses from show to show. I didn't know where we were or what I was playing half the time, but it meant no guard duty, no KP, plus you got to grow your hair a little longer. But then they sent me back to my unit. Everybody got rotated. Four months away and I wasn't much into soldiering. I was in pretty bad shape. This one lieutenant looked at me and said he'd never seen such a mess in his life. So he gets these three giant sergeants on me and they've got me right out marching around in the field. Those guys yelling out orders and me dragging my guitar and my gas mask around. It was pretty hairy for awhile. I guess all this is in my music, the rebellion. It all lands in there somehow. I was always a rebel as a kid, a loner type of guy. I hated all that gung-ho crap. All I wanted was to play guitar."

When the Army got tired of trying to whip him into shape, he dropped off his gas mask and headed back to Michigan. He started working joints in Battle Creek, playing for the folks who were spending their paychecks signed by Mrs. O'So-&-So of the Kelloggs Cornflake empire. "Big clubs, four hundred, five hundred people, all drinkers and fighters, everybody still kicking ass. Not me, though. I didn't like fighting. I still don't. Anyway, I met up with Max Crook, a keyboard player, and it started to happen right up there onstage. Ollie McLaughlin from WHRV in Ann Arbor came down to tape me. He's black so I made him come in the afternoon. I wouldn't have wanted him in one of those places at night; it would have been real bad. So he taped a couple songs and took them to Embee Productions and they flew me to New York. Man, I was only about twenty and I was a nervous wreck. Maybe that's why they said the vocals weren't good enough for a single."

He returned to Battle Creek, a little depressed but not about to quit. "I had all that drive. A record contract was an out, a chance to get out of the club thing. I said I was either getting out of it or I'd go into the carpet business. I had been selling them on the side so I could keep playing. Now everytime I see a carpeteria out here in California I say, man, that could have been me."

At the time Del and his band were going by the name of Charley Johnson and the Big Little Show Band and playing four nights a week at the Big High Low Club in Battle Creek. "I was looking for a new name. The guy who owned the carpet shop had just bought a Cadillac Deville; I said I had to get me one of those. And this other guy at the club was going to be a pro wrestler and call himself Mark Shannon. I really liked the Shannon part but Mark sounded like a detective. So I took Del from Deville and it came out Del Shannon."

After the first shot at recording failed, Ollie McLaughlin suggested he write an up-tempo song. "One night Max played a chord change I thought was great, A Minor and G. I said 'Hey, play that again,' and we went right into 'Runaway.' I already had the words but not the music. I'd been writing a lot but that one really struck."

So it was back to New York and the recording studio. "But they didn't want to pay for a plane so we drove an old Plymouth I had. The muffler fell off and the heater broke. We froze our things off. But we got there and cut 'Runaway' plus the flip in an hour and a half with a bunch of session guys."

It zipped up America's spine to the number one spot and Del hit the road, eventually touring as much as 250 days a year as he followed up with a string of successful singles including "Hats off to Larry" and "Little Town Flirt." But then in 1963, things got complicated. Del would say that was an understatement. "I realized I was getting ripped off. I sued for two years, at least two or three lawsuits trying to get what I was owed. I also started my own record company and got a few records out on it but my manager sent out thousands of telegrams telling the radio stations they'd be sued if they played any Del Shannon records. Eventually I got another contract with another record company, but I'm a fighter. I wouldn't take it. I can't see anybody screwing me. People warned me that my career would go right on down but I didn't care, somebody has got to fight these people."

The other matter to be taken care of was the quality of the Del Shannon sound. "You see, all the records I had done were recorded with session guys and it was getting stale; they just didn't have the gut feel I wanted. So I started working again with street guys, the guys who worked the clubs like I had, the guys who are right down in it, down in the dirt, down with the pulse of the people."

So with a new band and a new record company Del came out with "Keep Searchin'" which in 1965 made mincemeat out of Shirley Bassey's "Goldfinger" and the Kingsmen's "Jolly Green Giant" among others. "But then, it's not that I got lazy, I just wanted to take some of the pressure off myself and let some other people do the writing. I guess I was envious of guys like Bobby Vee who'd just go into the studio, the producer would hand him a song, and it would be a hit. But it just doesn't work that way for me. I tried it for a few years and I know it doesn't."

Then one night in the late sixties, Del and Brian Hyland were hanging around in the posh at the Palomino Club on the West Coast when Del decided enough of the muckamuck and they went down to a rock club called the Rag Doll. "There was a group onstage called Smith. They were playing rock 'n' roll and the chick lead singer knocked me cuckoo. I told them I would manage them and produce them and they said great. I was back in the streets again, with a street band, where I belonged. I picked out their single for them, 'Baby It's You,' which became a hit. But by that time there was another record company hassle and I wasn't around. But my energies were into producing and I don't like anybody to tell me there's something I can't do. So I took Brian Hyland to a record company and produced 'Gypsy Woman' for him."

In the early seventies Del decided to start performing again and went back on tour. He went back to England where he's always been big. "I've been going there twice a year forever except when I was producing. And Australia too. Rock music everywhere down there. For the last eight years or so I'll go on tour for six weeks and then take two

or three months off. I don't have to do it all the time because I have my own music publishing company too, Mole Hill Music. I remember one time a piano fell on me. They built this huge stage inside a stadium down in Atlanta and there were about thirty or forty thousand people there. It was real mixed show, Lesley Gore, Dion, Charley Rich, George Maharis, Ronnie Milsap, lots of others. At the end the emcee says everybody onstage to take a bow and we all got up there. It was pretty high up. Then the whole thing caved in. I hit the ground, looked up, and saw Milsap's piano coming down. I went to the hospital, but luckily it had just ripped my coat. But, man, I thought it was an earthquake."

Today Del lives about twenty-five miles north of Hollywood, canyon country, with his wife, and three teenage children. "I don't want to talk too much about my family. I want them to stay happy and free from the business. One of my daughters is interested in music. She's a little young yet. But if she wants to make it she's got to have tons of drive. It's got to come first in your life or forget it, you'll never make it. Girl friends get in your way. Boy friends get in your way. When I was in high school I didn't go with any girls because if I got them pregnant that would have been the end of my career before it had even gotten started."

Speaking of his career, "I'm writing new stuff now. I think the time is right now. I'm going back to the streets with the street guys again. When I try to do something I'm not then it's just insane. About ten years ago I actually tried to go psychedelic with an album called *The Further Adventures Of Charles Westover*. That was just silly. Right now I've been playing and laying some stuff down with Tom Petty and the Heartbreakers (Shelter Records recording stars), basic rock 'n' roll. I'm still a rocker at heart. The street is in my blood. So maybe something will work out with Tom because I want to get back in the studio again. I stayed out because I didn't think the time was right, but I think it is now and I think I'm right. If not then maybe next year. It's my life; it's been good to me and I don't have any reason to bitch. It's given me a lot of things and I think I've given a piece of something to rock 'n' roll."

Gene Chandler

Gene Chandler takes no prisoners. Interviewing him is like being run over by a tank. The man is fast-talking, freewheeling, hip-shooting, and smoking when he's not joking. Gene Chandler can make a half a dozen business deals in the time it takes to lick a stamp. When not holding court on the North Side of Chicago or playing tennis and racquetball, Gene is ensconced in the towers of Chi-Sound Records counting the money as it pours in from his new disco album *Get Down*. The dude has had more comebacks than Muhammed Ali since he cut his teeth in the business with "Duke of Earl." If you can't place the sound of Jerry Butler and Curtis Mayfield in any other city than Chicago, you also can't take Gene out of the Windy City. He's still single after all these years because, "I got too many things to do." As he says, "I'd rather stay in the Midwest where I've got power. You get lazy when you get to the West Coast and New York is too big, expensive, and verrry cutthroat. I'm in the middle."

In the early and mid-sixties, Gene Chandler set his appealing style of falsetto dives and swoops to a series of Curtis Mayfield tunes, which propelled him onto the scene as one of America's biggest black balladeers. His vulnerable reading of Mayfield's "Just Be True" later became identified with the whole Chandler persona, a wounded, misunderstood soul. This feeling pervaded everything from "Bless Our Love" through "To Be a Lover" and "Girl Don't Care." His ability to send the girls into hysterical pandemonium at Chicago's Regal Theater and Aragon Ballroom was one of the reasons he became a mainstay for Chicagoan Carl Davis's reactivated Okeh records, originally a label for "race" records. While Carl rescued Jackie Wilson's career in the late sixties with "Whispers" and "(Your Love Keeps Lifting Me) Higher and Higher" over at Brunswick Records, he continued producing Gene's hits "There Goes the Lover" and "There Was a Time" in 1968.

Gene Chandler was born Eugene Dixon on July 6, 1937, in Chicago. He later became Gene Chandler after his favorite actor Jeff Chandler because he thought "Chandler sounded romantic." His father, a steelmill worker in Gary, Indiana, took the five-year-old Gene to political picnics on July fourth where the youngster would sing "Danny Boy." After that early experience, he sang in the junior choir of his church and on street corners with various groups until the age of sixteen. About this time, he joined a group called the Gay-Tones.

"There was one girl and I was the lead singer. We used to sing at the schools and at a few talent shows. We happened to have won a talent show held at the Trianon Ballroom in Chicago. The contest was run by a DJ named Fitshoe. The prize was having the opportunity to sing on radio every Sunday in Harvey, Illinois. We would go out and sing two or three songs on the radio. We were excited because everybody was listening. When we got back to school on Monday everybody was talking about it."

Eventually, he joined the Du-Kays in 1957 right before he entered the service. He was stationed with the Airborne in Meinz and Frankfort, West Germany. It was in the Special Services, the entertainment corps of the military, that Gene realized that he wanted to become a solo act. But on his return to Chicago in 1960, the Du-Kays persuaded him to rejoin the group. At this time, Mrs. Bernice Williams heard them sing, liked their stuff, and became their manager and the cowriter of "Nite Owl" and "The Duke of Earl."

"When we went with Bernice Williams into a session, we cut "Nite Owl" and "The Duke of Earl." We put the "Duke of Earl" together in a rehearsal. We had this thing we did to open our chords, our throats. They would sing Do-Do-Do-Do. I had the idea for them to keep doing that

but bringing up the channels. It was Do, not Duke. Earl
Edwards was one of the fellows in the group. So it came to
me to have the Duke of Earl. I had no idea what or who
the Duke of Earl was. I knew it sounded royal. In any
event, I told them to begin saying Duke ... Duke ...
Duke ... of Earl and I began putting lyrics to it, just making them up. We were so thrilled with the song. And naturally at that time we didn't have any idea what a million-
seller was. But we thought it was a big record. So we left
my house from rehearsal and ran four blocks to Bernice
Williams's house, hollering we had a million-seller. She
eventually put some more lyrics to it."

Eventually, Gene and the Du-Kays went to Carl Davis, Gene's present manager and owner of Chi-Sound, and Bill "Bunky" Shepard, now vice-president of the national promotion for Twentieth Century Records, then Chicago talent agents starting a record company called Nat. The record company released "This Girl Is a Devil" and "Nite Owl" but passed on "The Duke." An A&R man named Calvin Carter at VeeJay Records was on the prowl for the publishing rights of the Du-Kays' material, heard "The Duke," flipped out, and tagged it a "monster." After a quick transatlantic buzz to the president of VeeJay, who was in Paris at the time, Carter bought the record, leaving Gene in a difficult bind. The Du-Kays' "Nite Owl" was climbing the charts on Nat Records while "The Duke" was being held up until he made up his mind whether he would make the leap as a solo act or stay with the group.

"So they gave me the choice of staying with the group or going with 'The Duke of Earl' as a single and leaving the group. I had to make a decision. It was a chance because the "Nite Owl" was really smoking. We finally had a national hit and "The Duke" wasn't released yet. I didn't even want to record "The Duke" because I wanted strings on it. I didn't even want Bill and Carl, when we first came to them, to hear it because I knew they were going to like it. They told me that if we didn't record this in that session, they weren't going to allow us to record anything. At that time, we couldn't afford strings so I was going to wait until the 'Nite Owl' record made it. We'd have the money on the next session to put the strings in. They told us, 'You are going to do it in this session or you're not going to do any of it.' I relented and it turned out to be a giant record."

Then in January 1962, with two hit records out, Eugene Dixon changed his name, not only for romance's sake, but also so that he could work as a solo while still being under contract to the Du-Kays. "I hadn't put any act together. I was so busy with the decision of which way to go, it hadn't happened. Things were going so fast that I had to make the decision because they wanted to release the records before the holidays. It all came upon me before I knew it.

'The Duke' was released the end of November and by December 'The Duke of Earl' was the number one record in the country. The record, 'The Twist,' was in the number one position and I knocked that out of the box. By January 1, it was number one. In less than a month and a half, the record was a giant.

"I hadn't tried to put an act together, even with the group. It came so fast that I got up onstage and did things that I did when I was a lead singer—a lot of movement and songs which I thought were exciting. I used to be a fan and sit back and watch. I knew what excited me. I tried to emulate some of these things. It got over for me. I became Gene Chandler at that point and took off."

After "You Threw a Lucky Punch," "Rainbow," "Man's Temptation," and "Soul Hootenanny," Gene went over to Constellation Records. They managed to secure the Impressions' Curtis Mayfield as a songwriter and arranger. Mayfield, who, at fifteen, had joined forces with Jerry Butler in the Northern Jubilee Gospel Singers and later the Impressions, developed a new, softer, and more complex sound than the blues dominating the Chicago scene on the South Side. Mayfield's younger and mellower side became perfect material for Chandler with "Bless Our Love," "What Now," "Nothing Can Stop Me," "Rainbow '65," and "Just Be True."

In 1964, Gene got into a dispute with the president of Constellation, who didn't want to release "Just Be True" with its Impressions harmonizing and the lush overlay of strings. Gene did want it out and refused to record for six months until it was released. "I had a hold on him because I was the only artist on the label who was selling for him. Finally, he gave in and we made a bet on the song. It turned out to be a big record for me and for them." In 1966, his record company folded and his master tapes were sold to Chess Records, which had been plying a roster of Southern-style blues, while Carl Davis, his manager, went off to round up acts for Brunswick which knew Chicago was a gold mine of exploitable acts. Gene got in the middle and found himself recording for both companies in a strange gentlemen's agreement which called for each label to alternate in their release of Chandler discs. But Gene found that by 1969 his well had run dry.

After four years, 1962–66, of playing the club circuit, Gene decided to switch over to the business end of music, starting two music publishing companies, a production company, and accepting the presidency of a St. Louis firm, Bamboo Records. The company was fifty grand in the hole and within months Gene's golden touch produced the big hit, "Backfield in Motion," which catapulted Bamboo into the profit margins. He followed "Backfield" with other minor hits until he ran into more business problems and soon found himself embroiled in a court case. With a string of companies under his management, Gene decided to add another, the Mr. Chan label, a subsidiary of Mercury.

It soon became time for a comeback try. He did it with his own production of "Groovy Situation" in 1970. "There are different feelings when a record takes off. With 'The Duke' it was so fast. I was barely out of it before I realized what a million-seller was. 'The Rainbow' sold a million over time. Then 'Groovy,' which I was proud of because I had produced it. In 1970, I also received a producer's award of the year at the NATRA convention with 'Backfield in Motion.' I beat out Gamble and Huff."

In the early seventies, Chandler found himself overextended on every front. "I was in the studio night and day, producing, arranging. I was with the acts showing them how to sing the songs, mixing, and I was moving. I was phoning around the country, checking with my jocks who were playing my records. I was backing up what these major record companies were supposed to be doing. I got off the ground from the years of friendships with jocks and they were willing to help me.

"I'm flying in and out different cities, working with acts who couldn't get flying because of certain things. It ended up that I didn't get the help I needed and my sound began to repeat itself. I recognized that. I didn't want to lose money for anybody so I got out of all contracts. So, one

day maybe I'd come back. They appreciated that. We closed all deals and I put my company in dormant and the publishing companies in administration which now freed myself from all obligations. I did nothing but travel around the country living off the losses I had invested in. By this time they were making money. The tunes would bring in something here and something there. I cut loose all the acts."

After a few years of keeping a low profile, Gene went to

Europe and Jamaica to record reggae music with Johnny Nash in July of 1976. The same year, he released "Tell It Like It Is," a moderate-seller and then "I Gotta Get Over the Hump." Finally, in the spring of '78, Gene's career came full circle back to the Master of the Chicago Sound, Carl Davis, his original producer and manager. Together they released "Tomorrow I May Not Feel the Same," which went aground because of bad marketing. Then Gene cut a disco record, "Get Down" and waltzed away to Europe and Africa on business, when it was released. On his return, he found that it had sold 100,000 after two weeks and that his star was once again on the rise.

"We have taken off like hotcakes. It's really a thrill to come back into the business with a bang like this. I knew I could come back any time I wanted. There were time and space between a lot of my hits like 'Groovy.' You never know but you have to feel comfortable and believe. You gotta believe. You have to remember what you've done in the past; it's an everyday learning process. You can never become complacent so that you feel you're so good anything will be popular. You have to deal with the times and the times says disco is happening. So a lot of people say they love it but it's out of my bag because they're used to 'Rainbows' and 'Just Be Trues.' But it's not out of my bag because money's in my bag.

"I'm happy about it. The whole thing and the movements I've made is due to my faith and my belief in Jesus Christ because I think he's very much responsible. I call him 'JC' because I talk to him real hip and don't say things like holy, holy, holy, because he's already holy. We talk together and I say I'm going to make this decision and this move. Obviously, I made the right move. He helps those who help themselves. I helped myself and we are smoking. What can I tell you?"

Johnny Tillotson

"If you're really small, people don't think twice about you. Everybody was playing football and wearing letter sweaters. I was very small for my age and couldn't participate in those sports which make you popular. That and living in a small town played crucial roles in the development of my personality and my career. I was the only singer in Palatka, Florida, and there was no one who could say I wasn't going to make it. Sometimes, the less you know about the barriers which can cloud your thinking the better. My desire was strong and I went right ahead to sing."

Every Saturday night in Palatka, one could listen to the beautiful, gentle singing of Hank Williams, who had risen from being an Alabama farm boy to a star at Nashville's Grand Ole Opry. "He had his great magic of handling the English language in such a simple way too make it more beautiful." A frail kid sitting on a porch in rural Florida and listening to "Why Don't You Love Me" and the classic "Your Cheatin' Heart" might imagine himself a singer, but could hardly imagine himself with twenty-three hit singles and concert dates as far away as Saudi Arabia and Japan. Such a kid was Johnny Tillotson.

Born on April 20, 1938, Johnny lived with his parents and brothers in Jacksonville until the day his granddaddy died. He was only nine years old when he was sent fifty miles south to care for his grandmother in the sleepy burg of Palatka. "I was sent to care for her because I was the eldest son. My job was to keep her company, not make money or anything like that. My parents stayed up in Jacksonville. Occasionally, my mother would come down to visit. In the summer, I got to visit my father. My going there took me completely away from my brothers and out of the family. Fifty miles to a kid is a long way."

"I don't know what started my creative spark. But I knew at the age of nine, I was going to sing. I always figured that if you did it long enough it would just work out. I managed to get a radio show at WWPF, which stood for Work With Palatka Florida. I'd walk down the street from my grandmother's house to the station and do The Young Folks' Revue. I sang all kinds of music, anything that was popular. Soon, I got a lot of recognition from the show. People would come up to me and say, 'I heard you on the radio today and you're really good.' If you hear enough of that and you're not told any different, you believe it. I remember I appeared on a talent show in Jacksonville which I expected to win. I didn't do very well, so I went back to Palatka. There I was still number one. In the beginning a setback like that can be very demoralizing."

In his early teens, Johnny went from his radio show to singing as a regular on the "Tobey Dowdy Show" in Jacksonville. The country variety show featured young talent and had a wide regional appeal. "I used to commute from Palatka to Jacksonville on a Greyhound. Even though I only got five bucks for the show and a bus ticket worth three something, it did put me in touch with television. That means a lot to me now when I host telethons and appear on shows like Sha-Na-Na." In 1953, the year Hank Williams died, Johnny at the age of fifteen got his big break, a television show of his own. He walked up to the station manager and just asked for his own show. "It's what you do when you don't know you're not supposed to do it." He had the show until college and built up a wide regional audience.

At the University of Florida, after hating business administration, he switched to being a journalism major so that he could maintain a good enough average to continue his show business career on the side. Throughout his college career, he played the fraternities, sororities, and all the school dances. Johnny's local popularity was soon to be transformed into a national phenomenon. He traveled to

Nashville and entered the Pet Milk Talent Contest. He arrived on the last day of the competition and walked away as one of the six national winners. After the contest, a record executive persuaded him to audition for Archie Bleyer, the president of Cadence Records and producer of such people as the Everly Brothers, Andy Williams, and the Cordettes. Bleyer was to be the first of several people whom Tillotson calls his mentors.

"It's very important for me to say to young performers today that you must have in all stages of your creative life somebody who motivates you and you really look up to, whether it be another singer, producer, or just a friend, someone to keep that creative spark going. Archie Bleyer was the greatest influence in my life. He believed in me and protected me. His belief in me was the key. He allowed me to live at his house and never presented me with a bill. I don't know why I was so special to him but I was. He was one of the most creative, honest, ethical men I have ever known."

When Johnny started cutting records in 1958, Bleyer brought him material to record. His first singles were "Well, I'm Your Man" and "Dreamy Eyes." As a consequence of Bleyer's influence on building his career, Johnny stayed with Cadence records for five years. As a performer, he adopted Bleyer's own philosophy about a hit song. "His idea is the same as mine today, that a hit is a hit because of the material. If the material is good and marketed well, then it will become a big hit and make money. It's always the song. The singer just interprets it."

Later that same year, Johnny began a friendship which would span his whole career. "The most amazing thing in my life has been my friendship with Elvis. I met him at his third concert in Jacksonville, then I sang a lot of his songs. When he went to Las Vegas, I was there on press night. We became very good friends within the space of time he had. We exchanged gifts and always talked a lot with each other. Elvis was different from the others. He was always gracious. There was no one quite like him. I loved Elvis very much." Ironically, Johnny's biggest triumph came at the University of Florida, when on a football field he did his Presley imitations before 45,000 cheering fans.

In 1959, after graduating from college, Johnny moved to New York City, where Archie Bleyer wouldn't let him walk the streets alone. There he started to record regularly and began touring the country with Dick Clark's Revue. From 1959 to 1961, Johnny released a string of hits including "Earth Angel," "Poetry in Motion," and "Without You." "We recorded 'Poetry in Motion' twice, once in New York where it didn't do anything and then in Nashville where it became a hit. I was excited with people like Floyd Cramer, Chet Atkins, Elvis, and Boots Randolph around."

During the height of his popularity, Johnny faced the problem of not being able to enjoy the Good Times era of music. "I wasn't out in front enjoying the era. I was enjoying being on stage, providing the entertainment. I was a teen star but there was a lot of loneliness involved. I dated very little and traveled a lot. I was having a lot of fun on-stage but in order to be there you had to compromise so much of yourself as a person. You had to contend with two different things—never giving up and the young people with the same desire to make it as you. You had to be willing to live in an apartment with no furniture, eat beans, and drink coke because you have that tremendous desire to write songs and act. If you really want to do it, beware. Show business is the big compromise. If you're ready for that, then you have to go for it and never stop because there'll always be someone dropping out, making it better for you."

Like Elvis before him, Johnny entered the Army in 1961 as a regular E-2 soildier. While in the Army, Johnny had his biggest smash hit with "It Keeps on A-Hurtin'," a song which has since been recorded by 120 different artists including Bobby Darin, Elvis, and Boots Randolph. "I got inspired by Hank Williams's situation and wrote the song. But I had no idea why it was such a hit. I had not experienced any of what the song talks about. A little later, when I grew up a bit, I knew why it was a hit. If you ever fall out of love with somebody or have any other very personal problems, 'It Keeps on A-Hurtin' fits any of them. When you hear their name, it keeps a-hurtin'."

Johnny's singing, which had started to gain popularity, suddenly stopped in the Army, even though he had a number of hits playing on national radio. During his six-month tour of duty and through summer camp, Johnny found an acceptance in the Army and a willingness by other soldiers to cover up for him when his body couldn't meet some of the requirements of combat training.

From the isolated, hermetic world of the Army camp, Johnny returned to the intense, lonely world of touring with his new songs "Send Me the Pillow You Dream On," "I Can't Help It," and "You Can Never Stop Me Loving You." He traveled to Japan and instantly became a big star there. Learning his songs phonetically in Japanese, Johnny sang his way onto the Tokyo charts with seven Top Ten hits in Japanese and three others in English.

By the time his next hit, "Talk Back Trembling Lips," came out in 1963, Johnny was making the transition from being a teen idol to a club act, headlining at the Copacabana and the Latin Quarter. At first the adjustment was difficult but the switch prepared him for the devastation of the American music scene when the Beatles arrived in February of 1964.

"If I hadn't prepared with club dates and taken chances, I probably wouldn't have made it. It was the most difficult period for the American artist to survive. It was very much in vogue to play British artists, not Americans, on the radio. We all worked and made money but to stay on top you have to have hit records. For everyone I know it was difficult. The only American artists who made it through the period were Bobby Vinton and Neil Diamond. But the Beatles were important because they changed the lifestyle of the world. They influenced everything—music, style, how one lives their life, politics.

"In 1964, I moved from New York out to California. There wasn't a lot of work and I was soon broke. At that point, Elvis recorded 'It Keeps on A-Hurtin' because he loved it." The royalties and exposure from Elvis's recording of his song revived Johnny's fortunes.

After club dates and some touring of England, Johnny settled into the Nevada scene as a regular star in 1970. Since then, he has headlined at The MGM Grand Hotel, The Landsmark, and The Hilton as well as playing regularly at other hotels in the Las Vegas, Reno, and Lake Taho area. Recently, he has toured throughout Saudi Arabia to entertain the oil technicians of ARAMCO, played the night clubs of London, and entertained NATO troops in Germany. He appeared on "Sha-Na-Na" singing his old rock standard "Poetry in Motion" and played at the Jim Halsey Music Festival in Tulsa.

The many changes in fortune over his thirty-year career have instilled in Johnny a professionalism and dedication which propels him past the sporadic lulls and dead periods that sap an entertainer's desire to continue in the

business. "My goals are always to have a very high opinion of myself, to be dedicated, to be disciplined, to enjoy what I'm doing. Today, I really enjoy the working, more than the money. Sure, I had more recognition then, but I'm very sincere when I do shows now. When I do the hit record segment, I don't walk right through that. Even though I had twenty-three hit records in the past, it is the past. I don't do a nostalgia show. I do the biggest things I ever had slowly because that's what people are looking for. I love what I'm doing. There's a chemistry that happens between me and people."

He credits much of his present outlook on life to various women who have influenced him—his present wife of one year, Karen, his acting coach, Laura Road, and a ninety-year-old woman, Frankie Murray, who taught him that age doesn't matter. As Johnny puts it, "Most of my friends are ladies. I enjoy and have learned so much from them because they're so strong and sensitive."

His present project consists of taking lessons at the Film Actors Workshop in Burbank, California, during the breaks in his singing schedule. The lessons are seen as therapy to make Johnny work harder in other creative areas and to fuel his desire to become hot again. "I took up acting because it's really a campy type of thing and with music it's great nourishment for other aspects of my personality. The classes make me more professional in all areas because I have to work hard to make this work and continue to grow. I love the growing part of life and California provides such a tremendous energy source. What would make me happy now would be to get the right combination of television and hit records. After all, the best press agent is a hit record."

Tommy James

The sun was rising the morning after election day, 1968, and Tommy James, twenty-one-years old, close to a dozen records already under his belt, sat with Hubert Humphrey awaiting the final tally of what appeared to be an imminent victory. After campaigning and writing speeches together for months, Humphrey had named Tommy for the office of President's Advisor on Youth Affairs. "It was the most exciting thing that had ever happened to me. We thought we had it and I thought I was going to Washington. I had all kinds of things in mind. I was really going to shake some heads, government-sponsored rock concerts, who knows. It looked like we were going to win the popular vote. We thought we had it in the bag."

Tommy was born Thomas Jackson in Dayton, Ohio, April 29, 1947. "I think I always knew what I wanted to be. As far back as I can remember, two or three years old, I was singing songs I heard on the radio and playing the ukelele. My parents tell me I was into it even before that. When I was eight, I saw Elvis Presley for the first time on the 'Ed Sullivan Show.' I remember the tremendous excitement he generated and I just said, 'Wow, that's it.' When I was nine my parents bought me my first guitar, a seventeen-dollar Stella, and I taught myself how to play."

A few years later Tommy started a band. "I wanted to play and I wanted to hear drums and bass. None of the people my age were into it so I ended up being the youngest in the group. The other guys were all in high school or older. They were the first Shondells. So I got my training very young and it was a good thing because when things started to happen later I was ready to handle it."

So by the age of twelve, Tommy and the band were already playing record hops, dances, college gigs, doing pre-Beatle rock 'n' roll. Even when not playing, Tommy was never far from music. He worked in a record shop all through junior high and high school. "I was about thirteen, working in the shop one day, and this guy, a DJ from a local radio station, walks in and says he's looking for a group to record some songs because he wants to start a record company. I told him I had an act together. I wasn't writing yet but we were doing all the stuff that was happening at the time. So we did a song called 'Hanky Panky' for him. That was 1961. It had been written by Jeff Barry, a good friend of mine now, and Ellie Greenwich. They wrote a lot of the early Phil Spector stuff. Anyway I had heard somebody else's recording of 'Hanky Panky,' I forget who, at some dance and the kids were going crazy. So we did it and it was released on, are you ready for this, Snap records out of Niles, Michigan, my home town. It bombed miserably for lack of national distribution and was more or less buried in the record cemetary."

All through high school Tommy and the Shondells continued doing local gigs. In 1965 he graduated, made a few personnel changes in the band, and took it on the road. "Then the story gets bizarre. It was about three months later, and all of a sudden, one weekend I was out of work and miserable, and I get this strange phone call, a fellow from Pittsburgh, a local promoter who had a series of nightclubs in that area. He had finally tracked me down in Chicago through the record store, and he says 'Hey, your record is number one.' I said, 'Who is this?' What record? I don't have any record.' He says 'Hanky Panky' and I just about. . . well, I almost hung up on him. After awhile he finally convinced me he was on the level."

It turns out somebody had picked up the forgotten record and played it on a local Pittsburgh radio station, and the switchboard lit up like the men's room at Grand Central Station. Since the record was not in stock anymore, somebody bootlegged eighty thousand copies and sold them all in ten days. "Hanky Panky" was clearly number one in Pittsburgh along with Iron City suds and the promoter wanted Tommy there. "By that time the original group couldn't be found. I needed a band to do the TV lip-synchs and the local dates and I needed one fast. I went pub-hopping around Pittsburgh until I found the guys. They became the Shondells who were on all the records. We really had to scurry. We were playing catch-up baseball, but we did the whole thing and recut the record. It started to break out so I took it to New York and sold it to Roulette Records. That was the beginning."

So suddenly Tommy found himself in New York City. "Hanky Panky" went just about number one in the solar system only eight weeks after the Pittsburgh breakout, a song and a sound that Tommy hadn't been into in five years. It was going to take some work to create the follow-up. "When I look back, though, starting from an early age things always seemed to fall into place. One thing always seemed to be a stepping stone to another. I didn't know it then, but when I was thirteen I was getting an incredible education in a recording studio, and at the record store I got to know all the trade papers. If that hadn't happened I wouldn't have known what to do with 'Hanky Panky' when I was eighteen. I guess the man upstairs definitely had something in mind for me."

He came right out with "Say I Am," which went Top Five and had another on the way when he bumped into Bo Gentry and Rich Cordell, songwriters then with Kama-Sutra Records in New York. "By that time I had my own office at Roulette and was in charge of my own production because there was nobody else to do it and I was having a pretty hard time. They brought up this tune 'I Think We're Alone Now' and I flipped over it. It became our fourth single and fourth gold record in a row. Then we went into 'Mirage,' 'Getting Together,' and all the early hits that became sort of synonymous with bubblegum. Let me explain. In the meantime, while we were having all these hits, the 1910 Fruitgum Company scored with a sound that was in many ways a cross between a lot of my hits, a slightly perverted version of my early stuff. The term "bubblegum" came from their name, and since we sounded so much alike I got tagged with it immediately. People ask if applying the term to me is an insult; well no, God bless it, really. If that kind of music, if my earlier hits hadn't happened, the later ones wouldn't have. It was part of the process of what was becoming my sound."

1968 proved to be a watershed year and not just in terms of the evolution of Tommy's sound. He was twenty-one, he and the Shondells were one of the hottest singles acts anywhere, and the country was busier than a one-armed paper-hanger keeping chaos number one on the nightly news. Tommy couldn't ignore it and became involved in the efforts to put ourselves back together again. "I started out doing Robert Kennedy rallies. We did five for him. As a matter of fact I was supposed to play that·night in Los Angeles but we were already committed to playing in Dallas at one of the World Teen Fairs which were like preludes to the big rock festivals. So we did the gig and this young lady from a newspaper down there was chauffeuring me around, interviewing me, and I said that before she took me to the airport I'd like to see where John Kennedy was killed. We went and I really freaked out. I stood right on the spot until the police chased me away. I flew home that night just in time to turn on the television and hear Frank McGee on NBC say there's been a shooting at Kennedy headquarters. And there I had just been in Dallas saying how could it ever happen again. I flipped out. I went into a state of depression I didn't think I was going to come out of. We were all dreamers, you know, and Robert Kennedy was the dream."

About three or four days later, Hubert Humphrey's office called Tommy's secretary asking if Tommy would do rallies for him. "I was still really stunned by the shooting, but it was anything at that time to keep Richard Nixon out of the White House. And once we got to know Hubert Humphrey we really loved him. It's strange. Out of all the acts he could have called he called us. The call came out of the clear blue sky, but that's what pulled me out of the depression. We played at every rally of his but three. So there I was sitting with him the morning we found out we lost. Words can't describe it, what you feel when you've really got it, really part of something, a chance to do something about what was going on at that time, and then . . ."

Soon after, Tommy reimmersed himself in music and decided to change his sound and produce himself for the first time. The result was 'Crimson and Clover'. "Basically, it involved a combination of two things I've always liked, sound effects and simplicity. We had a lot of things to play with. One of the first places all the space program technology landed was in the recording studio and electronic media. So I used it, created a new sound, and the record became the biggest I had had to date. All over the world. I was even getting gold records from countries in Africa. It began a whole new trend of music for me. I always let other people tag on the names because they will anyway. They were calling it soft acid."

Whatever you want to call it, Tommy followed up with another string of hit singles including "Sweet Cherry Wine" and "Crystal Blue Persuasion." By 1970 Tommy James and the Shondells had done eighteen gold singles and four gold albums. Tommy had also written and produced a hit for Alive and Kickin' called "Tighter and Tighter." At the age of twenty-three, Tommy decided it was time for a break. "Five years of craziness had gotten to me. I was really blazed. If I wasn't writing, I was in the studio. If I wasn't in the studio, I was on the road. And if not that I was setting up some new project. Frankly, I just got so fatigued, mentally, and so spiritually drained, that I just said time out. I bought three thousand acres of land in upstate New York and went into semiretirement. The Shondells went their seperate ways. I couldn't expect them to hang around to see if I was ever going to do anything again."

Tommy spent about a year and a half trying to digest where he had been before setting out again. "So many crazy things went down in the late sixties, music, politics, Vietnam. And for us to be so hot at the time and have access to the media. It just took the wind right out of you to be successful in that industry at that time. We spent six months of our lives totally dedicated to the presidential campaign. Hubert Humphrey and I stayed in touch for years, almost right up until the end. As a matter of fact he wrote the liner notes for the *Crimson And Clover* album and said some really great things about us. It was good for all of us. That was really one of the more fascinating periods of my life.

"But just look at all the history that was going down at that time, and what was going on in the music industry. Nobody was dancing. If you had the audacity to put out an up-tempo tune then there was something wrong with you. Those were sad times for the country and for the industry as well. Even though a lot of records were being sold, people were in pretty bad shape mentally. There was just an unbelievable amount of drugs in the music industry. There still is, of course, but at that time we were all guinea pigs and many of my friends literally did not survive, blowing their brains out, and if not that, then just turning into total burn-outs. And personal friends too, not just in the business. I consider myself a survivor of the sixties. They left their mark on everybody, but being in the business too, with all that shit coming down, and getting through it alive, I consider that a feat in itself."

In late 1971, Tommy was ready to come back. He was a little wary, wondering how much he'd forgotten in terms of studio techniques and production, but he came right out with his first solo effort, "Draggin' the Line," which went gold. He followed that up in 1972 with "Comin' Home," his second solo effort that turned out to be his last gold record as of 1978. In 1973 Roulette Records became K-Tel and Adam 8. "They started making more money doing cut-outs, you know, 'Order now and we'll send you a blender plus every record ever done,' than they were doing legitimate stuff. So the rug was more or less pulled out from under me. I became more and more unhappy and in 1974 I left."

In 1975 he signed with MCA and put out a single. "It bombed. Never before had I done a record that didn't

make the charts. I realized I was with the wrong company. They were also doing Elton John and Olivia Newton-John, and I got lost in the shuffle. Probably should have changed my name to John. So I left. I signed with Fantasy Records out on the West Coast. I did two albums with them and they tried to break them on FM radio, which was kind of silly. I'm from the old school that says until there's a demand for an album, with very few exceptions you shouldn't put one out. Because if the first single bombs, the album bombs, and you've wasted six to eight months of your life.

"One thing that's really gratifying is that during this whole time I never stopped doing concerts. We've bridged literally two generations with our music. It's great to see the little chickies and their mommas all screaming to the same song. I'm thirty-one now. Everybody thinks I'm forty-five because I started so young. But one of the nicest things about the whole trip is that even though it ended so quickly when I left Roulette and people were saying, 'What happened?,' we've still got an almost-cult following."

Right now Tommy has something in store to expand that following. "Just recently we went into the studio and did what I should have done three years ago. We just sat down and wrote singles the way we used to, Top Forty AM-oriented stuff. And while we were still excited we went right in and recorded them, as singles, not albums. We have a number of big labels interested. I don't think I've ever been as mentally, physically, or spiritually prepared as I am now, having the chance to do my own thing really for the first time in my life and utilize all the experience under my belt. Instead of playing catch-up baseball, I plan to be three or four runs ahead. And soon. We should have something out by the spring of 1979."

If that's not enough to keep him humming, Tommy is also going to be shooting a movie within the next year. "In 1977 I produced my own television commercial for an album of Tommy James and the Shondells' early hits for Adam 8. That thing went double platinum. The commercial was seen by some people in Montreal who are producing a TV movie called *On Camera*. They got in touch with me and I may have the lead. It could be a real milestone for me or it could be nothing. But there are a lot of things left I want to do, act, direct motion pictures, and, of course, in music, always my first love. All these things seem to be coming to a head now and I have a feeling that in the next year a lot of things are going to happen. I've only finished half my career. It was cut short for a lot of reasons. It would be a shame to waste all that time and experience. I'm just now beginning to appreciate everything that's happened. When it was happening it was like I was watching someone else's movie."

Gary "U.S." Bonds

Ike Eisenhower was motoring into his second term in a golf cart, Don Larsen was telling Bob Hope and the rest of us on prime time about throwing a perfect game, and a bunch of guys who called themselves the Turks were singing rock 'n' roll on a street corner in Norfolk, Virginia. Gary Anderson sang lead.

He was born June 6, 1939, in Jacksonville, Florida. The Andersons moved to Norfolk soon after. "When I was a teenager I really didn't know what I wanted to do. I never dreamed I'd be in music. I was momma's boy, that whole bit. The family had a little bread so I figured I'd just always stay with them. Anyway, that was her suggestion. She didn't want me to work, just sit there, you're my boy. Sounded okay to me. But I guess I always was pretty creative and that probably would have come out somehow."

It did. "We started singing in front of the market down the street from my house, just neighborhood friends, rambling around, rock 'n' roll. And singing acappella too, that was the only way to go. We sang everything, the Spaniels, the Turbans, the Coasters, the Cadillacs, the Drifters, Bo Diddley, you name it. One day this guy named Frank Guida comes up and says he's going to get a recording studio together and would I like to record for him. I said sure, why not, nothing else to do. But then I didn't hear from him. After awhile I broke up with the Turks. What did they go on to do? Time. At least I heard one went to jail for something. Some of them went in the service. Then I started singing lead in a rock 'n' roll band called the Sleepy King Band. Sleepy was the piano player. We played a lot of little joints around Norfolk, all those

Navy dudes from the base hanging out."

From there Gary went on to do a short stint in a local jazz band. By the time 1960 rolled around, Frank Guida had gotten his studio together and had his own label, Legrand Records. Gary returned to rock 'n' roll. "I went in with a group called Daddy G and the Chess Street Five and recorded a song called 'New Orleans' that was written by Joe Royster. But the next thing I knew the record was out and Guida had put his name on it. He put his name on all the records but he didn't do anything. Those guys were all good for doing that in those days. If they could write their name they put it on the record."

Gary also found out he wasn't Gary Anderson anymore. "It was Frank who stuck that 'U.S. Bonds' in there, without my knowledge. The record came out and there it was. I didn't feel too good about it. At the time it just didn't sound right. I'm still not sure it does."

Nevertheless, "New Orleans" was a hit in the fall of 1960. Gary followed up with a little-known single called "Not Me." "It was banned. The lyrics went 'Come over, baby, let's have some fun,' and somebody decided that was a no-no. The Orlons recorded it later on and I understand they had a hit with it."

In the meantime, Daddy G had recorded a single, "A Night with Daddy G," but it wasn't getting much response. "We were all in the studio one day, a bunch of friends, Daddy G, and the band, just sitting around drinking, having fun, and Daddy G says why don't you put some words to that damn thing and see what happens. So I went into another room and wrote down some words. Called it 'Quarter to Three.' We played it, taped it, and that was it. It sounded like hell but the next thing I knew it was out. It still sounded like hell."

A choice theory about the Bonds sound and in particular "Quarter to Three" comes from the "Rock Gallery" section of *The Rolling Stone History of Rock & Roll*. "Rumors had it Guida recorded Bonds in an open field next to an airport runway while planes took off—and given the blizzard of white noise that accompanied Gary's

hits, the story was quite credible."

As Gary tells the story, "Everybody was a little bit lit when we did it. It came out from fun. Maybe that's why it sold. There's the whole secret. You just get loaded."

Whatever the hook was, "Quarter to Three" was number one in the country in the summer of 1961. Oddly enough, it was only then that Gary went on tour. "You see, when people first heard my records, they hadn't seen me and they thought I was a white act. And during that time, if you were a black act, no matter what you did, you were labeled rhythm and blues. Even if you sounded like Johnny Cash and did Johnny Cash songs, you were rhythm and blues if you were black. And rhythm and blues was a small market. When we came out with 'New Orleans' it went right into the pop market, basically because from our sound people thought we were a white act. You can sell a lot more records in the pop market so the record company didn't want me out there. But when 'Quarter to Three' came out it was just too big, so they said okay, what the hell, here he is. So we'd go to play a club or a theater and all the people thought they were coming to see a white act. Man, were they surprised when I walked out. But it was cool once we started playing. Everybody has their little idiosyncrasies about what you are and what you do and what you don't do. Once you come out and show them what you're doing, it's okay, all's forgotten."

Gary started out doing theaters. Daddy G and the band, who backed Gary on most of his records, went out with him for awhile. "But they were older than I was, twice my age, so they couldn't hack it too good." Eventually Gary just carried Daddy G on sax and a drummer.

Their first gig was the Howard Theater in Washington, D.C., followed by the Royal in Baltimore, the Regal in Chicago, and the Apollo in New York among others. Dick Clark finally got a hold of him too, for the Caravan of Stars road show. "That was just plain fun. Of course I was much younger then and could go out forty days on the bus. When you're young you can take it. And Dick, he was cool. Most of us along on the tour had just gotten into the business. We didn't know anything about it and were just happy to get away, traveling and making some money. When I think back on that it gets a little foggy because, man, we'd get on that bus and everybody would have a case of beer. By the time we hit the Lincoln Tunnel it was all over. But I do remember Bo Diddley cooking chicken on the bus. He was always cooking. Bo could cook a chicken in a minute anywhere. He had one of those portable gas things and all sorts of other stuff he was always carrying with him. And then there was Ronnie Evans, the emcee guy for the Shirelles. That's my buddy, man. He's a nut, the funniest cat in the world. Between him and Bo, and the Coasters and the Drifters (Man, those guys!) you could really have a ball."

After "Quarter to Three" he and Daddy G wrote "School Is Out," then "School Is In." Both did well. Then he came out with "Dear Lady Twist," "an old song from the islands," which became a smash. "And that was about it, I guess. After that the bottom more or less fell out. We exhausted just about all the front music we could get out of that type of sound. It was time for a switch but the record company couldn't see it. They wanted us to keep doing the same old thing. And we did, bomb after bomb after bomb. The company just wouldn't listen to what we were trying to tell them. Then some time around the middle or late sixties I finally got a chance to get away from them. We ran into some hassles with that so I just cooled it on the recording end for awhile."

Gary stayed on the road almost continuously until the end of the sixties, playing rock 'n' roll shows, clubs, and colleges. "We played all the colleges. That was great. Hell, those kids didn't care; they were just glad to have you there. As soon as you walked in it was this way to the beer barrel and drink out of our tub here. I'd use house bands then. Just show up and they'd have a band and the beer ready. We'd rehearse for an hour or two, things we all knew, and then go out and do it, the 'Quarter to Threes,' your 'Knock on Woods,' your 'Midnight Hours,' throw in a little Sam & Dave and they loved it."

But Gary had never stopped writing and by the early seventies he was getting into the production end of the business too. He wrote a number of songs that were hits for other artists in the pop field, rhythm and blues and country and western. For example, "It was around 1972 and I did a country thing with Johnny Paycheck [of "Take This Job and Shove It" fame] called 'Friend Don't Take Her She's All I've Got.' It was nominated for a Grammy. It was selling in the rhythm and blues market too. Everybody was recording that doggone thing."

Since then Gary has been involved in all phases of the business. About six years ago he put together a band and has been touring every year. He's still writing and it looks like before long we'll have Gary "U.S." Bonds on vinyl again. "We're in the process of recording right now. We'll see what happens. Hopefully we will have a record out. Musically, we're doing a lot of different things, a little disco, some ballads, but not really any rock 'n' roll. I'm a little reluctant to get back into the rock scene. It's different from when I was having hits. In my day rock was less complicated, just straight on. I've done a few of the rock revivals shows, the Rich Nader things, but it's tough doing the oldies. You get that stigma on you. Gary Bonds? Oh yeah, 'Quarter to Three.' I hear a lot of the cats talking about how it's coming back, but I think they're dreaming. Probably because they miss it. But things change and you have to change with the times. You have to be capable of facing what's happening now and that's what I'm trying to do. I go out now and my show is a production thing, regular Las Vegas, nice suit, shine your shoes and sing pretty songs. Of course I'll do my old hits because the people want to hear them. But I show them what else I do too. Whether they like it or not, here it is. I'm optimistic about the record we're doing now. I hadn't been in the studio for awhile and I missed it. And I love the writing and the production stuff. But to actually record again is good, good for the head, settle the ego a bit, and if it does well, then great. So I'm hopeful."

Gary has been living on Long Island for about five years with his wife of sixteen years, Laurie, and his fourteen-year-old daughter also named Laurie. His wife currently sings background vocals with the band Gary takes on the road. His daughter plays drums in the school band, sings, plays the keyboards, and is a member of an award-winning dance troupe. "It looks like she's got the bug too. But I don't give her any advice. She says she's going to do it and doesn't want to know from nothing. I can understand that. It's good. She's young yet and she'll work it out for herself."

As Gary looks ahead to another stage in a career that has already spanned twenty years, he looks back with pride on his accomplishments and an uncommon understanding of what the business is all about. "I don't regret my career at all. I take things in stride. It happened and it was good. I got a chance to get around, meet a lot of people, and be creative. Whatever I've tackled it's usually been with pretty good success. And it didn't bother me that I wasn't on top forever. One good thing was that when all the guys in the original band and I parted it was on good terms. We're still friends and I see them all the time. I've never had a problem with people because I never screwed anybody. I was the one to get screwed but I'm not bitter about it. You can't be, man. It's life so what are you going to do about it, right?

"I guess I'm pretty much the same as I was then, a nut, going my own way, having my own fun. I always liked simple things, never got into the heavy stuff. Never cared about my status or anybody else's, still don't. I still like to hang out on the corner. It's no fun downtown, acting phony, saying certain things at certain times to keep people happy. Whereas I sit right down at the corner, say what I want, and the hell with it. I like that."

Johnny Maestro

Alan Freed, the son of a Russian mother and a Welsh-Jewish father, was the most vociferous advocate of rock and roll. He claimed to have coined the term to eliminate the racial stigma attached to R&B. Freed burst onto the New York airwaves in 1954 for WINS radio, where he played the best of R&B. Staging shows at the Brooklyn Paramount, Freed would skate across the stage in his outrageous sportscoat shouting, "Go, man, go!" (Later in December 1962, Freed became the only DJ subpoened and convicted in the payola scandal. In 1965, suffering from uremia, poor, and unemployed, he died a broken man at the young age of forty-three.) His shows and concerts revolutionized the music industry, influencing many white kids on the stoops and street corners to stop crooning and start harmonizing to the new rock beat. One of those kids was Johnny Mastrangelo, first of the Crests and later of the Brooklyn Bridge.

Born on May 7, 1939, Johnny Maestro was raised on the lower East Side of Manhattan on a street which no longer exists. Listening to Frankie Laine, Johnnie Ray, and the harmonizing sounds of the Moonglows at an early age, Johnny was inspired to become the only musical talent in his typically Italian family. Hanging around the park bench near the Alfred E. Smith housing project, Johnny sang with friends, eventually pulling down small jobs at local settlement house dances. There was a group with Tommy Gough, Jay Carter, and Harold Torres, who thought they might be something. Needing a lead singer, they snagged Johnny and became the Crests. The Crests went on to become the subject of street legends and myths across the Italian neighborhoods around the Bronx, northern New

Jersey, New York City, and Long Island. If you were hip, you knew a friend who knew a friend who had a distant relative who was a second cousin of one of the group's fathers. That was status.

The group's big break came in the same legendary way. A mysterious woman heard their reverberating echo in a Lexington Avenue IRT station and slipped them the business card of a local bandleader who might help them get out of the subway and onto the stage. Johnny recalled, "Everyone wanted to find a place where they could get a lot of echo. We went into bathrooms, the hallway in the project, or down in the subways to find a nice echo. That's when someone gave us a card with the band leader Al Brown's name on it. We went to him first to sing and he sent us to Joyce Records. They liked us. At his office, Al Brown asked the name of the group. So, someone, I forget who, said the Crests. So that's what we became."

Johnny Mastrangelo changed his name to Johnny Maestro and proceeded to cut two records with the Crests. They went nowhere. Joyce Records soon folded its tents and disappeared. A songwriter, Billy Don Smith, shunted them over to George Paxton, who owned Coed Records, a young firm without artists or records. They cut "Pretty Little Angel," which instantly became jukebox material in the New York area and secured the group a couple of appearances on Alan Freed's television show.

Before the Freed shows, the Crests got their baptism by show business fire with two appearances in Connecticut. In those days, the Crests looked like four head waiters in their waist coats and frilly formal shirts. "When we had 'Pretty Little Angel,' we did our first television show in Connecticut. It was a completely new experience for all of us. It was live but all you did was lip-synch the records. You couldn't make a mistake musically, but I couldn't tell you how nervous we all were. Between the shaking and the sweating, I guess we got through it all right.

"Our first real professional performance was at a theater in Hartford. We were performing with all the people we used to listen to—the Moonglows, the Flamingoes, and Little Anthony and the Imperials. They were a monster act back then with all the choreography. They were very polished and professional. We were just a street corner group. We got through it."

After recording "Beside You" and "Sweetest One," the Crests were handed a number from Paxton's large catalog of songs scarfted off the streets of New York from hundreds of hungry, hustling, would-be songwriters. In November 1958, Coed Records released "16 Candles," an almost-instant million-seller. From that point, the Crests winged the vinyl out in rapid succession, socking to the audience such hits as "Six Nights a Week," "Flower of Love," "The Angels Listened In," "Step by Step," "Trouble in Paradise," and "Journey of Love." "Isn't It Amazing," released in 1960, closed down the Crests' amazingly abbreviated but compressed career.

"I just enjoyed singing. Singing was an accomplishment for me. To sing with a group was an accomplishment. It happened so fast that we didn't get a chance to think about it. We knew that the record '16 Candles' was being played on the radio and it started to climb up the charts. We started doing promotion on television and going out of town to Connecticut and Philadelphia. We did Dick Clark's 'Saturday Night Show.' Once the record hit the Top Forty, we went around the country almost every day of the year. We'd do a three-month tour, then be off two weeks, then hit the road again on bus tours playing arenas and civic centers. It was a new way of life. But, once it started, it was natural. It seemed like that was the way it was supposed to be."

However, not all was such smooth sailing. In his book, *Rock, Roll & Remember*, Dick Clark recalls one time when the Crests committed a cardinal show biz *faux pas*. They were scheduled to appear on Dick Clark's live evening show to lip-synch "16 Candles" in the decidedly hokey set of a rowboat floating in an artificial, shimmering sea. Clark remembers that the rehearsal went well. That evening Dick Clark was in his position in the balcony, when he turned with outstretched hand to introduce the Crests.

Johnny Maestro (center) and the Brooklyn Bridge.

Picking up the cue, the camera zoomed down onto the stage and focused on an empty rowboat as the song came on. The Crests had long gone home, thinking that the dress rehearsal was the show.

The Crests continued the grueling, cross-country tours, playing with house bands wherever they went. In 1961, it ended as did their hits. Johnny went solo and recorded such Top Forty hits as "Model Girl," "What a Surprise," and "Mr. Happiness." Changing labels, groups, and acts for a few years, Johnny found that nothing was happening to his liking. The venue became one-nighters at the Royal Canadian and the Copa. The audience was there but the house bands weren't. Their knowledge was strictly limited to supper club material like "Walking My Baby Back Home." They were in the dark as far as Johnny's rock and roll career was concerned.

"My new manager booked me into these clubs. I went to the lounges in Wildwood. But he didn't tell me what I would have to do, or how to prepare for it. I had a whole bunch of rock and roll songs which I sang. But it wasn't the type of thing you'd do there. Coming from a rock and roll group into the lounge was a tremendous change. Eventually I watched other people and listened to the songs they were doing. Gradually I changed and tried it for a couple of years. But I didn't feel like I fit."

After switching bands two or three times, Johnny ran across the Del Satins, sometime backup vocalists for Dion, who were also stuck into the club circuit. Johnny liked their polished performance, intricate choreography, and tight harmonizing, but passed on the trio's invite to become lead singer in '65. The next year, he relented and joined them for a year, touring until he convinced them to split up the money pie and hire a whole backup band.

Their manager then contrived a Battle of the Bands concert on Long Island, which was simply a gigantic tryout for the Del Satins. A strong instrumental group with a brass section won their hearts with a unique sound which became the forerunner of the popular horn arrangements of Chicago and Blood, Sweat, and Tears. The band was called the Rhythm Method. "Good Catholic group," says Johnny. The union of the two groups created the Brooklyn Bridge.

While Johnny had continued recording since the Crests' breakup in 1961, it wasn't until late 1967 that he struck gold again with "The Worst That Can Happen." From 1967 through 1970, the Brooklyn Bridge recorded four albums, the least-known and most interesting of which was *The Bridge In Blue*, a platter of Loudon Wainwright songs. With the Bridge, Johnny reemerged on the major television shows like "Ed Sullivan," "Mike Douglas," "Jonathan Winters," "Della Reese," and "The Hollywood Palace." Starting as a regional success in the New York and New Jersey area, they opened two-act shows with the Four Tops and Beach Boys pulling top bill. Finally, after their gold singles and albums, they started up their own tours, taking as many as fifteen people on the road to the old haunts of the Crests.

But after 1970, the Bridge was torpedoed by frequent conflicts with their recording company and soon ceased all recording. Johnny, his wife Alma, and his three kids, Lisa, Tracy, and Brad, moved from their Staten Island home to East Islip, Long Island. The group pared down to Johnny, Fred Ferrara, and Les Cauchi of the Del Satins and a guitarist and bass player. When not boating in Long Island Sound, Johnny ducks into his studio at his home to lay down a few tracks. It's been two years since Johnny came off the road to concentrate on concert dates in New York area clubs, shopping malls, weddings, social affairs, and, of course, rock and roll revivals.

"It makes me feel good that I span two decades and can play that music. Of course, I'm getting older and looking to sustain myself with some secure thing. I'm still involved in playing. It's something I can do until I'm fifty. I'm enjoying myself now that I've stopped going on the road. We've all branched out into something else to make sure we have something in case we fall on our faces. But it doesn't look like it will happen soon. I realize that music will be here forever and as long as I can still do it, I'll be working."

Tommy Sands

"I don't look back with any bitterness at all. I try to be as honest as I can about myself when I do look back. There were some unfulfilled dreams. The direction my career has gone is a little different than I might have wished. But a lot of things that happened to me were beyond my wildest expectations. If I hadn't done some of the things that, in retrospect, I may wish I hadn't done or wish I had done differently, I wouldn't have been able to care for my family over the years or have been able to come back when I finally thought that I had rested long enough. If I hadn't had the television exposure which I might have wanted to change, I wouldn't have been able to come back. It's not many men who can leave a career for ten years and suddenly find that the door is still open and jump right back into it. I'm fortunate that those things I did for the first five years made a lasting impression."

Tommy Sands was a genuine teen idol, a young adolescent star known as much for his public image as his music. Starting with Ted Lewis's and Tennessee Ernie Ford's television shows in the fifties, Tommy paraded across the screen in numerous variety shows and teen-oriented films. His marriage in 1959 to Frank Sinatra's daughter Nancy further cemented his position as a teen star. But his image obscured his central position in the musical cyclone which whipped over the dreary, rolling scrublands of Texas in the early and mid-fifties and into musical history.

Tommy's roots are found in the countless dance halls, "fightin' and dancin'" clubs, and saloons which dot the Texan prairie landscape like oases in the Sahara. In the South of high school football, fundamentalist Baptists, dirt farms, oil and gas fields, county fairs, and truck stops, a group of musicians played something called rockabilly or rocking country, a music not quite country and western and not quite rhythm and blues. They filled the joints on Saturday night, when the "good ole boys" piled into parking lots with their pickups. A weary work week gave way to an orgiastic outburst of energy and celebration. The crashing cases of Dr. Pepper, Coke, and Sprite stacked outside with the rest of the returnables were drowned out by the string of musicians alternating turns at whipping up the crowd.

From 1952 until 1956, Tommy Sands, a transplanted Chicagoan, reached for his guitar to play country-western ballads for these crowds. Among those he toured with was a lone cowboy named Roy Orbison, dressed sinisterly in black. His eyes camouflaged by ever-present sunglasses, his hair in a pompadour framing his pale face, Orbison would mount the stage and sing "Only the Lonely." Johnny Cash sandpapered his way through "I Heard That Lonesome Whistle" or Carl Perkins sent the people stomping to "Blue Suede Shoes." A Louisiana boy, Jerry Lee Lewis, attacked the keyboards with his fists, feet, elbows, and any other part of his body which could defy gravity. Later, after Tommy had completed his sets, he would exit for an older fellow musician named Elvis Presley, who crooned "Blue Moon" and sent the locals dancing to "Heartbreak Hotel."

Born in Chicago in 1940, Tommy spent the first twelve years of his life living in Chicago and just outside Shrevesport, Louisiana. "My father was a pianist who played popular music and classical. He doesn't play professionally anymore but he still writes songs. When father was playing on the road, maybe seven or eight months of the year, I was living with mother and mother's relatives on a little farm outside Shrevesport. When he was not on the road, we lived in Chicago. This was every year for about twelve years until they were divorced. Then mother and I moved to Houston.

"I picked up the guitar at the age of five. I played at piano, drums, various string instruments like the banjo and mandolin; then I settled on the guitar. I was a very aggressive little kid. I used to sneak away, grab streetcars, and go audition for shows. I used to do that everywhere we went. I had the ambition early. I don't think a little kid thinks too much about where it would lead. I just enjoyed doing it. But, maybe, I was looking for wide, mass acceptance because I was alone most of the time. My only brother, who's eleven years older, was in World War II and pretty much out of the house by the time I was five. I was writing songs about the age of eight.

"The first job I ever got was on a radio show, a noontime country and western show that starred Pop Echols. Pop gave me my first job. It was a Saturday, the day I made the last payment on my guitar. I was ten. Once a month on a Saturday, we used to go into town on a bus and my mother would give me money. Once I made the last payment, I could finally take the guitar out and audition. I got my guitar, auditioned, and got the job.

"By the time Mom and Pop divorced and we moved to Houston, working wasn't just fun anymore. It was important economically, so I worked as much as I could and mother was glad. Every town we would go to I tried to get a job as soon as I could and as often as I could. Nina Vance, a director, was looking for a new little boy to star in an original play called *David Westheimer*. In Houston, there weren't a lot of kids acting at the age of twelve. She saw me on a TV show. So I auditioned and got the job. That's how I started acting, but I didn't do much more with it until Colonel Parker got me my first break with *The Singing Idol*.

"I worked with Colonel Parker from the age of twelve until sixteen. He saw me when I was working in a tavern in Houston. For about three years, he managed me and used to take me on the road every summer with Eddy Arnold and his other clients. Playing taverns and touring at that age was incredible because, we didn't know it, we were part of a group that was really going to pave the way musically over the next twenty years. There were Johnny Cash, Elvis, myself, Roy Orbison, Jerry Lee Lewis, Carl Perkins,

Scotty Moore, and Bill Black. I was pretty much younger than the rest of them. We were all working the same taverns, the same schools in Texas, and the Miss Teen Contest in Louisiana. We all met on Saturday nights at the Louisiana Hayride in Shrevesport, which was the main nerve center for all people who were uncategorized, neither country and western nor rhythm and blues.

"The first time I worked with Elvis was incredible. It was New Year's Eve 1954 in Texas, about a year and half before he hit it big. I then started working separately with Elvis down in Houston and on tours in the South. He influenced me very heavily. But about that time the Colonel and I were separating because nothing was happening to me. I guess I was too young. I recorded a couple of country and western songs I wrote for RCA Victor but none of them sold. I began telling Colonel Parker about Elvis. Finally, I guess, I whetted his appetite and he went and saw Elvis and signed him up. Probably, there were others talking to him about Elvis but we were talking almost daily about him. I was telling him I had never seen anything like him. The rest is history.

"I was briefly a disc jockey because I wasn't doing well in the South and needed the money to follow Elvis and my idol, James Dean, out to California. At this time, age fifteen, I worked for a few months, saved some money, and took off. I was out in California for a few months, playing a few little jobs, and had a few guest appearances on Ernie Ford's daytime show. But nothing happened and I was going to join the Army. I had already gone down and had the examinations for the Army when Colonel Parker called me. I hadn't seen him for a couple of years between the time he signed Elvis and Elvis became an international star. NBC had a deal with Parker to write a story that would parallel Elvis's life but by the time the script was completed Elvis was too hot. So they went through a lot of auditions, but it was pretty hard to find anybody at that time like Elvis. He was so unique. Colonel Parker remembered me and sent me the money to fly to New York to audition for *The Singing Idol*."

In January 1957, Tommy was propelled to stardom as the singing sensation on NBC's Kraft Theater presentation of *The Singing Idol*. In the show he sang two songs called "Hep Dee Hootie" and "Teenage Crush," the latter becoming his first hit. Later the same year, he recorded for Capitol Records "Ring-a-Ding-a-Ding" and "Goin' Steady." The only song penned by Tommy which became a hit was "Sing, Boy, Sing." The song came from the title track of the film score which Tommy and Rod McKuen wrote together. It was the first film for both of them. The album did well and was followed by such tunes as "Blue Ribbon Baby," "The Worryin' Kind," "I'll Be Seeing You," and "The Old Oaken Bucket."

Tommy had about four good years recording before he hit the downward spiral in his career at the age of twenty. The public image created by his appearances on variety shows led to the erosion of his following among fans who remembered him as part of the rockabilly scene.

"I never really had the career I think I might have if I had been a little older and a little wiser about my choices as far as work went. I was really a little too young to know what was happening and how to handle it myself. I really wanted to do much less of the variety shows and more of the serious dramatic work. The variety shows were really silly, where you did nonsensical skits. But it was the thing for a hit record artist to go on a variety show and act like a nut in some comedy skit he wasn't really prepared to do. I certainly was too naive to know how to handle that stuff. This led to a certain lack of consistency or credibility as far as the image I had already projected to the people who were buying my records. They had one image of me from the beginning which was an accurate one. I wanted them to believe I was as I saw myself—in the role of the singing idol. I couldn't have been handpicked better considering the type of person I am or was. It was the role everybody bought and then I followed it with all these roles which were at 360-degree angles from that. I'm sure it blew a lot of my fans away. They probably thought, 'Well, who the hell is this guy?' By that time, I was already on the downward spiral.

"I met Nancy Sinatra when I was nineteen. We got married that same year. I think my career was already going down at that point. Nancy was only sixteen when she came backstage at one of my concerts. She had just turned seventeen and didn't have a career when we were married. Frank Sinatra was kind of a vague name to me. I really didn't know what he did when I met Nancy. Being from the world I came from, you didn't listen to him a lot or Perry Como or Tony Bennett. I didn't know much about those people so I was too naive to idolize any of them then.

"I'm in the process of divorce again. I think this is about it for me and marriage. But it's been a good relationship this time. I can say I genuinely loved both ladies I married and I'm still very close to them. But I think the traveling and the touring has a lot to do with it. I'm on the road practically fifty weeks a year and was doing the same thing when I was married to Nancy."

The marriage to Nancy lingered five or six years until it dissolved along with Tommy's career in 1964. The much-heralded British invasion coupled with a rocky marriage sent Tommy Sands into a self-imposed exile on the islands of Hawaii. As Tommy vanished from sight, Nancy, after five years of trying to make the charts with a sweet singing style, acquired a growly, gutsy voice and climbed the hit parade with "Boots" in 1966.

For eleven years from 1964 until 1975, Tommy was first a beach bum, then a college student at the University of Hawaii. "I did all the great things that I never had a chance to do. For two years, I just hung around the beaches and climbed all the mountains. In 1966, I played Vegas for a month to pick up some money and then headed back to Hawaii. I wasn't sure what I was going to do with the rest of my life. I decided to go the University of Hawaii. I didn't start until 1970. I studied English because I had dabbled in writing ever since Rod McKuen and I had worked together on poems, songs, and a couple of screenplays. The notoriety didn't last very long. The other students were involved in themselves and after they had seen me for a few days, it was over. I was there every day and it became commonplace to have me around. The end result of school was that I had a great time. I graduated in 1975."

Another marriage, a constant trickle of offers to return to the music business, and enough rest started Tommy itching for a comeback. "When 'Happy Days,' Grease, and 'Sha-Na-Na' happened, I started getting hot offers. I was beginning to feel reenergized. When the offers really started pouring in, I had to look at it seriously. It was becoming an economic mandate. I went back on the road as a solo act playing clubs all over the country. I started out hiring a few girl singers, a conductor, and before I knew it a whole band. I do a lot of stuff that I always had done. I started out doing gospel as a kid in church, then went country, then rock, then to more traditional ballads. I now do a little of each throughout my show, plus a little acting,

a little mime, a little Charlie Chaplin thrown in.'' From his self-imposed exile, Tommy has returned to a full touring schedule, appearances in a number of made-for-TV movies, and a part with Fabian and Troy Donahue in the feature film *Avalanche*. Now he plays Reno and Lake Tahoe twice a year and after a twelve-year absence will be headlining at Caesar's Palace in Vegas.

Over a thirty-year career from the little farm outside Shrevesport through the barnstorming days in Texas to years wandering over the lush Hawaiian Islands and his return to show business, Tommy cites as the high of his life the morning his daughter Jessica was born two years ago. ''I waited a long time for that.''

Dion

In a rented house near the ocean, Dion lays down tracks with his band for a rock and roll album titled *Life Song*, a musical odyssey from his Bronx origins to the present. When he's not cooking up another exploration into his own psyche, he dashes down to the beach and paddles around in the pool with his daughters, Tane, Lark, and August. For the past eleven years, Dion DiMucci and his wife Susan have lived in Miami. After last year's "The Return of the Wanderer" (remember the 1961 "Wanderer," the lad renowned for his sexual escapades and his brutal dumping of chicks?), he has put together the first band of his twenty-one years of recording. Dion seems bent on remaining an enigma, plotting a career defying categorization or popular definition. His music and career have taken so many turns into dead-end alleys, open roads, and abrupt halts, that when you have a fix on the man, he skates off out of range and disappears behind the horizon.

He started his career as the fine tenor of Dion and the Belmonts and followed that stint with a solo career in the early sixties with the Del Satins as backup. After a brief return to the Belmonts from a fading solo career, Dion stopped dead in his tracks and vanished from the scene only to startle the public with his late sixties comeback as an acoustic guitar player and singer with "Abraham, Martin, and John" and the antidrug song based on his own experience, "Your Own Back Yard." Then, poof, Dion was gone again to recharge his batteries. Now the last three years find him at his most prolific and creative in over a decade.

"My past is a part of me. I know the last album, *Return Of The Wanderer*, was a conscious attempt to bridge the past and the present and bring it together for the people who stayed with me over the years through the many changes of music and styles. I know it's a problem because people tend to compartmentalize you. I'm not saying I have it made but I don't look at that past thing. It works for me, as you can see, and it works against me.

"When the new album comes out, and it's bitching, cooking, and full of life, some people will tend to say, 'Oh wow, he's an oldie, isn't he? But some people will give you the benefit of the doubt that he's alive, well, and living in the now. I feel fortunate that I'm still around and I'm very grateful just to be here doing what I'm doing. At one time of my life, I had mastered negative thinking and I didn't know why until I broke through that. I'll tell you the last twelve years have been the happiest of my life. Hey man, I got nothing to complain about."

Dion was born on July 18, 1939, in the Bronx. His father was a vaudevillian, a manipulator of marionettes, who played Radio City Music Hall, the Roxy, and the Palace in the Donald O'Connor and Gene Kelly days. "When he got out in the late fifties, that's when I got in." At the age of eleven, Dion made his professional debut on the Paul Whiteman radio show in New York. But it wasn't until he was seventeen that Dion broke into the recording industry and formed the Belmonts from a group of street corner singers out of Roosevelt High School in the Bronx, who hung around Belmont Avenue, Garden Street, and Prospect Avenue.

"I had gotten a contract through a friend who knew a friend who knew a friend who knew a friend who had started a record company. They said, 'I know a kid who sings' and brought me down there and they liked what I did. It was when rock and roll was in its infancy. This company tried to hook me up with some studio singers, 'Boop, Boop, Boop, Boop' stuff. They were these fifty-five-to-sixty-year-old types who were working the Four Aces style. I said, 'Wait a minute. You want to hear something. You wait right here. I'll be back Thursday.'

"I went back to my neighborhood. There were little

gathering places in the Bronx in the different neighborhoods. I got the best street corner singers. There were guys who were jocks and there were certain guys who would hang on the jukebox, literally hugged it all day, hung on it, and harmonized with every record. There was Freddie Milano from Mapes Avenue. So was Carlos Mastrangelo. Those guys were like Robert and Johnny. Angelo D'Aleo was from Tremont. I knew him because anyone who ever heard him sing knew. He always stood out. He had an exceptional tenor voice. I gathered these guys and we put together 'I Wonder Why' and went downtown. That was the start. We were the best street corner singers in the Bronx. I know it, man."

From their first hit, "I Wonder Why," in 1958, the Belmonts continued with "No One Knows," "Don't Pity Me," the Doc Pomus and Mort Shuman song, "A Teenager in Love," and their monster version of Rodgers and Hart's classic, "Where or When." In 1959, Angelo joined the Navy. Throughout their two and a half years together, Dion and the Belmonts became famous for their flair for arrangements on their records.

But Dion remembers their stage act as something less than spectacular. "We weren't a very visual act. We didn't do splits and steps because we were too damn lazy. But we sang our asses off. We were very creative on record and that's where we put our energy. There was a group around called the Mellow Kings and they could do splits. I loved to watch them but I couldn't do that. I had two left feet. I couldn't get the Belmonts to move. To tell you the truth, I can move pretty good. I like to move but I couldn't get them up in the morning to rehearse. Are you kidding? All they wanted to do was snap their fingers. That was cool enough. That's what they did. Everybody did what they wanted to. So we went out as a record act and did "I Wonder Why," "Teenager in Love," some things from our album *Where or When*, and then picked up some instruments and did an instrumental. Besides, in those days, you ran on for three numbers and left. Yeah, what act?"

Bobby Darin, who was older than Dion and the Bel-

Courtesy CBS Records

monts, was making a big splash and became a good friend
of Dion. "He was from East Harlem, down further from us.
He was a damn good friend. I did my first tour with him.
We ate, slept, and lived together for six weeks. He was
truly an inspiration in my life because there are people
who are damn healthy who don't do much more than sit
around and complain. He lived longer than he expected
to. He expected to die in his twenties because he had a
rheumatic heart. Here's a guy who had a bad hand dealt to
him and he made the best of it." After a mercurial career,
a reputation for arrogance and intense narcissism, Bobby
Darin became withdrawn in the mid-sixties, emerging
from seclusion to play an antiwar act, a dramatic change
from his Sinatra-style nightclub routine. Then in 1973, he
underwent seven hours of surgery for a rare heart disease
and died on the hospital table at the age of thirty-seven.

In 1960, after recording the standards, "When You Wish Upon a Star" and "In the Still of the Night," Dion went solo, leaving the Belmonts in good shape to continue without him. In the mid-sixties, they briefly got back together on a few albums which bombed miserably. Later, in 1972, Dion made one appearance at a revival show with the Belmonts. "We got together to share some memories but it was no kind of career move. It was just to get together and share some memories with old friends. I had to move on and stay in the now because I didn't want to go back." The Belmonts did go back to record the same year an acappella album, *Cigars, Acappella, Candy,* which proved that the kids from the white urban ghetto hadn't forgotten the streets after all those years.

Dion's solo flight got off to an auspicious start with "Lonely Teenager" and then in the fall of 1961 with his number one tune "Runaround Sue," which he wrote with Ernie Maresca of "Shout, Shout, Knock Yourself Out" fame, about a girl Dion later decided to marry. After "I Was Born to Cry," Dion's records grew erratic, suggesting his mind was elsewhere when he was in the studio. In 1963, he appeared to be playing out a string with "Be Careful," "Donna the Prima Donna," and "Drip Drop." His 1964 production of "Johnny B. Goode" suggested that, even though his act wasn't quite together, he was making a beeline back to the roots.

Dion then made a conscious decision to stop, regroup, and disappear into Bronx clubs where he experimented with blues-based material.

"I was in a bleak period of my life in the mid-sixties. I was searching for me. Everyone goes through that and the mid-sixties was the time for me. Thank God, I landed on my feet. I don't think I could have gone on without that breaking-through and growing. For me there's a joy in growing. I'd rather pack it in than not be growing. There were, of course, those unfortunates who, maybe, were born that way. I can't say I got through it because I was any brighter. It could have been me. Many times with too much of this or that. It was a matter of getting tapped on the shoulder. It was a "There but for the Grace of God" type of thing.

"A lot of people thought the British thing [the Beatles, Stones, etc.] blew a lot of people away. I don't remember it that way. It didn't knock me on the roadside. I remember stopping. It was a very conscious decision. It wasn't like anything overtook me. In fact, the British thing was very inspiring in one breath and intimidating in another. I'm dedicated to the living experience. When they threw that stuff over here, I wanted to grab hold of it and throw it back. It was frustrating because you wanted it to come out but it doesn't happen that way. It takes time.

"But at that time, I was getting into Lightnin' Hopkins, Leroy Carr, Robert Johnson, Bessie Smith. I was more into Dylan than the Beatles. I used to hang out at all those sessions when Dylan came up to Columbia. Kenny Rankin and I would come in and there would be all kinds of musicians. Tom Wilson was at those early sessions. I heard he died recently. It really shocked me.

"In 1963, I got turned on by John Hammond up at Columbia. He called me into his office and said, 'I heard you singing across the hall, "The Wanderer," "Ruby," and things. I noticed you have a real flare for the blues.' He turned me on to Robert Johnson and all the guys Paul Butterfield, Eric Clapton, and the Stones later did. All that stuff really turned me around. I went back to the apartment with an armful of albums.

"Greenwich Village at that time was filled with guys like Tim Hardin, Tom Paxton, and Dylan. I got hung up on finger-picking and got taken with filling the room with picking on the guitar. It sounded like bells or chimes. Something happened to me. I felt that it brought me closer to the roots of what I was doing. I had been doing it but I didn't know where it all came from. I had cut my teeth on Bo Diddley and Chuck Berry. That got me closer to where I was coming from. I got closer to the roots of my music and closer to what I wanted to say, closer to the guitar. I was getting out physically what I was feeling and thinking. 'Abraham, Martin, and John' was a result of working on those aspects of music."

From 1968 through 1970, when he released "Your Own Backyard," Dion followed the folk tradition of a man alone onstage entertaining the audience with his guitar and story songs, but, in a sense, he felt the need to put rock back in the repertoire. "That was a great period of my life. I just threw myself into it. I grabbed my guitar and had to fill the speakers for two or three hours a night solo. I made so many good friends in that time period— Jonathan Edwards, Jimmy Buffet, Melanie, and Bonnie Raitt. Just good songwriters. We'd trade off songs. It was a very simple time for me because all I had to worry about was putting new strings on my guitar and playing.

"It was simple but not easy. It got me out to people. Up to that point, it was a one-way street with audiences. I used to think, 'Dig Me,' and now it got to be a two-way street. Now when I go out there, it's a culmination of everything. I know what I'm doing. I enjoy what I'm doing and I have all that concentration left over to enjoy everybody.

"My senses were perking. But it's just another phase. It wasn't me to sit there with a guitar. It was only part of me. I used to sit there and pound on a guitar and sing rock and roll songs. I needed a rock and roll band."

After 1970, Dion cut a few albums for Warner Brothers which "didn't strike lightning from the sky" because he surrendered all control to producer-wizard Phil Spector, who was staging his own comeback at that time by ferreting out people who had grown up in the business with him—the Crystals, Dion, Bill Medley, and others. The second coming of the fifties and sixties didn't work out as planned. The music industry had become more complicated since the days of walking into a studio and cutting a hit record in two hours. Dion was stymied by the cobwebs of business confusions and artistic conflicts of will, which left him in the role of song interpreter, not the rock and roller he wanted to become. Dion became skewered by the revivals which pegged him into the Belmont days and the industry urging him to stick with the

David Michael Kennedy photo

successful products of the late sixties and early seventies. Finally, after two decades, Dion has a rock and roll band and continues on his unique musical and personal odyssey.

"I've been around for a while and I never had my own band. It was very frustrating. I had vocal groups but I never had a band. Now I have both—a vocal band. That's why life is so new to me. I've gotten a second wind with the band. I feel good about it. It's hard work but it comes easy. I just love rock and roll. It's not something you hand charts out for. My music isn't like that. It's homemade music. It's great that the confidence I have stays with me because the music doesn't get all knocked to hell when you walk out and everything you want to happen isn't happening. This band is self-contained.

"Hey, man, I am in the pool with my three daughters. I just ran three miles. It's such a great day. On top of that I'm free of pain. I got nothing to complain about. But I have a lot of growing to do."

Mark Dinning

In early 1959, Jean Dinning, of the famous singing Dinning Sisters, was in a small town outside of Chicago reading a magazine article about a disc jockey who was tired of parents dumping on their kids for being such a bunch of devils. He claimed that in his life he had met many teen angels. She turned that idea into a song that was recorded by her younger brother Mark and became an instant nationwide number one record. But some folks flinched at the story of a love-struck girl getting run over by a train while trying to retrieve her boyfriend's high school ring from a car stalled on the tracks. "Teen Angel" was taken off play lists of radio stations throughout the eastern United States, and was banned in England, of all places, that curious nest of musical hip that later presented the world with Mick Jagger proclaiming "I want it painted black," and Johnny Rotten of the Sex Pistols announcing "I wanna destroy." However, that didn't deter, and most probably stimulated, the five million people who've bought "Teen Angel" over the last twenty years.

Mark Dinning was born in 1933 in Grant County, Oklahoma. Endless flatlands steeped in dust bowl memories, folks working the land with one eye toward God and the other on the fates, and herds of cattle, with more cows than the towns had people, grazing beneath the icy glare of towering oil derricks. He was the youngest son in a farming family of five girls and four boys. His father was also an evangelist singer. "You know how it used to be in the old days, don't you? Well, different church groups were always looking for someone to lead the singing and maybe read some from the Scripture. Now my father wasn't a minister, but he was influential in the Church of

Christ down there and he could sing too, so he was always being asked. And all his brothers, they were all evangelist singers. But basically they were farmers."

When Mark was still too young to go along to the church meetings, he stayed home with an eleven-year-old babysitter named Clara Ann Fowler who would later change her name to Patti Page. "I was just a little tyke then, and she was the little fat girl down the street. I don't hardly remember, but she was always telling my ma how she wanted to be a famous singer. She and her sisters were working for the McCormick Deering Company, tractors, singing songs for them on the radio. They were called the McCormick Deering Sisters. Then they sang for the Page Milk Company and this little girl took the name Patti Page from that. She really hit the big time with that 'Tennessee Waltz.'"

Around that time, Mark's older brother Wade took three of his sisters, Lou, Ginger, and Jean up to Chicago to audition for the KFH Barn Dance radio show, and they played with the likes of the Hoosier Hotshots, Pat Buttram, and Les Paul and Mary Ford. They went on to have a gold record of their own, "Buttons and Bows." "Oh yeah, people were constantly reminding me about my sisters, asking when was Mark going to get up and sing too and all that kind of thing. But I was just a bashful little kid. They even got Ken White, the Dinning Sisters' A and R man, to come down to the farm and try to audition me, but I was so embarrassed I stood behind the door. I was only about thirteen."

By that time, the Dinnings had moved to another farm in little Orlinda, Tennessee, near Nashville. With all the music in the family, they were always trucking down to the Grand Ole Opry where the Dinning Sisters would be playing with folks like Roy Acuff and Snooky Lansen. "Well, believe it or not, the only thing I wanted to do then was raise turkeys. I was about sixteen and I already had about 200 of them. Only trouble, they kept dying of the blackhead. I'd have a perfectly healthy bird and go out the next morning and he'd be staring, toes up, toward the sky.

They have medication for it now, whatever it is, but they didn't have any cure for it then. Darned if I knew what caused it, but it sure did take them away. That kind of dampened my blanket."

Then when Mark was seventeen, his father bought him an electric guitar and amplifier. He started off playing folk songs. "I always loved Burl Ives, his type of singing. And I always liked Patti Page too. So I did little things here and yonder, just playing little places, like with my brother Ace. He was playing at the Boots and Saddle Club in Bowling Green, Kentucky, and he'd call me up and I'd sing with him. That was a real nice place. Don't think it's there anymore, but it was kind of the elite club in Bowling Green, and not country either, strictly tuxedoes, even the band in tuxedoes, all high mucky-muck."

Just after graduating from high school, he married a girl from Kentucky. "You know how ignorant you can get." They had a son who was nine months old when Mark was drafted into the Army. "First I went to Fort Knox. Then they said I could go to Germany but I turned that down because they said it was too cold. Damned if they didn't send me out to some camp in the Mojave Desert. It was 120° in the shade and we were forty miles from the nearest town, which wasn't any bigger than the one I'd left. I was the communications chief for the 723rd Tank Battalion. The tanks would go running around in the desert, bust up their radios, and I'd have to fix them. Communications chief means I was a slave with a title."

Mark took his guitar out with him, and, as there wasn't much of a crowd, usually ended up picking for the coyotes. "But sometimes the general would have me down to his place to play at his parties. He was only a one-star. I guess he must have screwed up somewhere or he wouldn't have been out in the desert. His damn swimming pool dried up on him when I was there and there wasn't enough water to fill it again. But he was always throwing parties. He'd promote somebody or some damn thing and then he'd throw a party. I'll never forget one time I had a weekend pass and this Lieutenant Somebody comes up

and finds one tiny little loose button on my fatigues. He pulled that sucker off and restricted me to the barracks. Boy, I hated him. But the general was having one of his parties so I got to go over and play. And he had a good-looking daughter too. But I was scared of her. She was bad news, being so pretty, and all these men around. All a man had to do was ... well, you know what I mean, and he'd end up down in the grease pit. They poured all the garbage down this chute into a pit, and if you messed up on her you'd end up down there cleaning that thing out. A real sweetheart job that was. Nobody'd speak to you for weeks because you couldn't get the smell off you. So you didn't want to make no trouble with the general's daughter.''

So Mark would hang around the dried-up pool singing folk songs, ballads, and a lot of Elvis Presley for the officers basking in their Mojave notoriety, and he'd be thinking about playing for a different audience. He vowed that when he got out, he'd get himself a recording contract "come hell or high water."

Mark got out of the Army when he was twenty-three and headed straight for Nashville where he auditioned for Wesley Rose of Acuff-Rose. "Well, he called Mitch Miller right up over at Columbia Records. But he said I just missed because Mitch had signed up that day this guy named Johnny Mathis. I said dadburnit because I knew he and I sounded a lot alike. But I had said I'd get a contract and I got one six weeks later with MGM. First I wrote a thing called 'Shameful Ways.' I don't even have the record anymore. The other side was called 'A Million Years.' I recorded it in New York City, damned if I know where, damned if I could ever find the studio either, but it was somewhere downtown, whatever downtown is there."

In late 1959, Mark then recorded "Teen Angel" for MGM. "I don't know what happened. One of those one-shot things, I guess. But, man, that was something else. I didn't know how to handle it hardly. Number one on *Billboard*, number one on *Cashbox*, just number one all across the nation. I couldn't believe it, just thrilled the hell out of me. I don't know why, but some people thought it was too bloody or something and a lot of the radio stations stopped playing it. Me and this promotion man from Acuff-Rose had to go out and change their minds about that. We went to Detroit, Baltimore, Philadelphia, and all those cities, and what we'd do was wine and dine the record librarians at the stations, the ones who decide what gets played. We'd be real cordial, take them out to dinner, try to get them drunk and persuade them to sign a peace treaty vowing they'd play it a thousand times a day or something. Well, not really, but you know what I mean, just be real friendly and let them know we cared. It worked because they started playing it again. They just out-and-out banned it in England. Do you believe that with some of the stuff they got coming out of there?"

Meanwhile, Mark was touring all over the place. He

went down to Australia to do shows with Jerry Lee Lewis, Larry "Please Mr. Custer" Verne, Fabian, Frankie Avalon, the whole crew. "That was back when we were all doing those package shows. The second time I went down, I really loved that place; I followed Mel Torme at the Embers Club in Melbourne. It was real nice, but they bombed it the week before I got there. I guess it was the Melbourne mafia. Probably didn't like the way things were going at the club. They blew the whole front off of it, but we played anyway. They had this stage with a pool in the middle of it, a little decorative thing, but it was deep. One night I'm singing and leaned against the rail around it. I heard that thing go 'creak' and jumped back just in time or I'd have been in it."

In the States, Mark did all the clubs and live shows, and

estimates he was on Dick Clark's TV show about fifteen times. "And then there was the time I was playing a place called the Seven Points in Atlanta and I got this letter about going to Philadelphia to do the 'Dick Clark Show,' and about how a limousine would then take me to Allentown, Pa., for some other show. By the time I got up there, my God, it was about ten below and the snow was flying. This guy comes into the studio, says the car is ready, and we go out and here's this '47 Plymouth station wagon with no heater, busted-out back window, and the other windows won't roll up right. We had to ride that sucker all the way over the hill. It was full of old papers, all kinds of crap, and I never saw the like. Sure was a poor limousine if I ever saw one. If somebody'd said, 'Hey, there's Mark Dinning,' they'd have said, 'Naw, that's an imposter; he'd never get in a baggy-looking car like that.'"

"Another time I'm standing on the corner, I think in Times Square, and I asked this newspaper guy for the time because I wanted to go see that movie *Baby Doll*. He starts yelling 'Jesus Christ' this and 'Jesus Christ' that, and 'Can't you see?' He points up at this building and the whole building is a clock with giant hands on it. Hell, I didn't know. I wasn't from New York. But he keeps saying 'Jeeeeesus Chrrrrrist,' kind of chewing it on out of his mouth."

After "Teen Angel," Mark did "A Star Is Born," which sold just under a million, then "Lovin' Touch" and "Top 40, News, Weather, and Sports," all of which did okay but things were starting to slow down. "You know, if you don't come up with a hit right after the first one, people start to lose interest. 'You're only as hot as your last record' is the way the saying goes, I believe."

Nonetheless, he continued touring, doing all kinds of clubs and shows around the country. "I've been to some kinds of places! I bumped into Buddy Knox recently. He had a big hit with 'Party Doll.' Well, it'd been a long time but we recognized each other. In fact, he looked right at me and said 'The Merry-Go-Round, Louisville,' which was the place where we had played together. It was a strip joint, really something. We're up there playing and I don't know how many girls are running around the place naked except for a little g-string and things on the ends of their toochies."

Mark also remembers the places he played out in the rural areas of Virginia and the Carolinas. "I loved it out there, and I mean that was really *out* there; can't get much more redneck than that, everybody stomping around saying, 'Shoot, get the goddamned show on the road,' just saying 'Shoot' all the time."

Today, Mark lives in Jefferson City, Missouri, and is "very happily married to a beautiful blonde," his second wife, Polly. "I try to stay home as much as possible without going totally broke, just take it easy, fix the porch, drive around town, and go shopping, things like that."

Still he's on the road about half the year, playing clubs, lounges, and resort hotels around the South and the Midwest. For awhile he was doing current popular music. "But now people are asking for the old nostalgia things, and hell, I'm full of those. I do the nostalgia shows too and they're great, seeing all the old people and having a real good time. And like all exrecording artists, I'm still hoping to get another record deal. I just signed with a company to do 'Teen Angel' again, but we'll have to see about doing anything else."

When Mark's on the road these days, he does a one-man show featuring an automatic rhythm and percussion machine, and a bass amplifier with a peddle attachment that he plays with his feet while simultaneously singing and playing the guitar. "Usually nobody asks me for a light when I'm playing."

Bill Medley

Bill Medley of the Righteous Brothers was born on September 19, 1940, in Santa Ana, California. He grew up in L.A. where his father was Chief of Communications for the Sheriff Department and moonlighted at the Rendezvous Ballroom as the light and sound man. Throughout junior high and high school, Bill would go down to the old ballroom and sit onstage watching stars like Fats Domino, Nat King Cole, and Little Richard set up. At thirteen Bill started getting into music by listening to the records of the Doo-Wop groups like the Flamingoes and singing along. "I did that for about seven years. Literally, my training was those records." Bill and a friend fused the California art of cruising for chicks with music by warbling as the Romancers, a dubious duo who rode around in cars and sang to girls as a come-on. "That didn't work but we did learn how to sing. That's when I started doing a lot of writing and arranging."

By nineteen, Medley had formed a group called the Paramours. His first tenor quit as the group was preparing to record its first song. Bill tapped a singer by the name of Bobby Hatfield from the Variations. A year later, Johnny Wimber, another local singer, decided to form a new quartet with Hatfield as the first tenor and Medley as bass. Backed by a drummer and guitar player, the new group played "toilets," usually appearing at a hangout called John's Black Derby in Santa Ana. After six months, Johnny dropped out, leaving the two front singers as the leaders of the group. Singing R&B, the duo drew good business to the Black Derby because of the unique black sound they had in 1959, when whites didn't sing black. But they were soon fired.

"Bob and I were going to stop and put together a show group for Las Vegas. Now at that time, around this area, Las Vegas was the epitome of success. It was the best place in the world to work for money and exposure. Vegas didn't have the stigma of being plastic."

Medley had in his mitts a tune he had penned called "Little Latin Lupe Lou" and wanted to record it with Bobby Hatfield. Since the Paramours had gone the way of all flesh, the duo needed a name for the act. "We didn't want to call ourselves the Paramours. These black friends of ours would come into the nightclub and watch Bobby and me. At that time, if you wore a neat coat, they said it was a "righteous" coat. If they liked you, they called you 'brother.' Out of the five guys in the group, they called Bobby and me the 'righteous brothers,' which really meant 'good friend' to those guys. So I said, 'Let's not use the Paramours anymore; let's use the name Righteous Brothers.'"

The Rendezvous Ballroom, the old haunt of jazz and big bands, had been rejuvenated by the infusion of Dick Dale's surf music into its cavernous hall. The Righteous Brothers' record had gone nowhere, gathering dust at Dressons' and Gracie's. Needing money, they agreed to work the Rendezvous for twenty-five bucks apiece. Singing "Little Latin Lupe Lu" to a surf beat, the Brothers built the house attendance up to two thousand kids. Constant requests from the audience for their record and complaints about its scarcity led Medley and Hatfield to distribute it themselves to the various local record stores. "We told the stores, 'If you sell them, you sell them. If you don't, sail them.' KRLA, the big radio station, used to call the stores to find out what was selling so they could add to the playlist. When they called Gracie's, she said, 'By the way, there's one damn record, "Latin Lupe Lu," by the Righteous Brothers which sold 1700 copies this week!'" KRLA took the song and used it as background music for the promo ad of the station. The number of call-ins convinced them to put it on the playlist where it immediately took off.

From 1962 through 1963, the Righteous Brothers were strictly a California act playing a string of one-nighters at local clubs, making good money off their next two West Coast hits "My Babe" and "Koko Joe." Finally, after a zealous agent's salespitch, the Righteous Brothers were put on the first Beatle tour starting in Washington, D.C. in 1964. "We got the job with Jay and the Americans. You can imagine the situation. All it said was 'Beatles Concert.' They didn't mention that you would have to sit on those hard benches an hour and a half before you saw them, or in those big stadiums where the kids crushed themselves to get up front. We went out there doing thirty-five minutes right before the Beatles came on. There was a lot of clapping, 'We want the Beatles.' The West Coast was neat because we were known. On the East Coast, the Righteous Brothers could have been a disease. We got along great with the Beatles. They were terrific guys, real gentlemen, but the situation became impossible. So we left in the middle of the tour which, as far as a career goes, was really the wrong thing to do. But everything we did from '62 through all our career, every mistake turned to gold."

Fleeing the din of Beatlemania, the Righteous Brothers went back home to shoot a pilot television show, "Shindig." It became a rating grabber for ABC and propelled the duo onto the national music scene. Featured every week as regulars, Medley and Hatfield lasted the whole run of the show and in the process getting massive national exposure. In October of 1964, they sang "You've Lost That Lovin' Feeling" on the show and, consequently, had a number one national chart topper. As a result, the Righteous Brothers became the first group ever to have three albums in the Top Fifteen at the same time. Though dwarfed by the gigantic success of "Lovin' Feeling," their recording of the Carole King tune "Just Once in My Life" also went gold as did "Ebb Tide," "Unchained Melody," and "Soul and Inspiration" recorded in 1966.

Taping "Shindig" on Thursday nights, Bill would fly out every weekend to play 5,000 seaters with Glen Campbell as the opening act and return to L.A. for eight-hour mara-

Righteous Brothers Bill Medley and Bobby Hatfield.
Wide World photo

thon recording sessions with Phil Spector. Besides the performing, Bill had to pen more material, arrange new songs, and produce all the albums. Phil did the singles. It all took its toll. "I got married in 1964 and my son was born in 1965. I had a new baby, a new wife, a new career. We were on the road all the time so it was a tough time to get married. There wasn't a private life. You kissed it off. If you went out to dinner, you knew you were putting yourself in that situation where people stop and want autographs. I felt it came along with the turf but it was pretty impossible at times. So I would come home from the road and still didn't have time to produce, write, and arrange. I fell apart from fatigue. In 1965, I was thrown into the hospital with a nervous breakdown."

After a brief layoff, imperceptible to the public, the Righteous Brothers continued to open doors for other rock groups by being the first to play a major hotel in Las Vegas, the Sands, the "Tonight Show," and the Coconut Grove in Los Angeles. The Coconut Grove is said to have concealed from the industry the box office figures of the

Righteous Brothers' concerts because the management of the club didn't want it known a rock and roll group had shattered every gate in its history.

In the meantime, Phil Spector arranged a tour with the Rolling Stones in England for the sole purpose of sinking Celia Black's cover version of the Righteous Brothers' "Loving Feeling." Black, then under the tutelage of Beatles manager Brian Epstein, managed to rocket up the charts with her version. Spector didn't think so kindly of it. With the requisite press conference attended by the pouting icons, Mick Jagger and Keith Richards, the Righteous Brothers opened the English offensive against Black and promptly blew her disc out of the water. At a farewell party for the Righteous Brothers thrown by none other than Epstein himself and attended by the Beatles and Stones, Epstein warned them, "OK, you guys win this time but next time remember I own this town." The mock bravado was followed by Epstein's tentative offer to manage them, a proposition which ended with Epstein's death in 1967 from a drug overdose.

The popularity of the Righteous Brothers was a result of their adaptation of a black sound, the tremendous production quality of their records, and a polished stage act, rare for the young performers of that time. "We always carried our own nine-piece band and sound system. We wanted to make sure we were heard right. At that time Bobby and I were performers, talking and joking with the audience. Some of the acts weren't even good enough to be up there singing. So they would just stand up there. We were doing something that the audience had never seen before. Bobby and I would do comedy and really powerful ballads. We were making them laugh and trying to hit all the emotions. I think the Righteous Brothers were Bill and Bob like Dean Martin and Jerry Lewis. We were total opposites. He was short. I was tall. I was dark. He was light. I was a bass. He was a tenor. But we aren't opposite in personality."

From 1966 until their breakup in 1968, the Righteous Brothers churned out "Go Ahead and Cry," "On This Side of Goodby," "Melancholy Music Man," and "Stranded in the Middle of No Place," but all failed to grab the brass ring. "The reason for the Righteous Brothers' downfall was that I didn't have the time to produce properly." But when they did break up in 1968, they had over three million dollars worth of jobs on the books, concert dates before 12,000 at a pop, and an offer to become the first rock and roll group to have their own television show. "I knew that I would have to become involved in signing some pretty long contracts. I felt like I had 100 percent to give. I had to try and go it alone or else get so far locked in I could never give it a shot."

In 1968, his marriage collapsed and his wife took custody of his son, Darren Lee. His record label MGM was on the brink of bankruptcy, sliding in a new president every week. His first song as a solo, "I Can't Make It on My Own," was ill-advised and badly timed. His bold, controversial "Brown-Eyed Woman," with its racial overtones, broke new ground in the recording business by becoming one of the first singles ever to reach number one in both L.A. and New York only to bomb everywhere else, an unheard-of phenomenon. "Peace, Brother, Peace," a minor hit, indicated that Bill stood on the brink of happening again or taking the dive into oblivion.

The stress and depression Medley felt was increasing with the advent of hard rock and its rewriting of show business stage etiquette. "I love the music but that just wasn't my style of performing. It was a crazy period for me. Basically, I was a rock and roll or blues singer. I tried to walk a fence that was impossible to walk. Every now and again I would get pushed into different situations—rock and roll or a MOR in Vegas. I had offers from some pretty 'go' people to grow my hair and beard and wear Levi's and t-shirts. People would say, 'Come on, man, go one way or the other.' I really didn't fit in with either one. That was when in Vegas long hair meant you were a doper. If you wore a tuxedo, you were plastic. I had no way to win. If you told a joke in your show, it was 'Tah-Dah' show business bullshit. I didn't know what the hell to do."

Financially, Vegas saved Medley's life, providing an income of $300,000 a year for his shuffling along from gig to gig. A second marriage quickly dissolved in 1972. Medley soon blew out on the depression and tenseness, the result of seeing his private life and career slip away. At A&M records, under the production of Herb Albert, Medley cut a comeback single which promptly was shelved when James Taylor turned the same song, "You've Got a Friend," into a hit. Another disappointment for Bill came when the creators pegged him for the leading role in the TV series, "Then Came Bronson," the ongoing saga of a motorcycle-riding hippie figure who lays gentle vibes on everyone he meets in his travels. His agent, without Medley's advice, ruined the deal by jacking up the asking price. The part went to Michael Parks and the show went on for a modest but popular run.

From 1972 through '74, Medley's voice, once a nimble instrument of three octaves, deteriorated into a gravelly half-octave range. "I thought I was finished. I'd find myself down on the pier by the beach crying and asking God, 'What are you doing? I don't understand?' The depression and the tenseness started to nail me. Overworking and going onstage being so uptight goes right to the vocal chords. I was going onstage and sounding like crap. When I was in Vegas, the other stars around town would come in and see me because I was working the lounge late at night. Now I sounded like crap and I knew it. I could feel them staying away. They tried to be more supportive. 'Come on, man, why don't you rest?' I literally blew myself out. It might have been another way of dropping out."

Meanwhile, Bobby Hatfield had started the New Righteous Brothers with Jimmy Walker, formerly of the Knickerbockers. The reincarnation soon failed and Hatfield went solo. In 1974, Bill was reunited with Bobby who also was playing Vegas at the time. The reunion was a calculated move to survive. "When I went back with the Righteous Brothers, it would have been fine with me if it had ended then because I thought I was dying. I thought I was absolutely finished. If Bobby and I could have made three million apiece and put it in the bank, I would have been satisfied. That wasn't my total motivation but it was in my mind. I knew that Bobby could use two or three million himself."

To this day Bill counts as his best friends the guys who he went to junior high with. He lives in Villa Park where he was raised and pals around with his former classmates who have become mortgage bankers, real estate salesmen, and swimming pool cleaners. In 1974, when he needed some support, it was his old high school choir teacher, Jack Coleman, who came to his aid. He began a long process to reconstruct Bill's blown-out vocal chords. At the age of thirty-five, Medley took the first vocal lessons in his career at an accelerated rate of six times a week for eight straight weeks. "My vocal chords had been literally reset. So he had me go back to the beginning of 'La-La-La-La-La,' which I thought was total BS because nothing was happening. Finally, it started breaking through."

At the same time, Bill went through intense psychoanalysis to "see whether I was playing a mental trip on myself. Basically the shrink pointed out what probably was happening and allowed me to sit down and think about it and say, 'Yeah, that's exactly what's going down to put so much pressure on my voice.' He gave me confidence and straightened things out."

After the reunited Righteous Brothers scouted around for a new producer, they signed with Dennis Lampert and Brian Potter of Haven Records, where the duo recorded "Rock and Roll Heaven," an instant hit which helped ease the pressure on Medley. "And I said, 'At least I can sing a song that sold a million records. At least I'm not totally through.' 'Rock and Roll Heaven' was a good production and a good commercial record. But it wasn't necessarily Bobby's or my favorite song."

The Righteous Brothers seemed to have been transformed into a polished Mutt and Jeff act, a shadowy rerun of the sixties success days. While Medley had regained his voice at new strength, he floated through the act, drifting further away from his goal of singing simpler, more story-oriented material. The group finally dissolved again. "It was inevitable. It got to the point where we were acting onstage. We were copying what we used to do. We were reliving the past, not going toward the future at all."

At this time he also played a character named Bible Bill, a religious truck driver in Andy Griffith's favorite North Carolina town, Mayberry. The series was a Griffith spin-off called "Goober." It was promptly put into mothballs.

Medley's life at his beach house as a bachelor and weekend father came traumatically to an end when his first wife, Karen, was murdered in a rape attempt at her house. Luckily, that day, Bill had his son Darren Lee with him; otherwise his son would have been home. Medley had to stop playing the disappearing, big hero act of a visiting father and build a new home in Orange County, where he now lives with his son and a married couple who help out with the household chores.

"It took me a good year to adjust. Karen was an absolutely beautiful, beautiful woman. She was one of my closest friends. I was very bitter and hurt. Having Darren come live with me made me a lot stronger. I had no idea what an enormous job it is to raise children. I would just step in and say, 'This is my boy' and disappear. I took a hard look at it. I knew that my son needed me to be strong and happy, not necessarily rich and famous. I really felt that if I wanted to be with him all summer, I could not work then and hang anybody else up. So I decided I'd get back to what I.had set out to do. I wasn't doing it just for me but for him and me. He needed me and that's a terrific feeling."

A few years went by with Bill writing new songs at a rapid-fire rate but with no outlet for recording. His old friend Glen Campbell offered to produce him as did childhood buddy Brian Wilson, the reclusive genius of the Beach Boys, who hoped to end his own hermit's existence by producing Bill. But Kenny Rodgers, another compatriot from the early days of the First Edition, had impressed Medley with his simple, honest production of "Lucille."

"I said that's what I have to do this time out. If I'm going

to go down in flames, I want to go down doing me, not what a producer thinks of me, or doing an ego trip. I love to sing the blues because it's basic and honest, but I write songs that are more country than anything because I'm very bottom line."

The negotiations with United Artists dragged out until Kenny Rogers personally negotiated Medley's contract with Jerry Butler, Nashville's premier producer. For his comeback *Bill Medley* album, he flew to Nashville with ten songs, six of which he wrote and cut, such songs as "Lay a Little Loving on Me" and "Statue of a Fool."

"I've enjoyed the fact that the Righteous Brothers had such a nice impact on records. There is a certain amount of admiration and respect which really helps you. When a cameraman on a television show says, 'Boy, that was great when you did . . . ,' it makes you feel great. I don't have any idea about what's going to happen to me. I've been shuffling along and always had the right people interested. That's really nice even if nothing ever happens."

Paul Petersen

Under the automatic Southern California sun an instant city named Los Angeles has, among other things, the well-documented habit of launching various earthlings, for better or worse, into a realm called stardom. Paul Petersen, at thirty-three a twenty-five-year veteran of the star business, has been there and back. By the time he was twenty he had played the role of Jeff Stone on the "Donna Reed Show" for eight years, and as a recording artist had had a number of successful singles including "My Dad" which was a number one record during 1962. Paul candidly discusses the rapid rise to the limelight and the jarring confrontation with reality that followed. He is proud of the fact that he was able to summon the strength and the presence of mind to survive the journey and achieve success in another field. However, he is dead serious when he says that fame in the star business "is not a career, it's a sentence."

Born in the Los Angeles suburb of Glendale, he spent his very early years in Iowa. When his family returned to L.A., where his father, mother, and grandfather would work for Lockheed, he was already, at the age of seven, taking voice and dance lessons. "I started to make the rounds, taking all the lessons children get treated to. It was mom's idea pretty much straight through. Some mothers believe that you improve on God's gifts or at least try. Thus I became a pretty fair country singer and dancer and did the usual recitals the teachers set up to show off what they've taught their youngsters. Next came the quasi-professional things that occur in California—talent shows, Veterans Administration shows, et cetera. Then one day I was taken to an open audition, in other words a cattle call, at Disney Studios. I got a job as one of the original Mouseketeers. I was nine. But three weeks later I was fired for conduct unbecoming a Mouse. At that age I didn't understand that kid actors can't be children. Somehow it was decided that my nickname would be 'Mouse.' I detested it. But the casting agent at the studio, a very ponderous fellow, insisted on using it so I called him 'Fatso' and socked him in the stomach. Walt was lurking somewhere nearby and I was promptly fired. I'm the world's first ex-Mouseketeer. Timmy and Mickey Rooney Jr. were second and third. But obviously that wasn't the end. You have to understand that the work ethic is absolutely paramount in my family, and having been canned from my first job the only answer was more work."

Continuous interviews and auditions led first to commercials, then to small speaking parts, and then to larger roles on TV shows like "Playhouse 90" and "Lux Video Theater." Somehow he usually ended up playing orphans. Movies followed, including a featured role in *Houseboat* with Cary Grant and Sophia Loren. "Then before I knew it I was called in on another cattle call and got the job as Jeff Stone on the 'Donna Reed Show.' And there I was from age twelve to twenty."

During those years Paul was exposed to millions of people every week but his personal experience was almost totally restricted to the inner world of show business. For youngsters, that meant the standard Hollywood variety school replaced public school. "I took three hours of school per day, usually just me and the tutor. The largest class we ever had was with two other kids. Sometimes Shelly Fabares, of course, and Lee Aaker from 'Rin Tin Tin' and others. Obviously, there's no way I can compare it to public school, but you do miss learning the social skills. You never really find out where you sit in the larger pecking order. It's one of the perils of working in the industry. College was a bruising experience. It all had to be conducted off campus because whenever I tried to go to classes the notoriety was just too intense."

In 1962, a seventeen-year-old Paul Petersen was handed a recording career by the people behind his television career. "I had no control over it. Shelly and I were both asked to record for Colpix, a division of Columbia Pictures which owned Screen Gems which was the production entity of the 'Donna Reed Show.' They brought in writers, arrangers, and producers. The first one I did was 'She Can't Find Her Keys.' I heard recently that in some Top Forty radio station poll it was voted worst record of 1962. It deserved it but I sang it on the show and it was very successful. And then I had 'My Dad' [written by Barry Mann and Cynthia Weil] which was a number one record. After that things sort of petered out. People found us out, I suspect. When you're on television and thirty million people tune in every week you can sell a lot of records. But that doesn't mean they're very good records. Still I know that Shelly is proud of 'Johnny Angel,' and I'm kind of proud of 'My Dad.' After all, it is a Father's Day standard. However, in my case I would use the term 'recording artist' advisedly."

For Paul the sixties came in two distinct installments. During the first half, "The only thing outside of 'Donna Reed' and singing was personal amusements which came in two categories, cars and girls. Not exactly in that order, but fast cars and faster ones. I was very visible and had a lot of money in my pocket. It seemed that the good times would last forever. However, it's very difficult to be objective about something while you're doing it."

The second half began when the "Donna Reed Show" went off the air in 1965. "Every year after that I worked half as much as the year before. The Beatles were here, we had half a million men in Vietnam, the late sixties had arrived. Somebody supersquare like Jeff Stone didn't have much of a place. But Paul Petersen was definitely not Jeff Stone. I was part of my generation. Things got hot then, a little thing in Chicago in '68, the music, the people waking up to a different form of consciousness. I was involved, had the money to support movements and I did. I supported the SDS and I supported Donna when she was

Paul Petersen with Hayley Mills in 1965. *U.P.I. photo*

cochairman of Mothers for Peace. I did what I could. It seemed to me that the right answers were with the people who were under thirty at that point. And if it meant getting high or wearing your hair long and looking somebody in the eye and telling them they're supporting that man's lie, then fine. I lived that and I was particularly keen about it because I felt and still feel that the 'Donna Reed Show' played a role in all that, a show that says, 'Let's ignore reality and make believe mothers wake up beautifully dressed and there is always a solution to a problem and the country is always right. The show hardly addressed the questions that were being asked in families at that time. I guess in some ways you could say I was making up for the years on the show. Which isn't to say, however, that I didn't have a good time doing the show. Who wouldn't have? But I would have enjoyed it more had I known the difference.''

As the decade drew to a close, Paul was in the midst of a divorce from his first wife, had gone through most of his money, and had to come to terms with the rest of his life. "I had made a lot of money and had acquired those things I thought were important and found they weren't. I had squandered, blown, and otherwise dissipated my funds and learned a lot of lessons along the way. I don't regret that at all. But by the fall of '69 I had this creeping realization that I had excess baggage hanging around my personality and outlook. I had no real goal because it had always been supplied from without."

But then, inspired by Stephen Crane's *Red Badge of Courage* and his own deep commitment to the antiwar movement, Paul sat down to write a story called "Honor" which turned into a six hundred-page manuscript. "It was as much about Vietnam as about me exorcising my own ghosts. I was really proud of it." About that time he was turned down for a part on the "Marcus Welby Show." He was furious, and immediately churned out a script for the show on speculation. They bought it. "So suddenly I was a writer and admitted to myself that until a significant period of time had passed there was going to be no work for me in Hollywood. The people who knew me and knew my work were not the people who were operating Hollywood, still aren't, and probably won't be for five or ten years."

So Paul stuck with the typewriter. His first book was on high-performance driving and had been requested by Simon & Schuster. They liked that one and asked what else he wanted to do. He showed them a novel he had started called *The Smuggler*. They liked that enough to turn it into a series of books based on a James Bond-type figure cavorting through the seventies. "Of course I went on to do other things, but by that time I had another paid apprenticeship in another creative field. I appreciated that. Writing is intensely personal and not at all frantic. I don't require recognition. The recognition comes from me when I finish a manuscript. I like for people to buy and enjoy my books but the fact is that I'm doing it for me and

I love it."

In 1970 Paul moved to Connecticut to concentrate on writing. Then in 1977 he played a part in creating the concept for a "Donna Reed" reunion show with all the original cast. Two days after the show was sold to ABC, it was discovered that Carl Betz had cancer. Two weeks later, as Paul watched the moving vans leave his driveway headed for California, Donna called to say that the cancer was terminal. "All I could do was follow my belongings out to California where my family is. As much as I miss the people and the enduring relationships I had in Connecticut, there's nothing like love, especially if things are going to get difficult."

Carl Betz's death was a heavy blow to the whole cast. It's doubtful whether a reunion show will come off now. "It harmed us all. It hurt us in the heart. Our television family is most unusual. We accepted the adjacent reality of being a family and not really being a family. We had famous six-hour lunches together at the Bistro in L.A. all the years before I left for Connecticut. We did it every month and we reinstituted it when I returned. We care for each other. There are very special elements of our lives which only we who served can understand and appreciate. There are special and powerful emotional ties after twenty years."

Paul feels that there is a real difference between people who have known stardom and those who haven't, that fame has a staggering effect on the lives of those who've experienced it. "I admire and respect people who have been in the business for more than three weeks. I don't pay attention to the ones who come in as hot flashes and then disappear. I've been around for twenty-five years and I respect survivability in this industry because that's the only thing that counts. It's difficult to explain to civilians what happens when your circle of effect contracts rather than expands as you grow older, especially when you start young. It's difficult to explain to an ordinary person, an outsider, what being famous is all about. There is no consideration of age. You're not old and famous and you're not young and famous. You're just famous. The distortions visited upon the developing personality by fame are many and severe. Attached to fame is the idea of privilege and that's an error. I had to tear down the person I had constructed out of so many artificial elements and start fresh. Writing was my means. It was a conscious decision that required all the will and concentration I could muster. There were many failings along the way. Nevertheless, I would like to think that I went through the process and came out the other side a human being with some connection to reality while retaining pride in the work I had done. Never mind that for some time I had adopted a television personality and had suddenly raised my level of amusements artificially high. The fact is that there is as much cause for pride as bitterness."

Now living in California, Paul continues to concentrate on writing. In 1977, Dell published *Walt, Mickey and Me* in which Paul treats the Disney empire in depth. He occasionally receives offers for acting jobs too. "And I accept them. I'm always delighted to work as an actor. It's something I know how to do. I don't go after the work, I don't feel I have to compete. But if it's there, fine. It's like a bartending job to me now. That's probably a result of the years after 'Donna Reed' went off the air. I wanted the work then and some guy who two weeks earlier was selling cars in New Jersey is asking me what have I done."

Speaking of cars, just recently Paul went in with a pal on a limousine service, Superstar Limousine. "Holy smokes, we're having a good time. We cater almost exclusively to the music industry and I've really been piling up the stories. People reveal themselves in a limo. I've found that people hire one either because of vanity or paranoia. Really goes to show you."

After having looked back over all the years, Paul left us with these final words: "Have some consideration for the people who served. There's nothing more painful than someone looking at you and saying, 'Gee, I used to love you.' It's the most distant praise in the human vocabulary."

Tony Williams

For aficionados of early rock recordings, the creme de la creme of the period is the so-called Doo-Wop form of R&B vocal harmonies represented by groups like the Orioles, the Falcons, the Spaniels, the Flamingoes, the Moonglows, and other groups named after zoo creatures, things that fly and go bump in the night, cars, and any other usable objects. Most were wondrous one-shot deals producing memorable novelty hits like "Speedo" ("Some people call me Speedo but my real name's Mr. Earl") by the Cadillacs and a saloon favorite, "I'm Not a Juvenile Delinquent," by Frankie Lyman and the Teenagers.

In 1955, the same year that "Rock Around the Clock" was released, a group vaulted onto the Doo-Wop scene and held center stage for the rest of the decade. They were the Platters, by nearly unanimous decree, the most popular vocal group in the country. By the time their recording days were over, the group had collected sixteen gold discs and had knocked out four number one songs, including the first Doo-Wop single ever to hit number one nationwide, "The Great Pretender."

Their nonpareil of a lead singer, Tony Williams, was born in August of 1928 in Elizabeth, New Jersey. His mother was a full-blooded American Indian and his father, Ed, was a black man with a prosperous business laying lawns for the wealthy in the suburbs of northern New Jersey. Both parents were divorced and married again, providing Tony with a slightly unwieldy set of kin, eight sisters and two stepbrothers. His sister, Linda Hayes, sang at Harlem's Apollo Theater and had one hit record, "Yet I Know," the sequel to Bill Mabins's "I Don't Know." A brother presently teaches classical guitar at St. John's University in New

York.

Tony began by singing in his mother's choir at the local Baptist church. "My parents were very religious, very spiritual. I think they were religious fanatics. It was pretty strict when growing up."

While his vocals with the Platters now seem effortless and graceful with a natural wide range, Tony over the years has studied at the Essex Conservatory of Music, with a black woman, Liola Carter, whose father sang in Leipzig, the Luigi, and Paul Thompson in LA, who taught him the operatic voice. Except for the rocking gospel music in his mother's church, Tony, like the Platters' baritone Paul Robi, started out on the very disciplined singing of classical materials and the old standards like "Danny Boy." This would play no small part in Tony joining a group. In the early fifties, it was hard to book a black tenor singing "white."

While his family constantly moved around northern New Jersey, Tony appeared in various amateur shows at Elizabeth's Liberty Theater, the Newark joints such as Laurel Gardens, the Adams and the Bradford theaters. Once a local DJ, Bill Cook, the manager of Elizabeth's Roy "Ebb Tides" Hamilton, ran an amateur contest on TV with the prize of appearing at the Mosque in Newark. Tony copped the honors and went on to win the prestigious Amateur Night at the Apollo.

To pay the bills, Tony delivered furniture along the Jersey Shore, tallied stock at the foundry of the Singer manufacturing plant, covered missiles with tarpaulins at the Raritan Arsenal, and became a cam milling operator. Tony played a three-year gig for the Air Force at Lackland Air Base in San Antonio, Guam, and Clark Air Force base in Manila. During the week, he was a sergeant in charge of supplies, on the weekends the lead singer for the squadron band. He returned from the service to Jersey, was married, and had a son, Derrick, who today is in the Air Force.

"I couldn't get the break in Jersey that I wanted. So my sister on the strength of her record took me to California.

I had just quit a job and they were calling me a fool because you could make about $42.00 a day. They thought if you quit a job like that, you must be crazy.

"Out there, I did a show at the Club Alabam on Central Avenue and saw Herbie [Reed], Alex Hodge, Joe Jefferson, and Cornell Gunther of the Platters, Cornelius [later lead for the Coasters] was singing lead then. We met because I won the amateur show there. It all passed by for awhile. I went back to work at Douglass Aircraft where I was a form block maker. You had to read blueprints and things of that nature. I had to stay there for approximately a year or eight months. Cornelius had quit and they wanted me to try out. I said, 'OK.' They were breaking up anyway. I tried out and they liked me."

Unlike other vocal groups of that era, The Platters didn't originate from the same neighborhood. They came from across the nation. David Lynch, the second tenor hired after Tony's audition, was from St. Louis, Missouri. Herb Reed, the big bassman and early organizer of the Platters, hailed from Kansas City, Missouri. Paul Robi, the conservatory-trained baritone, came from New Orleans. Zola Taylor, then fourteen and already formerly of Shirley Gunther and the Queens, was the only group member from Los Angeles.

Tony's sister introduced her brother to Buck Ram, a songwriter for the Ink Spots and the manager of a group of Fremont High School (LA) kids named the Penguins, who took their name from the friendly arctic beast on the old Kool packs. Buck wasn't enthused about signing Tony up as a solo act because the people didn't exactly crow for a black tenor singing "white" or so he thought. Tony told him about his fronting the Platters and arranged an audition. Buck liked what he heard and signed them.

In 1954, Ralph Bass, a producer for Federal Records, then a subsidiary of King, whipped up a Platter cut entitled "Only You." It didn't take off. But Buck Ram had something up his sleeve. The Penguins had recorded a big hit on Dootone Records called "Earth Angel" and had generated interest from Mercury Records. Ram refused to

The Platters circa 1958. *U.P.I. photo*

sign the group with Mercury unless he got a two-for-one deal which included the Platters. As Tony says, "It was connivingly done." But as a harbinger of the Platters' own management problems, the Penguins had to surrender all rights to their hit record and subsequently never recorded another.

In the summer of 1955, Mercury rerecorded "Only You." A disc jockey named Bob Salter in Seattle, Washington, started banging the record and it took off. Unfortunately, its writer, James Creegman, now a New York photographer, has reportedly never received royalties. In October of 1955, the Platters released their most remembered tune, "The Great Pretender," which had been bought by their manager Buck Ram from its creator Alanzio Taylor for twenty-five dollars. It went on to become the number one nationwide on all charts, the first Doo-Wop record ever to do so. From then until 1958, the Platters with Tony on lead pumped out hits after hits with such notables as "My Prayer," Buck Ram's "Heaven on Earth," "You've Got the Magic Touch," "Twilight Time," and "Smoke Gets in Your Eyes."

With a string of national hits, the Platters started playing Vegas at the Moulin Rouge, then an interracial club showcasing black performers. Tony recalls, "Immediately, the money went up when we had the hit records. The first club we played in Vegas was the Moulin Rouge, which Joe Louis had something to do with. The audience was black and white but the performers were black. The strip wasn't too open then. This was in 1955.

"After we played the Moulin Rouge, we came back to play the big room at the Flamingo. At that particular time, you still couldn't be staying in the hotel. We were just peeking through. Guys who had been up there for quite some time like Epstein and Nat King Cole could stay in the hotel. But they couldn't gamble. No black people could gamble. Now, of course, everybody's gambling and the place is wide open. But then we had our dressing room outside the hotel. When we played the lounge, we had to go into the kitchen after we finished the set. You had four to six sets a night. That went on all night long."

The reception and treatment of the Platters was considerably different in Paris where many black American jazz artists like Charlie "The Bird" Parker, Charlie Mingus, and Miles Davis cavorted with writers James Baldwin and James Wright. De Gaulle's Paris hosted black artists at La Coca Trix's Olympic Theater. The Platters played there and around Europe drawing enthusiastic crowds. The last time they played the Olympic in 1958, they were joined by Josephine Baker for a charity affair attended by the entire French political hierarchy.

It was the relationship between Buck Ram and Tony which formed the drive behind the Platter sound. "At that time, we were inseparable. As far as our veins could go, we could see one another and understand one another. It was like a marriage. We would be in the room some nights, talking about different things, and he would tell me what songs he wanted me to do. Then he would tell me how he thought the song would go.

"But then I would put my inflection on the thing. He

would fight me to the end. 'It won't go that way.' We had all kinds of arguments. On the session I'd turn a deaf ear to him and do it the way I thought it should be. Usually, I never waited for my playbacks. Then he would hear it back. I'd come back and look at him and he'd say it would go. Because it's the song, the story, what you can tell. With the embellishment you can get behind it, the feelings, forethought, the song becomes you."

But that close relationship had an underside resulting in nearly eighteen years and twelve lawyers battling Buck Ram for the rights to the Platters' name. On June 6, 1960, Tony left the group to become a solo performer. He is supposed to have introduced his replacement at the Copa Club in Newport, Kentucky. Ten days later, Sonny Turner premiered at the Lotus Club in Washington, D.C. But the Platters weren't the same.

The dispute over the use of the name and royalty payments forced the group to dissolve and fragment into three different versions of the Platters. Zola Taylor fell on rocky ground, suffering personal problems and facing destitution until she formed a group of her own. David Lynch with nine children took alcohol for a time as did Tony. "All of these things pressed into one another because alcohol is a helluva thing. It turned my life upside down."

The responsibility of the Platters' demise affected Tony the most. He soon suffered a few nervous breakdowns from the strain of the breakup. As Helen recalls, "If you're not working, you can't pay the bills. That got to Tony. He thought, 'Here I am, I took the Platters to this man, and how could he turn on me like that and on everyone else.' Things got pretty rough."

As Tony recollects, "I've been through a lot of situations where I didn't think I was going to make it. I've seen things happen that would destroy a household. You have to play the shots the way you see them. According to how it goes down, I've got to live. I'm not going to live scared. I can't and will not. I've had five strokes. I've had a few nervous breakdowns. But if it hadn't been for Helen, this woman, my wife, the most beautiful person I know, I think I'd have gone off the deep end. She stuck by me when things were very dim and I couldn't see. Helen was in my corner. I had gotten to the point where I was getting angry with Helen and wondering why these things were happening to me. I didn't know why this girl stayed with me. She was trying to tell me, I love you. She was trying to take me away from all the stuff which was destroying me. I feel like I had to go through that vicissitude of life, that phase of life. What I was telling Helen was I have things to do. I'm put here like anyone else. I see things that no one else can see and that's for me. Can it be included in your scope of living? When it took that light, I said, 'This girl is trying to show me something, the best.' The greatest thing in the world is understanding."

With Tony's relationship with Buck Ram severed, Helen, then Zola's replacement in the Platters, became his manager and his wife in 1962. Helen then began a crusade to regain the use of the Platters' name and for the restitution of funds to the Platters. She succeeded in 1964 to sort out the royalty problems.

In the early sixties, Tony began doing a solo act with his old Platter standards. In Japan, Tony was backed by four Japanese singers called the Kingtones, who perfectly imitated the original voices of the group. As a consequence, Tony's records over there became big hits. While there, Tony worked the circuit with Nat King Cole. Helen remarks, "We worked together in the Far East. We worked some fabulous clubs, the Geisikaya Circus, which was run by the Japanese Mafia. They own the best wherever they go. They have sumo wrestlers, the biggest guys you've seen in your life. When we would close, Nat would open. When we would open, Nat would close. We played the whole Circus together one year. We stayed at the Hotel Okuru, which at that time was called the Ichiban Hotel, which means the number one hotel." Then Tony traveled around South America in 1962 and 1963. "I met Frankie Lyman in the airport when I was going into the airport and it was kinda tough." It got tougher for Frankie who died five years later of a heroin overdose in a Harlem apartment. Tony continued as a single act playing New York Clubs like the Safari with Little Anthony. But, "the people always associated me with the group."

Helen recalls an aborted attempt to reunite the Platters, "In 1965, we wanted to get together as many as we could of the original Platters. People urged Tony to get the original Platters together. David had a big drinking problem then. We took Zola and Paul and two other guys. We stayed a long time overseas that year. The Beatles have much more sense. When you put old men onstage, it's not the same. They wanted to remember them the way they were. We went over and, Honey, it didn't work. It was a very, very bad tour. I'd never relive it again. Each one of us came back on separate planes. That's when we found out there would be no reunion.

"A guy in Manila took us to a restaurant like the Three Sixes in New York, overlooking the whole of Cebu City where MacArthur was. He took us on the town that night because he knew what we were going through. He said, 'I know what's happening so when you come again, you and Tony come with a group! That's when I got the idea for a group."

Tony states, "Well, why don't we start a group and see how it works? The people are used to the voices behind the act. So we started a group for the Larry Marshack Show at the Academy of Music [in Booklyn]. We needed a couple of months so the people could learn from the records. We got the musical director who had traveled with the Platters, [Earl Warren and Mr. Raymond Jones]. Helen rehearsed until we got the sound almost the same. From 1967 on, we called it Tony Williams and the Platters, then Helen and Tony Williams and the Platters, and now Helen and Tony Williams and the International Platters."

Meanwhile, Zola Taylor has her own group and Paul Robi with his Argentinian wife tours Australia. In 1976, the confusion between the groups led to a widely reported news item that Tony Williams had died of a drug overdose. In fact, it was the lead singer of Zola Taylor's group who died, but the foreign press filed the report as saying the lead singer of the Platters had died. Naturally, the U.S. papers took this to mean Tony. After a frantic filing of notices in the industry papers, Helen cleared up the matter.

Since 1968, Tony and Helen have built up an extensive network of overseas dates, allowing them to play the Far East and Europe for about eight months of the year. Helen attributes their ability to sustain their careers without a record in eighteen years to the everlasting appeal of the Platters' sound. "Wherever you go, they recognize the Platters because the records are still selling today like they were when they were made. They sell on television and radio throughout the world. When you mention the Platters, children say, 'Oh, I'd love to see the Platters.' Since 1968, most of the places we play are discotheques where all the kids dance and the older people sit around and watch them."

With Helen as the troupe's mother and major cook, whipping up full-course banquets on hot plates in hotel rooms around the globe, the International Platters have played some of the more bizarre concerts to date. They've played with the Ray Bloch Orchestra before 6,000 of Hyannisport's more well-heeled inhabitants in an airport hangar emptied for the occasion; in a soccer stadium in Yugoslavia filled with 18,000 cheering fans; at state fairs where they ride in ticker tape parades like VIPs. Their caravan has played virtually every officer's club on the globe as guests of the Pentagon.

The topper has to be their concert on a nuclear submarine under the ocean. Helen remembers, "There were 350 boys down there. We have the greatest guys in the world on those submarines. They are not at all like people above water. They don't know any race or prejudice. We had dinner with the guys as if we were members of the crew. Everything they cook they make themselves, even the ice cream.

"I always like to joke and kid with the boys down there. When Tony went to get a haircut while we were down there, I said, 'Do you know how to cut this style hair?' The

Tony and Helen Williams and the "International Platters" today.

captain said, 'Come with me.' He took me in the green room and there was a soul brother. Then he took me around and there were six more soul brothers. He said, 'See, we're not like people who live above water. We're all brothers."

But Tony observed there were pitfalls involved with the date. "I told Helen and her mother that when you're going on deck, wear pants, because when they climbed up the ladder through the hatch, all the guys would crowd around and look up at her. I said, 'Change into some slacks. We don't want an abandoned ship.' "

Tony's long exile from recording may soon be over. Tony and Helen will soon record the old tunes on a new disco beat as Helen and Tony Williams and the Twilight-timers.

"There are a lot of things I can see now at fifty. I'm proud of my age. When I used to shoot dice there was a thing I used to say, 'A lotta little people never reach forty years old,' then boom! I got it. The point is to make something out of yourself. Be someone. Do something to have people remember you by. I have gone the whole gamut. Yet I feel I have to far to go. I also know that where I live, there is a multitude behind me."

Bobby Vee

Robert Thomas Velline was born April 30, 1943, in Fargo, North Dakota, an unlikely launching pad for a young man who would land a spot in the teen idol hall of fame by the age of eighteen and go on to record nearly thirty albums in a pop singing career that is now into its twentieth year.

There was music everywhere in the Velline household. His father, now a retired chef, was a honky-tonk piano player. Two older brothers played guitar, trumpet, and trombone. But it was his uncle, a saxophonist in many of the thirties and forties' big bands, who provided the initial inspiration. He helped him buy his first sax and Bobby studied the instrument through junior high school. By that time he was also getting into older brother Bill's guitar. Bill gave him some lessons and soon they were getting together with a couple of other guys from Fargo to play. "We were really just flogging our instruments, having fun, but learning. We started getting together on a regular basis to practice, in basements or anywhere we could find. We were playing rock 'n' roll, Buddy Holly, Elvis, Jerry Lee Lewis, Little Richard, and the Everly Brothers. But there weren't many bands in the area and not much of a scene, so the only place people would see us was when we practiced in the basement of Morehead State College."

Bobby's group had only been rehearsing for about three or four months when on February 3, 1959, one of rock 'n' roll's first tragedies provided their big break. A plane carrying Buddy Holly, the Big Bopper, and Ritchie Valens to a rock 'n' roll show in Fargo crashed in a cornfield in Ames, Iowa, killing all aboard. As Bobby tells the story, "Nobody even knew we existed at the time. The afternoon before the show, the local radio station was asking over the air for bands to fill in the show. Dion and the Belmonts were going to be there and some others, but they needed more. So Jim Stillman, our bass player, just called up and said, 'Yeah, we have a band and we're excellent and we'd love to come down and do it.' They said fine and suddenly we only had a few hours to get our act together. First we went out and bought matching uniforms. They were incredible. Sleeveless sweaters with buttons down the front, white shirt, black pants and angora neckties, black-and-white angora neckties that we bought for a quarter apiece at J.C. Penny. I never did get the knot out of mine. I ended up having to get it cut off my neck.

"So we went on down to the show and the producers didn't have the faintest who we were. There was a disc jockey there to emcee and he informed us we would go on first and asked what the name of the band was. We were all supposed to have thought something up by the time we got there, but it turned out I was the only one who had. So we all just looked at each other until I just came out with 'The Shadows' and everybody said fine, yeah, that's great. Ten seconds later, 'Ladies and gentlemen, the Shadows,' and the curtain opened.

"In some of the bios done on me they say I was the only one who knew any of the songs, which was basically true. I guess I was the only one in the group who took it halfway seriously. It came naturally to me or something so I ended up doing the singing, by chance really more than choice. And I didn't even really enjoy it at the time. But we did it. Didn't even get paid. We certainly didn't think anything would come of it."

Not so. In the audience that night was a local promoter, Bing Bingston, "the local Hollywood contact, well, he owned the drive-in theater so we figured that was pretty close. It turned out he also booked platter parties and disc jockey record hops. He asked if we were interested in doing dances and things and we said sure. He booked our first paying job on Valentine's Day, eleven days after the plane crash, at a high school dance in Breckinridge, Minnesota, about fifty miles from Fargo."

So at the age of fifteen Bobby was a professional. "It paid sixty dollars, fifteen a piece. We jammed ourselves and all our equipment into a '51 Oldsmobile, drove down, played, and drove right back. It was February and I ended up in the back seat freezing underneath the bass drum."

Bing Bingston continued to book dates for them, mainly school dances. They were all too young to play clubs. Bill Velline was the oldest at nineteen. "The school crowds were pretty well behaved. They still are up in that part of the country. But we were really quite an attraction because we were one of the few bands around. The kids would dance for awhile but always come back up near the stage to watch."

Four months later, the band went to Minneapolis to cut a record. "I had written some songs. I had always been writing, poetry, songs, whatever. So we took one of the songs, worked it up, and it sounded pretty good. Bingston let us go down and cut it along with a few others, four songs done in three hours, all two-tracked. The first one, 'Suzy Baby,' came out on Soma Records, a Minneapolis label which specialized in polka music of all things, in September. The flip was an instrumental written by my brother called 'Flying High.' It was distributed in the tri-state area, Minnesota and the two Dakotas. We went around to all the radio stations, Sioux City, Sioux Falls, Duluth, Bismarck, and introduced ourselves. It was such an oddity that there was a local band they'd bring us right into the studio, interview us on the air, and play the record while we were sitting there."

The single became number one in the regional market and the group started hearing from the large record companies who wanted to put it out nationally. They listened to the various deals that were offered and decided to go with Snuff Garrett and Liberty Records, Snuff eventually becoming Bobby's longtime producer. "Suzy Baby" hit the national charts and Liberty decided they would sign Bobby to a separate contract, and the band to another. It would seem that Liberty was more interested in Bobby as a solo act than they were in the band as they already had

United Press International photo

an instrumental band under contract called the Ventures.

Then Snuff Garrett had Bobby do a song called "What Do You Want," a number one single in England when recorded by Adam Faith. Unfortunately, a few other people had the same idea. Bobby's version on Liberty came out simultaneously with five others. The effect was similar to half a dozen debutantes showing up at the Waldorf wearing identical gowns. The thunder gets spread a little thin.

Then in 1960, with Liberty Records willing to give this seventeen year old another shot at the top, and with Snuff Garrett at the controls, the Bobby Vee sound was created. First Snuff took Bobby down to the studio in Clovis, New Mexico, where Buddy Holly had recorded. They cut an album side's worth of straight-ahead rock 'n' roll numbers. Then they went to Los Angeles and laid down six more songs but this time with Bobby solo-backed by a full orchestra. Snuff liked the Los Angeles session better so they cut six more songs there. "Snuffy was happiest with full orchestra and the big arrangements so that's what we used on the album. It was called *Bobby Vee Sings Your Favorites*, all songs from the fifties. But I was kind of disappointed at first because I was really excited about the straight-ahead rock we'd done in Clovis. I had always been a rock 'n' roller."

The album came out, and "Devil or Angel," the single that was issued from it, hit the Top Ten. They followed up with "Rubber Ball," a novelty tune written by Gene Pitney, and Bobby had another hit. So they put another album out with both singles on it barely a few months after the first album. "We put out so many albums. In the early sixties we were putting out four a year five years in a row. Back then we could cut one in two days, four songs in three hours, take a break, then four in the afternoon, cut four the next morning, and you've got an album. Take the best song and that's the single. That's why I had time to tour eleven months a year, which I did. As of now I've put out a total of twenty-seven albums and there were probably three or four that were never released."

So Bobby Vee was a major recording artist, a teen idol touring all over the United States and leading the pre-Beatle American invasion of England in person and on the charts and he was still waiting for his driver's license. Then in early 1961 Bobby was in the studio to record a number of singles including "How Many Tears," which had been written by tunesmith mainstays, Gerry Goffin and Carole King. They came out to the West Coast for the session and during a break Carole sat down at a piano and played a few new things that she and Gerry had written including "Take Good Care of My Baby." "It sounded fantastic so we cut it almost immediately. It seemed obvious that it was there, that it really had it."

It did. It soared to the top of the chart and was number one in the nation for three straight weeks in the fall of 1961. For the next four years, with Snuff Garrett producing, Bobby worked at an incredible clip, record after record, album after album, all landing somewhere on the charts, and touring worldwide, Europe, Australia, the Far East, and the U.S. "Japan was pretty hysterical, fans swarming the hotel and all that. I think I did my first color television show over there some time in the early sixties. I had my own special with all Japanese guest artists including one little girl who sang 'More Than I Can Say,' a song of mine that she had a hit with over there. I also remember playing a coliseum in the Phillipines with the Ventures. Thirty-six thousand people. Everybody could get in. The ticket prices started at a nickel and went up to a dollar. And of course England. I've gone there at least once a year since 1960. I actually saw the Beatle thing coming in the real early sixties. Snuffy and I were over there when 'Love Me Do' came out. I thought it was incredible. It reminded me of the Crickets. Snuffy tried to buy the American rights to it and bring it back to the States but the price was too high."

Of course the Beatles did make it over and so did the Dave Clark Five and the Stones and Herman and so on. The impact and effect on the careers of American artists were immense. "Through the latter part of the sixties I was really kind of groping for direction. I had split with Snuffy Garrett in about 1965. We had done so many hits I was in the habit of thinking that you just put a record out and it would make it. But the music was changing."

Bobby did have a few successful songs in the late sixties though. "Come Back When You Grow Up," a simple little song that a disc jockey friend in Oklahoma suggested he record, came out and didn't seem to be doing much until it was realized that it was selling well but only in way-out-of-the-way markets. So they took out an ad in *Billboard* advertising the song as number one in Billings, Montana, and number one in Spartensburg, South Carolina, and number one in all the other podunk places it was selling in. It started slowly after that but eventually sold two million records.

Nonetheless, Bobby decided to sit down and reevaluate the situation. "I was doing clubs and working with big bands and big arrangements and not really enjoying myself. I have always seen myself as a rock 'n' roller even though my music has always been pop. I decided to get back in touch with the reason I got in the business in the first place and got a band together to tour with. Once again I was a lead singer in a band. That's the way I like it and I still am. Since that time I've become involved in the production of other groups' records and my own, which I'm still recording. Now basically, production is really where my heart is. One of the biggest pleasures for me has always been working in the studio, making the records and now producing."

Today Bobby lives in Bel Air, California, with his wife and four children ages seven through thirteen, all who are studying music, and all by their own choice. "That's one thing I wanted them to discover for themselves. It's been a great source of joy in my life, and great sorrow too, but if they develop a talent for it they can take it with them wherever they go. Like any other business it takes a lot of hard work and there are disappointments. It's not all gold records and the 'Ed Sullivan Show.' But I don't have an axe to grind with anybody. I loved everything I was doing, came out of it with some good friends, and the record company was as straight with me as any company in this business could be. I think that about covers it."

Dave Clark

In 1963, Dave Clark was sitting in an audience of three thousand people at the London Palladium watching Judy Garland strut her stuff in the filming of 'I Could Go on Singing'. He was a paid extra. A year later the Dave Clark Five were on-stage at the Palladium before a packed house, top of the bill.

He was born December 15, 1942, in Tottenham, a suburb north of London. His mother was a teacher and his father worked in the post office. "Same as any other family in London we lived week to week. We weren't rich but I had a great childhood. A lot of love, caring, and good times. There were no restrictions put on me, which was good. I was always advised but allowed to make up my own mind, which I think is important for a child."

After Dave finished school he started off as a draftsman, then had a job in property. "But my yearning was always to be an actor, a childhood ambition. I always admired James Dean and Laurence Olivier. So I packed everything in to be a film actor."

Dave began as an extra, then became a stuntman. "If you went to one of the movies I did and sneezed, then you missed me." The first movie he was in was a horror film called *The Brain*. Directed by Freddie Francis it was about a group of scientists specializing in keeping a brain alive indefinitely. "I heard that they were looking for people and I managed to join the union. I was picked out for a crowded ballroom scene. I'm dancing with this girl. The maniac has escaped and the police are after him. I kiss the girl I'm dancing with and the maniac runs into us and knocks us over. Very corny. I got paid embarrassment money. It was crazy; you used to get three pounds a day as an extra. I didn't get very rich that day."

He went on to appear in over forty films before the DC Five went professional, including *The V.I.P.s* with Elizabeth Taylor and Richard Burton, and *The Victors* with George Hamilton. "We hadn't made any records yet so I was just one of the hundreds."

The DC Five was formed in order to finance a trip to Holland for the soccer team Dave played for, the Tottenham Hotspurs. "One Easter we were invited to play a Dutch team but we didn't have enough money to get there. We decided to form a group, four other guys on the team and myself, in order to get it. Mike Smith had studied classical music since he was four or five. Lenny Davidson had been playing guitar for five years. So had Rick Huxley. And Denis Payton had been on sax for about that long. I was the only one who hadn't played before. But we needed a drummer. There was a drum kit at the Salvation Army that I bought for ten pounds and I learned to play listening to rock 'n' roll records, Little Richard, Bill Haley, Elvis, late fifties, early sixties rock 'n' roll. I enjoyed it actually. So we ran all these dances until we had enough money for the team to go."

For the record, the Hotspurs were victorious by a score of three to two. When they returned, mission accomplished, Dave figured that that was that as far as the band went. "But when we got back there was a letter waiting for me from Buckingham Palace. What had happened was that while we were running the dances we had business cards printed up offering our services at gigs. The mother of a friend of mine worked at the Palace and had been distributing the cards around. The letter was a request for us to play at the annual staff Christmas Ball. I thought it was a joke and ignored it. Then a footman came around for an answer. It was for real and of course we agreed to do it. We didn't have the money to go down by taxi so we took the subway, then got a taxi just around the corner from the Palace, put all the equipment in it, and were driven to the gates. This was before we'd made a record or anything. It was really a publicist's dream. It was

The DC 5. Dave Clark is bottom left.

lovely to be able to say we played the Palace. It almost
sounds made up but it really happened.''

It was certainly enough to keep the group together.
''We expected instant stardom but that didn't happen. We
did gigs all over for awhile and then decided to play at just
one place, The Royal, which was actually a huge ballroom.
That's where we really started to draw crowds and make
our name. Sometimes they'd have as many as six thousand
people a night. All of a sudden everybody started to get
into it.''

But still they didn't have a record. Nobody seemed to
want to record them. Well, if Dave could get a whole soccer club to Holland, he could get a record out. ''I was still
doing some film extra work and some stunt work. There
was one movie with Anne Baxter and Adam Faith, an English pop star at the time. I can't remember the name of it
but I got 120 pounds for crashing a car in it. It wasn't really
difficult because these things are always timed and
planned. It sounds good but there's nothing heroic in it.
In those days I had studied karate and unarmed combat

and knew how to take a fall, car crashes, barroom brawls. All the guys in the group were still working too. Denis was in electronics. Mike was in insurance. Rick worked in a music store, and Lenny worked in an engineering firm."

So Dave put the 120 pounds into having the band record a single, "Do You Love Me," a song originally done by an American group, the Contours. He produced it as well. "I took it to EMI. They flipped over it and gave me a very good deal. The record did well but actually we were covered on it. A group called Brian Poole and the Tremeloes were just coming off a number one record and were looking for a follow-up. Somebody sneaked them a copy of our record. They did it and it came out two weeks after ours. Since they were following up a hit, the record shops only stocked their version. And I said, 'Well, I guess that's about it.' Their version did get to number one in England and fortunately ours got to number nineteen. However, in the rest of the world our version was on top. Then we followed up with 'Glad All Over' which Mike and I had written and it went straight to the number one spot."

"Bits and Pieces," another song from the pen of Mike and Dave, came out next and blew out the British barges as well. Within days humankind was lining up for the DC Five, top of the bill, at the London Palladium. Meanwhile, Ed Sullivan had his sensors groping the here-and-there for some hot licks to keep the kids moist before their moms and dads settled in for the alien horse shouts of the Flying Cadenzas and other trained seals. "They got in touch with us through the record company in England and I didn't want to go. We were just hitting it off in England, and to be perfectly honest, I didn't know who Ed Sullivan was. Well, they called back and offered us a fortune and it was stupid not to go.

"The strange thing was that on that first show he announced after we had played that we would be on the following week and of course everybody went crazy. But he hadn't asked me and we were committed to play in England on that date, so I said sorry we can't do it. He said he realized he should have asked me first but he would appreciate it if we would do it. As far as our commitment in England, they would pay for it, buy it all out. I said okay and I guess because I was totally honest with him, not playing any games, and because I didn't come on with 'Yes, Mr. Sullivan, no, Mr. Sullivan,' we got on very well together. A lot of people hated him but I always found him a gentleman. So we came back for the second time the next week. It was fantastic. We had come in an unknown the first time and when we returned there were thirty thousand people out at Kennedy Airport. That was the power of the 'Ed Sullivan Show,' really incredible."

At that time, Murray the K, frenzied DJ and self-ordained "Fifth Beatle," gave the Five a further boost. By the time they were here to do Sullivan, they had three singles, "Do You Love Me," "Glad All Over," and "Bits and Pieces," all on the British charts. The Beatles had made their debut on "Sullivan" the week before and Murray, quick as a cat and never far off the bandwagon, leaped on the Five, banged all three singles all over the air waves, and boom, they were all hits in America. On the strength of that plus the prime-time exposure care of Sully's weekly living room invasions, the Five became the first English group to tour the States in the spring of 1964. The Beatles didn't tour until the summer.

All this and Dave was still managing the group himself. "As a matter of fact, we were the only group ever to have two number one records and to have topped the bill at the Palladium and on 'Sullivan' and not have a manager. I eventually brought in an agent because it got to be too much, but at the time no one wanted to know about needing somebody else. I guess you could call it controlling one's destiny creatively. And of course when you hit up everybody wants to jump on the bandwagon. We always said we wouldn't go professional until we had two records in the Top Five, so the boys didn't pack in their jobs until we had the second one. I didn't want it to be a flash-in-the-pan thing. I also wanted it to be a top-of-the-bill act. It would have been stupid to do it just for kicks. Everybody said we were crazy. Now they look back and say it was a shrewd move. Sure, you can say that after it happens. But you only hear of one's successes, you never hear about the failures. And I said that as soon as the enjoyment goes then we'd pack it in.

"But the group took off so fast we were just interested in enjoying that, riding along with it. But making the right moves, moves with the long term in mind. Even when I didn't have any money I'd do something if I thought it was the right move. I'd have played the Palladium for fifty dollars instead of some other spot for five thousand. You have to look at it as a long-term thing. If you do the right things for your career, the money will come later. If you go for the quick kill, then you don't last long. That was always my philosophy. And if you do things well, put on a good show, make records to the best of your ability, not getting cheap about it, then you're giving people value for their money and I think in the long run it will pay off. Fortunately, for the DC Five it did. In those days you sold records and we did, over forty million which is a lot even by today's standards."

With such incredible success, the Five was constantly on the road. "We were very lucky that we hit it off so big because we really toured in style. I mean, coming from a working class area in England to America with your own private plane, it was incredible. I enjoyed every minute of it. But after a time it becomes repetitious. In those days you play for only maybe thirty minutes and people would only want to hear your hits. I can understand their point of view, but for us it's not really much of a challenge and it becomes monotonous. You go around, then you do it again, and everybody's asking how did it all start. I used to get asked that a thousand times a year. And, you know, I was in the States twenty times and all I really saw was the plane, the hotel, the stage, the hotel, back out the kitchen to the plane, and on to the next job. I would go back to England and people would ask what's America like and I'd have to say I couldn't tell them. The first time I really saw it was on a holiday I took in 1969. I grew a beard so I wouldn't have to worry about being recognized and I real-

ly enjoyed it.

"But when we were doing it the audience response was fantastic, the fan hysteria. We were always locked in the hotels, couldn't go anywhere, kind of like being in the Army, I would guess, but without having to get your hair cut. We had a lot of close calls. In Long Beach, California, we finished a show and the people thought we were going to come back on and do another encore. When we didn't they were laying under the limousine so we couldn't leave. We were totally surrounded by thousands of kids. They started climbing all over the car and caved in the roof. We were on the floor trying to hold it up with our feet. I remember getting the bill for that one; the insurance company wouldn't cover it.

"I also got knocked out a few times. One time we were in Sweden and I got hit in the head with something while we were onstage. There was a trickle of blood down my forehead and then I was out. Somebody had thrown a stone or a rock with a note reading 'I love you' attached to it. Another time, in Cleveland, a girl jumped out of the balcony of the theater we were playing and landed right on the stage breaking both her legs. She tried to crawl up my drum kit.

"When we arrived in the Phillipines the people went berserk turning over cars and breaking windows. It was a little frightening. We were all given our own little armed bodyguards and locked in the hotel except when we went out to play to a quarter of a million people in two days.

"But we always said we would take it year by year. And in fact we only toured for about three years before we stopped enjoying it. We played most places around the world and I really loved it. People say to me that I must have hated it to stop when I did, but I tell them I wouldn't have missed it for the world."

The success of the DC Five continued unabated until the boys decided to disband in 1970. "In the latter part of '69, I had been offered a scholarship to study drama at a college that Laurence Olivier runs called the Central School. We had hits out, but I figured I couldn't do both. And the boys wanted to get into their own things. So we decided to pack it in while we were still on top. That was nice.

"So I carried on studying drama for three years, six days a week from nine in the morning until ten at night. Loved it. Since then I've just taken off around the world a bit getting myself back to normal. Recently I've written a screenplay for a motion picture. It's a thriller and a black comedy at the same time, black comedy in the English sense. In America, I guess, you would call it more of a caper. I'll be producing it myself, but I won't be in it because I'm really too close to the story. It's my baby, so to speak. And although I have no ambition to record again I want to get involved in a bit of production. Music is my life and I'll always want to be connected with it."

When we talked to Dave, he was living temporarily in California working on the film project. "My base is really England, but the last six months have been the first time I've lived here and I love it. I'll be going back to England soon, but America's always been my second home."

Sheb Wooley

Sheb ("Purple People Eater") Wooley will tell you his "maiden" name is Shelby and that he was born in 1921 on a small hillside farm in Ericka, Oklahoma. At his father's farming and ranching operation, Sheb and his three brothers pastured steers for other ranchers in the neighborhood. Putting the spurs on and saddling the steers, they would buck as many as twelve head a day apiece. Although he never got to be a professional, he played a small town area as a cowboy. Until, "I found out there was an easier way to make a living than falling off them damn horses."

Around 1932, while listening to the Grand Ole Opry and the Light Crust Dough Boys from down in Fort Worth, he knew he was smitten by the guitar. He discovered his neighbors had an old guitar, so he talked his father into trading the shotgun for the beaten-up old instrument. Once it was in his possession, he and his dad would play a few chords, his father being a fiddler.

For the next five years, his "growing-up period," Sheb worked local dances with a fiddler player. "They usually had a country dance out in the country at somebody's house. They would strip all the furniture out. They'd make up ten gallons of home brew a week ahead. One guy was assigned to make the beer and by Saturday night it was finished. Everybody would pitch in a quarter or a half dollar. They'd bring it to the party and fill up the water bucket with it.

"We'd make a few bucks, sometimes a few dollars apiece on Saturday night. They charged twenty-five cents per set and each person had to chip in. You could dance all night for twenty-five cents. A lot of times we had a bunch of drunk people. People do get on with it a little bit. It makes us great lovers and great fighters. Everybody got drunk and was somebody. But I don't remember but two fights over six years."

As a student at Plainview High School in Plainview, Oklahoma, Sheb had a band called the Melody Boys. They had a local radio broadcast for an Elk City station selling baby chicks for the Magnum Hatchery. After "one of those teenage marriages" at nineteen, Sheb got side-tracked from music for awhile and worked as a welder on defense contracts at a shipyard in Long Beach, California.

After the war, Sheb went to Nashville with a sheaf of songs he had penned for the country stars. "I thought it would be so simple. Like, here's five I'll give Eddy Arnold, here's another five for Ernest Tubbs, here's another for Roy Acuff. Of course, it didn't work that way at all." However, he met Jim Bullit, an announcer at WSN, who planned to start a record company. He did and Sheb was his first artist recording "Oklahoma Honky Tonk Gal" and "I Can Live on Without You."

While the records sold few copies, he hustled up a job at WLAC. "I went over there and said, 'Hey, I would like to be on your radio station. You don't have to pay me, if I don't have to pay you. I'll announce where I'll be appearing and let me sell a picture or song book." During his two shows, the first starting at 4:45 in the morning and reaching across the continent to California, he hawked eight by ten glossies of himself, the "Long Tall Singing Cowboy," with the words of a song printed on the back. "I'd just sit there and open envelopes and take the quarters out of them and send the pictures out." While playing the local schoolhouses, tobacco barns, and granges around the Nashville area, he printed up pictures of himself with Eddy Arnold and Ernest Tubbs into a songbook, even though his relationship with Arnold consisted of mowing his lawn while he was on tour. Sheb soon lost his job when the musicians' union complained that Sheb was making tran-scriptions of his own music on the radio show and publish-ing them in Chicago without paying for them.

From Nashville, he cruised down to Fort Worth and Dallas, where he fronted a band and did commercials as the Calumet Indians. His job was similar to the Light Crust Dough Boys, selling Calumet Baking Powder, a General Foods product, through a mix of entertaining pop songs and periodic commercial spots. He sold the baking powder for three years on a "bobtail" network, a loosely organized group of fifteen stations which reached into the rural areas. "After 1950 that folded or I folded and I went to the West Coast."

A fellow in Dallas had slipped Sheb the name of a Hollywood agent. When he got out there, he called him up, and set up the appointment. He walked into Ray Cooper's office with his big cowboy hat on and said, "Hey, I want to be a movie star." After three months in Hollywood, R'y put him into a play with a Western theme at an actors workshop. From that flop, he got a screen test with Warner Brothers, who were scouring the countryside for new faces to appear with Errol Flynn in *Rocky Mountain*.

Sheb got the part of a heavy in a bunch of ragtail soldiers coming across the South after the Civil War. For seven weeks, he worked in Gallop, New Mexico, shining in his attempted rape of Patricia Wymore, the heroine of the flick. Help from Flynn, described by Sheb as "a hard booze fighter and nice guy," got him good footage on the production and helped him to continue his film career.

Over the years he has appeared in forty-eight films including *Boy From Oklahoma*, *Little Big Horn*, *Hellgate*, and *Distant Drums*. However, the year after *Rocky Mountain* saw Sheb in his most memorable role as the drinking heavy at the railroad station in *High Noon* with Gary Cooper.

"I wasn't setting the world on fire in the picture business, but I was eking out a living. I was recording but no one knew it. The records were selling about 15,000 but then every record sold something. Now you can have a record sell only fifteen."

In 1953, he picked his guitar up again and struck out to play clubs like the Phoenix in the Los Angeles area. His song writing became his mainstay with Hank Snow's 400,000 seller of his "Mexican Joe Met Joliet Blond" and Teresa Brewers's gold rendition of "Too Young to Tango." While he had a chart record himself, Sheb continued making films, appearing in *Giant* with Rock Hudson, Elizabeth Taylor, and James Dean as one of the friends of the Benedicts, the ranchers who hit it rich. Hudson and Wooley grow old together on the plains.

In late 1955, he wrote and recorded "Are You Satisfied?" which went gold and had eight different cover versions over the years. 1958 was the pivotal year for Sheb's recording and acting careers. In February, he and a youngster by the name of Clint Eastwood started work on a pilot television show called "Rawhide." The show ran as a series for six years, the first four and a half of which Sheb played Pete Nolan, the scout of the cattle drive. In May of that year, he recorded "The Purple People Eater," which became a number one national chart topper. But he was so tied up in shooting "Rawhide," "I couldn't even get free to do all the appearances.

"Actually, I guess it was an accident. A songwriter friend of mine told me a joke his kids told him one day when they came home from school. 'What has one eye, flies, has a horn, and eats people? It's a one-eyed, one-horned, flying people eater.' Those were the jokes kids were telling around. I said, 'Hey, that might make a song.' I wrote the thing. I wasn't sure I was writing a song. I was just having fun. I had a session coming up with MGM. I was going to go to the Beverly Hills Hotel to meet the president of the company. I get down there and I had this thing at the bottom of my guitar case.

"I was singing all my songs, mostly ballads. He said, 'Well, OK, but what else do you have?' 'This is really the bottom of the barrel.' And I showed him this 'Purple People Eater.' The president said, 'Why don't you sing this?' I said, 'Well, OK.' After we had done it, the people in charge of sales didn't want to release it. They said, 'We don't want to be identified with this. We're Metro Goldwyn Mayer!' The company was on its ass. They were about to go broke. That summer they told me that 'The Purple People Eater' put them back into business."

He followed with "Sweet Chile" in 1959 and "That's My Pa," a number one country hit, which marked his return to Nashville. Still appearing on "Rawhide" and making films, Sheb remained in California, first living on a twenty-two acre ranch in the San Fernando Valley, and after 1964 in the Old High Valley near Santa Barbara where he raised race horses. From time to time, Sheb had a family. His only child, a daughter Christie, sings in Nashville and is a student at Ventura Junior College. Sheb is currently married to his fourth wife.

After "Rawhide," Sheb went out on tour working the package shows in big auditoriums, fairs, and clubs. But, as for country nightclubs, Sheb says, "I've tried to stay out of the skull orchards. Every entertainer needs some fill-in dates. You're out there so you might as well pick up the loot. But I don't particularly like to stay around inebriated people or a bunch of drunks." Through the sixties, Sheb toured U.S. bases in Korea, Okinawa, Vietnam, and Taiwan as well as in Germany and Spain. "But they don't do that anymore because they don't have the slot machines. They used to have slot machines in the clubs and that was a big contributor to their revenues. They don't have as much money to pay entertainers as they used to."

Sheb Wooley has recorded hundreds of albums, fifteen of them in the guise of his alter ego, Ben Colder, a drunken character he created in the early sixties, who sings parodies of hits. Under that name, Sheb has done such parodies as "Son, Don't Go Near the Eskimos," "Almost Persuaded Number 2," "Harper Valley PTA Number 2," which sold 300,000, and his take-off on Kenny Rogers's "Lucille" called "Lucille Number 2." Unfortunately, in 1963, the people down under in Sydney, Australia, who were expecting Sheb's country hits, didn't take too kindly to the appearance of Ben Colder. In the middle of his concert, Sheb found himself standing on a revolving stage set up in the old stadium built for the Australian boxing championships. His voice was being drowned out by the rain pouring down on the tin roof and his act was being received by an audience rapidly turning into stone. He finally had to revamp the entire act before total disaster struck. He says, however, that, "they were courteous." Cold but courteous.

In 1968, he played the bases in Vietnam near the fire zones where audiences sprinkled applause between their screams of "mortar incoming." At one such base, Sheb had a memorable experience paralleling the way the war was going. "I had a little trio. When we rehearsed I told them, 'We'll open with "Rawhide" because a lot of people will recognize that. You guys start singing the theme "Rollin', rollin', rollin', keep those doggies rollin', Rawhide!" You keep singing that over and over and I'll bounce out onstage.'

"So this particular night before the show, I had to take a leak. I go back over there and I heard the band 'Rollin', Rollin', Rollin'.' I realized, 'Good Lord. They don't know any more than that.' Well, I rushed it and made a mistake. I had the tourista trots and messed my pants. I had to take off my boots and my clothes while the poor band is still onstage 'Rollin', Rollin', Rollin'.' They had been up there eight to ten minutes just 'Rollin', Rollin', Rollin',' along. That was the longest introduction in the world. I had to get cleaned up and onstage but the show went on."

After 1969, Sheb joined up with Buck Owens and did the first pilot of the "Hee Haw" show. But the slough of concert dates and recording obligations forced Sheb to pull in his horns, cut down on touring, and drop the "Hee Haw" show. "I realized that I didn't need as much as I was making. How many cars can you drive? How many beds can you sleep on? I simplified my life and got rid of the race horses. That cut down on lots of dates right there."

In the summer of '78, Sheb moved from California to Old Hickory Lake in Nashville, where he owns a sound studio called The Music Mill, some real estate, and an office building off Music Row, the heart of the country western music business. "I haven't been too bad a businessman. But I had one loser. I lost $100,000 on a land deal in California in 1964. I was going to shoot my eye teeth out. But I've done pretty good." He still tours around the clubs, recently working with Dolly Parton's sister Stella, and keeps Ben Colder alive jibing the contemporary chart busters.

On his success as a songwriter and singer: "Well, I don't know. I think I have a knack. I started early. I wasn't good but I kept writing. I had a little bit of talent and lots of sweat. And it worked."

Steve Alaimo

"If you're a star, you can't get away with being a normal human being. If you have a hit record, people will crowd around. When you're on television, you're a box of soap. You can't be rational and be an entertainer; it doesn't make sense. The whole business doesn't make sense. It's the only business where people will work for nothing just to be in it. You have to eat, drink, and live for the moment you make it. I didn't make it because I didn't have the desire. I had the ability, talent, knew the right people, and got all the breaks, but I never really wanted to make it. I'm relieved and thankful I'm not an entertainer. I know so few who are happy. A star has to deal with being put on a pedestal and then later being knocked off. It's tough to sustain longevity. It's easier not to have gotten to the pedestal."

Steve Alaimo is best remembered as being a regular on Dick Clark's "American Bandstand" and "Where the Action Is" and having sung "Everyday I Have to Cry." Along with his old buddies Henry Stone and Jack Kratish, Steve presently owns TK Productions in Hialeah, Florida. After deciding that "it ain't no good," Steve hung the mike in the stand for the last time and strode offstage to form a miniconglomerate of record labels. Since 1969, Steve has devoted himself solely to the production end of hit records, spinning out everything from white gospel sounds to disco music.

Born in Omaha, Nebraska on December 6, 1940, Steve is the son of a general practitioner and the eldest of eight children. At the age of five, his family moved to Rochester, New York, where for many years he lived just six blocks away from jazz artist Chuck Mangione, a fact he only discovered after years in the music business.

At the beginning of his musical career, he was a sax player interested in the blues, but soon he wanted to sing rock and roll. His guitar playing he owes to his uncle. "The first time I picked up a guitar was because of my Uncle Sam. Italians always play guitar or mandolin. In those days, the family spent the summers at our house in Canadaigua in the Finger Lakes region of New York. At night there was nothing for the kids to do, so the family would gather round and sing songs with Uncle Sam on the guitar. I watched him and soon we played little old Italian songs together. From there, I decided to get into Elvis's songs. Elvis was the first person who made me want to sing. I stole my music from three people—Elvis, Ray Charles, and James Brown. Actually, nobody really originated anything. If you throw in Sinatra and Sam Cooke, you can nail everybody in show business down to these people. After the Italian songs I learned from Uncle Sam, the others were much easier to play."

In his senior year of high school, Steve formed a group called Steve Alaimo and the Redcoats, which consisted of two guitars, a bass, and drums. "Everybody said we couldn't make it because we didn't have a sax and piano." That year the Redcoats played various bars and lounges in the Rochester area. "The first place we ever worked was the J&L Lounge, a small little bar on a relatively raggedy street, then Three Rivers in Syracuse, and Club 86 in Geneva, New York, a real godforsaken place which used to be a gambling joint."

After a brief stint at the University of Michigan, Steve transferred to the University of Miami to further his pre-med studies in the hope of joining the long line of doctors in his family. He graduated from Miami with a B.S. in chemistry and received offers from various medical schools. But Steve and his Redcoats had become a regionally successful band, playing dances and record hops with Charlie McCoy's band, the Agendas. Working as a promo man for Tone Record distributors, Steve hooked up with many record people who later were to become valuable contacts in his producing career. During this time, he dabbled in the production end of the business and discovered a twosome who later were catapulted to international fame as the singing duo of Sam and Dave.

Around 1960, Steve did a favor for a man who eventually became a lifelong friend and booster—Dick Clark. "Dick was producing a show at the Miami Exhibition Hall with fifteen or twenty-five acts including Fabian, Connie Francis, Duane Eddy, and the Everly Brothers. When they entered the hall, the musicians union demanded that Dick have a twenty-five piece orchestra, because all 'variety shows' under the union agreement were supposed to have X amount of musicians. Of course, none of the acts had sheet music. They were rock and roll acts. We were a jukebox band in those days and knew all the performers' songs. So we backed up the whole band. It wouldn't have gone on otherwise. Dick never forgot that. When I had 'Mashed Potatoes' out, he gave me a shot on American Bandstand. Today, he and I are still doing projects together but on a totally different level."

In 1961, the Redcoats' wide range of material again paid off with an eleven-month gig at Eden Roc, a posh Miami Beach Hotel used to the likes of Frank Sinatra. The twist was happening and the hotel wanted a group who could play for the current rage in the lounge called "Harry's American Bar." "Harry, the manager, didn't know what he was buying but he hired me because everybody told him that the twist was happening. We did Ray Charles, James Brown, Little Walter, Muddy Waters, and Sam Cooke, all black artists. There we were, the hottest thing in Miami, doing R&B and calling it the twist. Nobody in the audience knew the black artists so it was an original act. All the material was new to them."

In 1963, Steve recorded his gold single, "Every Day I Have to Cry," and followed up its success with a tour around the country, performing with such people as Lou Christie and Paul and Paula. Then the bottom fell out of the American music scene with the British invasion. "In 1964, my agent told me to go back into nightclubs and do

the big band stuff Sinatra was doing. They changed my whole image, put me in a tuxedo, told me to cut my hair. They said that I couldn't make it with long hair singing the rock and roll sounds I had been doing. So I cut my hair and sang songs like 'Accentuate the Positive' and 'Day in Day Out.'" Steve worked the little club circuit, playing resort areas like the Catskills and quickly tired of the routine.

In 1965, Dick Clark was putting together a pilot television show for a series he was trying to get aired. The show would later make history as "Where the Action Is." With his career waning, Steve suddenly was rescued by Dick Clark who remembered Steve's popularity from "Bandstand" days. As Steve recalled: "He made me the star of the show and hired a backup band for the show. Eventually, that band ended up being the stars of the show. That wasn't the way it was originally planned. They were Paul Revere and the Raiders. So I returned to the nightclubs but this time playing the funky music I thought the audience really wanted to hear. It worked."

With a revamped act and his old repertoire, Steve headlined with the Fifth Dimension in the main room of Caesar's Palace, and later at the Copa and the Caribe Hilton in Puerto Rico. While those years were lucrative, Steve admits that he probably should have gone to Europe. "My act probably would have been big there. My problem was that I was years ahead of my time."

In the late sixties, before his recording career slacked off, Steve tried out his dramatic skills in three, less than sensational, films, *The Wild Rebels, The Hooked Generation*, and *Family*. Steve comments that, "all can be seen on your local television station which plays horror films." *The Hooked Generation* released in 1969 is a certifiable bomb starring Jeremy Slate and the prizefighter Willie Pastrano. The story is a bewildering saga of narcotics peddlers massacring their way through Cuban contacts and Coast Guard patrols. As a respite from their drug transactions, the desperadoes kidnap the usual group of innocent local victims.

Luckily in 1969, Steve returned to Miami to start TK Productions as a full-time concern. His business partner Henry Stone had produced Steve's first hit, "I Want You to Love Me," on Marlin Records, one of several labels Steve would later come to own. After being produced by the likes of Bob Crewe, Burt Bacharach, Luther Dixon, Tommy Boyce, and Bobby Hart, Steve concluded that he had tried one too many times for stardom. "All my agents and producers were always trying to do the right thing in my career. They took a shot and were wrong. I am not in any shape or form disappointed. Henry and I had been in production off and on for years. We decided to give it a go and go all the way. We got hot, we got lucky, and we did the right thing. We've done very well."

Today, when Steve gets together with old friends like Al Cooper, Frankie Valli, Steve Stills, and others who come from certain eras, he says it feels like "crossing into different time zones, like being in a time warp." During a taping of a recent Dick Clark "Good Old Days," Steve vis-

ited with other stars from the fifties and sixties who hadn't adjusted to the loss of stardom. "They all seemed to be lost, just doing what they always had. I felt that I was where everybody really should be. It was discouraging." But he understands the appeal of the spate of rock revival nostalgia shows because, "compared to what followed, those were good clean, fun days. Happy days like the show says."

In 1972, the year he last performed in public, Steve married his wife Candida. They live in Coral Cables with their daughter, Lindsey Anne. Her birth, Steve claims, is the "most amazing thing that has happened to me." Knowing his joy over his daughter's birth, the great songwriter combo, Mac David and Jimmy van Heusen, wrote a song celebrating the event, appropriately titled "Lindsey Anne." Even though Steve produces hits as a routine affair these days, he still fantasizes about another hit record, the song about his daughter sung by a Sinatra. Until then, he'll have to be content with having produced eight of the top thirty disco hits last year.

Dolores "Dee Dee" Kenniebrew

So which was your favorite girl group? Did you melt with the Chantels "Every Night"? Count "A Thousand Stars" with Kathy Young and the Innocents? Open up the Marvalettes' address book and dial "Beechwood 4-5789"? Drop by the "Chapel of Love" as guests of the Dixie Cups? Hang around with the Ad Libs at the shopping center waiting for "That Boy from New York City"? Pin a medal on the Shirelles' "Soldier Boy"? Shake your finger with Patty and the Emblems at that "Mixed-Up, Shook-Up Girl"? Go "Walking in the Rain" with the Ronettes? Or maybe even lock your bedroom door, slip into a leather vest, and have the Shangri-Las gun your private engines with "The Leader of the Pack"?

Everybody knew that perfect love was just around the bend, boy-and-girl utopias in the back of the bus, throbbing passions beneath the party lights, desire on the turntable. For the uninitiated, these girls charted the route to that first roll in the golden hay of teen heaven. Obviously Mom and Dad and Sister Mary Beth down at St. Cecilia's weren't much into handing out helpful hints. For the lonely and the ugly, they filled the gap and broke the mirrors with a soaking-wet wall of sound that could transport any plain or wanting Jane into the realm of love consumated in furs and chiffon. Because when the Shirelles sang "Tonight's the Night" they weren't talking about getting to first base. This was home run derby underneath the bleachers. Aunt Ethel would sit on the divan in her housecoat flipping through *Reader's Digest* and smile benignly when little niece Lois would put on the Jelly Beans begging "I Wanna Love Him So Bad." She'd have a reassuring vision of Wally Cleaver carrying Lois's books home from school and Thank God she didn't get taken in by evil Elvis packing his behind in leather on the "Ed Sullivan Show." But if Aunt Ethel had ever figured out what the Jelly Beans had on their minds, or on little Lois's for that matter, she would have split her girdle.

But she didn't. These songs were wrapped in such elegant, well-crafted packages by producers like George Goldner and especially Phil Spector that desire became endowed with innocence and made safe. And there were no rocket-launcher guitars, no devils in daughter's woodpile with a megawatt axe. This was the sound of lust and longing draped in pristine sentiment by a wall of warmth and raised to a level not of this world.

Dolores "Dee Dee" Kenniebrew was fifteen, and along with the other teenage Crystals a student at Wingate High School in Brooklyn when Phil Spector, nineteen-year-old boy genius, super producer and budding enigma, overheard them singing in a studio rehearsal hall and decided they would be the first artists to record for his brand-new Philles label. His production credits already included a string of gold including "To Know Him Is to Love Him" by the Teddy Bears and "Pretty Little Angel Eyes" by Curtis Lee. According to Dolores, "We had been singing in school and this manager guy was taking us around trying to get us a recording contract. It was fun just rehearsing, but we really had no expectations. But then Phil came along and we cut a record a month later. The record was 'There Is No Other,' which was written by the brother-in-law of one of the girls. He had a little daughter named Crystal. That's where we got the name. We wanted to keep it simple, not the Four This or the Five That."

The single started out well and the girls made the record hop scene to promote it. "We'd lip-synch the records, hop in the car, go down the road, and do it again. Now when I think back, we were probably pretty crappy, but there was nothing to compare it to so we were probably quite all right. Then after awhile we did the same thing on Dick Clark's television show and then with his Caravan of Stars bus tour."

Everybody tells the story of when the bus broke down outside of a redneck saloon in Virginia. The beer-flushed denizens mistook the troupe for freedom riders and started picking out their pool cues for a little lesson teaching. Supposedly that didn't stop Dolores from walking in to use the facilities and order some food. When the waitresses refused, she went to the grill and cooked hamburgers for everybody on the bus. Then six guys pulled into the parking lot wielding clubs and axe handles. Dolores and the girls immediately broke into "Mine eyes have seen the glory of the coming of the Lord . . ." when the guys were walking toward the bus with menace on their minds. Luckily the Highway Patrol pulled up in time to restore a semblance of sanity and the bus rolled on to the next show. "You know I've heard that story about me so many times, but I just don't remember it happening, I really don't. A lot of silly things did happen but what can I tell you?"

Meanwhile, the law says children have to go to school whether they're stars or not. "I had to go to one of those show business schools. When you were on the road you had to do it by correspondence. I remember Patty Duke and Bernadette Peters went to that school, but it's not like they taught you anything there, and plus, I really missed gym and some of the other things."

And what did Mom and Dad think of their little girl flying off to stardom in the Phil. Spector machine? "My father didn't really have much to say. I think he's seen two shows in my whole career. As far as he's concerned opera is the only thing worth listening to, or close to it. Mitch Miller was about as far as he would go. My mother was okay. She could have worried, but she just said, 'If I haven't taught you anything by this time then what the heck?' Plus we always had chaperones until we were of age so not much was going to go on when I was away."

Then in 1962, an incredible blend of talents was some-

The Crystals circa 1964. *Wide World photo*

how brought together and the result was a number one record, "He's a Rebel." It was written by a tight-lipped mystery named Gene Pitney who the year before at the age of twenty had multitracked his voice into a hit called "Town Without Pity" and was known in some circles as the Boy Air Raid Siren. It was produced, of course, by Mr. Wall-of-sound and maniacal knobmaster, Phil Spector. And the Crystals sang it, right? Well, yes, but in the annals of rock history from Norm N. Nite to *The Rolling Stone Illustrated History of Rock 'n' Roll* it has been well-documented that Phil took Darlene Love, at that time with the Blossoms, and had her sing lead with the Crystals when the record was recorded in 1962. But when we asked her about it Dolores seemed a little miffed. "Murray the K started all that. I didn't even meet Darlene Love until 1964 when they were taking the photo for the Christmas album. Murray the K was putting on some Christmas show and there was some kind of blow-up between him and Phil. Phil never booked or managed us but apparently Murray the K wanted him to get us on his show. I never found out exactly, though, what it was all about. Phil must have said no or whatever and they had a hassle. At that time Darlene Love was with the Blue Jeans and Murray the K wanted them to sing 'He's a Rebel' on the show. But they didn't do it."

We leave it up to the reader to sort it out. If you can get by the electronic sensors, guard dogs, and electrified fences that surround his California mansion, maybe Phil can tell you how it was done. Nonetheless, "He's a Rebel" became a rock milestone and conjured up some powerful imagery in millions of heads. One image in particular that points up the fervor of the girl-group genre's sound comes from *Scorpio Rising*, a film made by Kenneth Anger in 1964. In one shot Jesus is riding along on an donkey (taken from Cecil B. DeMille's *The King of Kings*) accompanied not by the Vienna Boys Choir or the trumpets of time marching onward, and not by the adorational drone of disciples or the whistling winds of history, but by the Crystals' "He's a Rebel."

Between 1962 and 1965, the Crystals jettisoned the charts with a string of hits. Who could forget the air-hammer force of "Da Doo Ron Ron" or the saucer-eyed ecstasy of "Then He Kissed Me"? But then by late 1965 the Beatles and company had successfully invaded our shores and the girl groups and the soaring Spector had some stiff competition. "I often thought that England was in terrible financial trouble and our country was trying to give them all the support they could. But they sent over some of the worst crap I've ever heard in my life. And when it hit I said, 'What?!' Some of those things were totally ridiculous. What is it? It was a lot of promotion and England was in."

Also, the Crystals were in the middle of a money fight with Phil Spector that would eventually land in court six years later. So the Crystals split up. A year later Dolores and two of the girls got it back together for about a year. "Then we all took a shot at marriage. I'd been working for six years and I was ready to settle down. I lived in Brooklyn, then St. Thomas, then back to Queens again."

It was 1971 when she returned to New York, separated from her husband and about to go to court with a claim against Phil Spector, a claim which Dolores lost. "I don't believe there's anybody around who can say they got the money they were owed. We got a few royalties but not all.

And it's hard to prove. The burden of proof is on you. Well, I took it to court for what was supposed to be a jury trial, but suddenly it was just the judge, and he sat there reading newspapers the whole time.

"You know, whenever a black group started getting somewhere they got screwed. They got taken because they were ignorant and because the government and the law didn't care about them until their taxes were due. What kills me is that when I go to England I see that they respect their artists. Over here you don't get it, not from television or anywhere else.

But Dolores is one tough cookie. After having separated from her husband and having to deal with the court and money messes, she got the Crystals going again with two of the other original girls. "When I'm separated, I work. And music's my business. I grew up with it and it's like my second nature."

So the Crystals worked for three years until 1974 touring the country and abroad. Then one of the girls got pregnant and the other tired of the grueling pace and both quit. Undaunted, Dolores auditioned many girls until she chose two who are now, along with Dolores, the present Crystals. "Where are the other original members now? Pat's somewhere in the Far East where her husband is stationed in the service. Barbara's husband is in the service and they live in North Carolina. Mary lives in Brooklyn. And Lala is married to a jazz drummer, lives in Teaneck, New Jersey, and has four kids."

Today, the Crystals, led by Dolores, are alive and well and busy. They regularly tour the U.S., Canada, Bermuda, and Europe. "I like Germany a lot, the cities, Bonn, Frankfort, they remind me of New York before things started going down. The spirits of the people are up over there. They're intelligent and much better informed about world affairs. And their clubs aren't hurting financially like ours. They still have money to spend and get dressed up to go out for an evening. They're very relaxed too. In this country, there's only the outward appearance of being relaxed. Underneath everybody is uptight. I've really had it with New York, the weather, the dirt, the attitude. I like Atlanta. It's newer, cleaner, and I see young people down there doing well. That's encouraging. My sister lives down there and I just might join her."

In the meantime, people still want to hear the Crystals. "People want to remember when they were teenagers. Those days had to be good. They were carefree, no worries, no children, no bills. So now when they're older and have a little money they want to come out and see us and reminisce about those times. It's funny too because I guess they expect to see some fifty-year-old lady up there. But I'm only thirty-three. So they have children of their own; they're getting into new phases of their lives. But those days were a part of their lives they will always cherish, the dances, the hops, the good times, and I was part of that."

Freddie   Cannon

Revere is a two-story town with a glimmer of a skyline. It is a seaside suburb of Boston with a decaying amusement park off the boardwalk. Nearby, a greying elephant of a roller coaster sits long condemned. Dividing the residential areas of Revere is Route 15, a garish neon strip of donut shops, hamburger joints, used car lots, and supermarkets. Down the highway is the greyhound race track, where New Englanders indulge in their favorite pastime, betting on wiry hounds as they chase a mechanical rabbit. Revere is only a few short stops on the MTA subway system from Boston's North End, the compact area of squat red brick tenements, historical churches, and open markets, where the first wave of Italian immigrants settled. Frederick Anthony Picariello lived in Revere from the age of twelve until he became Freddie Cannon, the rock and roll star.

His father, Fred, drove a truck during the day and became transformed at night into Freddie Carmen with his orchestra of reknown, playing lead trumpet on the slow swing songs in vogue at weddings, socials, and family gatherings in the area. Like his father, Freddie became a trucker, first delivering mattresses and bedsprings, then graduating to a paint route for a local hardware store. He also had a band, Freddie Carmen and the Hurricanes, which played the record hops at the amusement parks, ballrooms, and high school gymnasiums for the various radio stations around Boston. Frederick Picariello cultivated a gyrating, throbbing stage presence and yelled "whoos!" into his songs so that they sounded like explosions. Unlike his father, Freddie managed to parlay his musical talents into a twenty-three-year career which now finds him a thirty-nine-year-old grandfather living with his family in Tarzana, California. He lives down the street from the Edgar Rice Burroughs's estate in the town named after the famous Apeman.

While a student at Lynn Vocational High School, Freddie got his first electric guitar, a Silvertone cheapie. He practiced on it for two years before he revealed his act to the public at the age of fifteen. The Hurricanes with Freddie on rhythm guitar and lead vocal, pedaled their Chuck Berry rockers around the area. "Every record hop I did for free. I never got paid, not even gas money. I was just so excited about playing in front of thousands of kids. They paid a buck a head. Three or four thousand kids would come to the gymnasium and a disc jockey would play for about twenty minutes. We would then come out and play live. The kids would go crazy. Then the records were played again. It was like a giant disco. We were doing Chuck Berry-type of music, rock and roll, the mid-fifties thing. I would get exposure on the radio and that was enough."

At sixteen, Freddie joined the National Guard for a five-year hitch, an act slightly leeward of the law. But Freddie did it because "all my cousins were in there." While he was in the Guard he met a fifteen and a half-year-old girl, Jeanette, whom he would soon marry. With high school finished, Freddie drove his trucks and rocked at the hops during the weekends.

In his late teens, life looked rather predetermined for Freddie. With his son, Billy, on the way, he would work his steady job, raise a family, and get his jollies by performing at social functions. But one day, when he returned home from work, his mother Annette showed him a poem she had written entitled "Tallahassee Lassie." "She likes to write words down. She still does but there hasn't been anything since. She said, 'Why don't you get the guitar and try to sing this?' " When he did, the result was his first hit record.

Later, Bob Crewe, one of the Philadelphia Sound's ring-masters, seized on the gimmick of songs written about

Southern places and helped Freddie turn out a quick string of gold with "Okefenokee," "Way Down Yonder in New Orleans," and "Chattanooga Shoe Shine Boy."

In the spring of 1959, Crewe saw Freddie perform and offered to collaborate with him on a demo disc of "Tallahassee" for Swann Records of Philadelphia. According to an early publicity blurb, Crewe was taken by Freddie's ability to project "his own dynamic personality to the audience." "I only played a little guitar and slowly broke away from that. I may be a white Chuck Berry without a guitar. I just use a mike and stand up there singing. Elvis was an inspiration from the standpoint of how big he was. Every time I turned on the radio I would hear his songs. I could relate to Elvis onstage. I felt freer when I didn't have anything in my hands. When the crowd isn't with me, I won't leave the stage until that crowd is rocking. That's the type of enthusiasm I try to create during the show. I'm not doing anything but projecting myself and getting down with the people."

By the time "Tallahassee" returned to Boston for test-marketing, Freddie discovered that his name had been changed from Carmen to Cannon by Dick Clark, a man whom he had never met. Dick Clark had advised Bernie Bennett of Swann Records that Cannon was catchier than Carmen. He was right.

The Cannon demo appeared on the consol of Arnie Ginsberg, a disc jockey for WMEX in Boston. "Arnie was the only one in Boston who played it. He really banged the record, playing it ten times in a row. If he hadn't played it, the record wouldn't have been anything." The phones rang off the station's walls. On the strength of that one-day response Freddie quit his job and became Freddie "Boom Boom" Cannon. The "Boom Boom" was a nickname coined by Ginsberg, when he heard the pounding bass drum on the record.

As the record shot to the national charts and the demands for record hop appearances increased, Freddie's mother wrote a letter to the Pentagon pleading for her son's tour of National Guard duty to be ended. The letter apparently worked. Freddie got an honorable discharge and hightailed it out on promotional tours. He returned for his bon voyage appearances at the local hops. This time he got paid. "It was a real thrill to get good money."

He fanned out from Massachusetts over the entire East, concentrating on one-nighters in upstate New York where the record busted big. Four months later, he drifted South where the crowds loved the Southern themes of Freddie's first hits. "The crowds were fantastic because all the people initially thought before I opened my mouth that I came from the South. They would come up to me and the minute I opened my mouth say, 'Uh, oh, he's an Easterner. A Yankee.' They knew it right away."

In April of 1959, when he played his first "American Bandstand," Freddie finally met the man who gave him his stage name. "It was a thrill to be on his show. I dreamed one day that I would be on the show and meet him. Just to walk in there, I was scared to death. It was the hottest show in the country. There was no home in the United

States that didn't turn on the television set and catch it for, at least, an hour. For me, to be on there, a little kid from Revere, Massachusetts, was something else. I never dreamed it would happen. I was nervous and did it. Every time I got more and more relaxed but I still would get those little butterflies in the stomach."

"Tallahassee Lassie" broke into the international roster of Top Forty hits prompting a European tour for Cannon. "The best gig for me was the first time I went to Europe in 1959. First we went to England and over to Holland. I was the king. I had a number one record. I had four songs and all of them were on the charts. When I went to Holland, they went out to pick me up. The cops came out with a red carpet and threw it out. There were thousands of kids at the airport. It was like a president coming in there and the Beatles coming over here. It was a fantastic feeling."

In the late fifties and early sixties, the DJ more often than not made a hit record, providing the potential was in the wax. Regional jocks had specialized audiences for their favorite music, a loose and free-wheeling format where a record could be "banged" ten times in a row without complaint from the station manager. Then a jock didn't obey a tight programming schedule based on heavily researched popularity charts and didn't mimic the sanitized ad copy. He was a raving lunatic, shouting at the high decibels of the music he played. The screaming, bulging-eyed man behind the microphone had a divine and arbitrary power over the fate of the record. Many succumbed to accepting payola while others shot their bolts in various promotion stunts, which rivaled the more bizarre antics of the *Guinness Book of Records*. Some were buried alive; others threw money off the tops of office buildings into the streets. Giveaways and record hops were their standard appearances. Freddie Cannon realized their power early and spent a good deal of his time on the road cultivating their friendships.

"I mainly concentrated on upstate New York where the record busted so big. I just couldn't get out there, thanking disc jockeys. Throughout the early years with records, the more records I had, the more popular I would get. Every place I'd go, there were always people greeting me at the airports. I became friends with a lot of disc jockeys around the country. Things that paid off. Even to this day, when I don't have a record, there are all these radio people. Even my wife is amazed by it. Guys come up to me and say, 'Do you remember when I met you twenty years ago.'

"I kept a good relationship with them because you never know when disc jockeys move from radio station to radio station. They've been awfully good to me. Don't offend them, don't insult them, don't lie to them because when you do, you hurt yourself. That's what I never did. If the record wasn't any good, I would say to them, 'Don't play the record, it's no good!' They respect you for that. There are a million guys I could thank. I can't thank radio people enough."

The jocks did all right by Cannon. From 1959 until 1964, Freddie's driving beat carried him over sixteen hit records sporting such esoteric titles as "The Muskrat Ramble," "Buzz Buzz A-Diddle It," "Transistor Sister," "Teen Queen of the Week," "Palisades Park," and "Everybody Monkey."

Dick Clark's magic bus carried the boy from Revere from the Steel Pier in Atlantic City to the state fairs of rural America. Despite an infectious stage presence, with his lean 5'11" body and wavy brown hair prancing and jerking across the stage, Freddie Cannon was always called on to blast the show open or appeared buried in the middle. Freddie finally got a chance to close a show at the Allentown, Pennsylvania, fair. "There must have been 30,000 people there. Outside the fairgrounds was a portable stage set up on a race track. The people were in the bleachers. Dick Clark was the emcee. Dick said, 'I'm going to let you close the show.' I really got excited. It made me feel like a superstar. I had 'Buzz Buzz A-Diddle' at that time in the Top Ten. In Allentown, it was number one or number two so I was thrilled with closing the show.

"I did all my songs and the show was almost over and I

got to 'Buzz Buzz.' Half the people had binoculars because they were so far away from the performers. The binoculars started to move. The sunlight glared off the glasses going away from me to the left down the track. They had released the horses. The race was on. Nobody cared whether I was on stage or not."

During the late fifties and sixties, a large teen star booking agency, General Artists Corporation, booked rock performers on regional tours through their various headquarters in major cities. One of the biggest agents, Frank Barcelona, signed Freddie up for a lucrative spin around the Midwest flatlands. "The jobs were such that you drove five hundred miles a day across the farm fields in the midsummer, when it was about 112 humidity with the mosquitoes diving down at you. They put me in a laundry truck. I had to travel with the band. They had made the laundry truck as comfortable as they could. There was a bed in there which was sealed off. It was like a tomb. All heat, no air-conditioning. I thought I was going to die. I banged on the door for them to let me out. They couldn't hear me because the motor was so loud. I thought they were trying to kill me. So I said, 'Let me out here.' They finally left me off in the middle of some farm field. I got a ride to the airport, got a private plane, and came back to Chicago. I said, 'I quit' and got sued for the rest of the dates. I claimed I was sick."

Since his last hit in 1964, "Abigail Beecher," Freddie has dabbled in record promotion, worked every summer with the Dick Clark tours, and played Vegas and Tahoe. Residing twenty minutes out of Los Angeles with Jeanette and his youngest son, Johnny, Freddie still stays close to Del Shannon and Dick Clark. His eldest son, Billy, twenty-one, is in the Navy and operates a Southern rock band, Backslide, out of Norfolk, Virginia. Billy has a son, Anthony, and Freddie's daughter Connie has a son, Patrick.

As Freddie says, "My wife and I feel younger now than when we didn't have the grandchildren. Some performers are afraid to admit it because they think that people will consider them old. They act ashamed. I think the music business is such a self-conscious business that it keeps us young all these years because I'm always talking music, discussing jobs and shows. The atmosphere alone can keep you like that.

"The biggest thrill was to be able to make a small dent in this business, enough to make noise, and make millions of people happy listening to my records. They're still following me today. I thank everyone who helped me and the guy upstairs because the chances of making it are one in a billion. It's an honor that you can always hear a Freddie Cannon record somewhere."

Bill Pinckney

"I'm Bill Pinckney of the 'Honey Love,' 'White Christmas,' 'Steamboat,' 'Fools Fall in Love,' 'Such a Night,' 'Soldier of Fortune,' 'What'cha Gonna Do,' 'It Was a Tear,' 'You Promise to Be Mine' Drifters. The name Drifters started in an apartment in New York with a bunch of us— myself, Clyde McPhatter, and David Baughn. Out of fifty or one hundred names came the Drifters. David said, 'Since everyone seems to drift from one group to another, why don't we call ourselves the Drifters?!'

"I was in the Drifters from 1953 until the last of 1958. The original sound was gospel, the soulful spiritual sound. We were doing soul music before they were calling it that. We created rock and roll, R&B, and soul because whenever Clyde McPhatter sang a song, it touched you all the way through the heart.

"At the first of 1959, the Drifters came out with 'There Goes My Baby.' They weren't the Drifters. They were the Five Crowns with Ben E. King singing lead. They adopted the name which had already been established. The Drifters had been out five years prior to this with hit after hit, hits upon hits. Any group with a good sound could release a record and call themselves the Drifters and keep on sailing. Some groups call themselves the Drifters and they've never sung or recorded under the name. They think it's a gravy train. 'If the people don't know no better, I might as well get me a group. People are buying anything, so we'll sell them something.' To keep down the confusion, I don't try and fool anybody. I'm Bill Pinckney and *his* Drifters."

On December 5, 1978, in Columbus, Georgia, Bill was joined onstage by Archie Bell and the Drells, Maurice Williams and the Zodiacs, and the "I'm a Girl Watcher" Occasions. It marked the twenty-sixth anniversary of the Drifters' formation.

Bill Pinckney, the big bassman and sometime lead, now tours all year 'round with his own Drifters along the Carolina coast with the Drells and the Coasters, and the Saudi Arabian oil fields entertaining the ARAMCO technicians; they play concerts in the Northeastern cities which feature the Five Keys, the Rainbows, the Jewels, and the Clovers, as well as numerous benefit shows for VA hospitals, prisons, and narcotics abuse programs. The group now features Bill singing baritone lead with a trio of singers and a backup band with son Bill, Jr. on congas. His twenty-six-year-old daughter lives in Miami, singing gospel like her pop did. Bill occasionally entertains ideas of getting his daughter and his son into a new group and striking out from under the Drifters' umbrella. "I would drop the name but it's the only thing I've known for twenty-six years. Why drop it? I'm making a decent living. I'm working all the time. The people enjoy it. It's amazing when the people see me come out there at my age and tear them up."

Bill Pinckney was born on August 15, 1925, in Sumter, South Carolina, the hometown, he quickly points out, of former New York Yankee second baseman Bobby Richardson. Today, his home alternates between Atlanta and Sumter. He sang gospel in the choir when he wasn't throwing a baseball. "It's only now that there are young singers coming out who haven't had a chance to sing in church. Most of all black singers—Sarah Vaughn, Dionne Warwick, Della Reese, and the male vocalists—came from the church. That's why they have such great feelings behind what they do. Years later, they put so much more into it. When you were singing gospel in those days, there were no rehearsals. You had to have you. You didn't have any instruments, maybe a guitar. You only had one microphone, two at the most. There was no rehearsal before showtime. You just go in there and do it. Then it was more or less the individual."

Bill Pinkney (center) and his "Original Drifters" today.

Raised in Brooklyn and Manhattan, Bill joined the Army at the age of seventeen and spent the next four years from 1942 to 1946 in the European theater. He's a veteran of the most grisly battles of World War II—Bastogne, Normandy, Rheims River, and Saint-Lô. "I was in all of those. I'm lucky I came back. Somebody's prayers were with me." Returning from the service, he stayed in South Carolina until 1949 when he decided to migrate up north back to New York. "Don't ask me why.

"I stopped singing when I played baseball. I didn't play in the majors but I played with the New York Blue Sox and the Pelicans. I started off in Central Park with the Pelicans. Back then you did it all. My best position was on the mound. I had a good arm. As a kid I won thirty games in one year. We traveled around New York and Pennsylvania, New Jersey, and Connecticut. When I stopped playing baseball, I came back and started singing again with some gospel songs in New York."

While traveling around the New York gospel circuit, playing churches and ballrooms, Bill met Clyde McPhatter. Clyde was a seventeen-year-old native of Durham, North Carolina, who had launched his career as a choir boy in the Mt. Calvary Baptist Church. He had been singing around New York for five years when Billy Ward tagged him as the lead singer for the Dominoes. While the group was known as Billy Ward and the Dominoes, it was Clyde who introduced the electrifying singing style of postwar black gospel to popular music, creating what has since been called "rhythm and gospel." His combination of the gospel style with straight blues, his funky phrasing, wails, screams, and trading phrases with his background singers in echoes of the call-and-response practice of the black church, dominated the smash hit records of the Dominoes from 1950 to 1953. He sang lead on "Do Something for Me," "I'd Be Satisfied," the sobbing "Bells," where he breaks down in tears, and "These Foolish Things." But disgruntled with his lack of billing and his conspicuous anonymity on all the records, he quit the group in 1953 and was replaced by an unknown Golden Gloves champion named Jackie Wilson.

That same year Clyde came back to New York from Detroit and looked up his old friends, the Civitones, on the gospel circuit. Together with Bill, Andrew, and Gerhard Thrasher, he formed the Drifters. The Drifters immediately pulled down a recording contract with Atlantic Records and went on to fire out the Jesse Stone song "Money Honey," later a hit for Elvis, "Such a Night," "Lucille," the sizzling "Honey Love" replete with gasps, grunts, and suggestive sighs which made DJs a bit skittish, "Bip Bam," and the Irving Berlin classic, "White Christmas."

But in 1954 Uncle Sam caught up with Clyde and he went into the service, occasionally coming home on leave to record as a solo act. When Clyde McPhatter was discharged he continued as a solo with "Seven Days," "Treasure of Love," "A Lover's Question," and "Lover

Please." But the fire and spark was gone and after an erratic decade as a solo artist, Clyde McPhatter at the age of thirty-eight died of a heart attack in 1972.

With the Thrashers, guitarist Jimmy Oliver from Buffalo, and Bill, the Drifters continued with a boy from 126th Street and Lexington Avenue in New York (David Baughn) replacing Clyde. "He sounded so much like him. He didn't have to do any recording but just sing the songs that were already recorded and had been released." Bill continued as the engineer behind the Drifters' continued success.

"After David, I met a guy in Cleveland, Ohio, in 1955, when we were doing a job at the Circle Theater. His name was Johnny Moore. He asked me for a job and I hired him. Now I had two lead singers but David eventually quit and we carried on with Johnny who recorded 'Adorable' and 'Fools Fall in Love.'

"It wasn't as tough then as it is now to get an act together. Actually the hardest thing was recording. They didn't have many record companies. You found your best singers on the street corners and in the hallways. You could have a dynamite group on the stoops which didn't need anything but a microphone. You go into rehearsal and the guys were ready from the hallway or the stoop. So they thought the only thing they had to do was audition and find out whether they could get a recording. Back then, I realized one thing—you could hardly get onstage without a record. The main thing was getting a record contract.

"Most of the acts playing the Apollo were recording acts except for the comedians and dancers. The same was true for the Capitol and the Brooklyn Paramount. The people who were playing the Apollo back then were Ruth Brown, Ray Charles, Roy Hamilton, Chuck Willis, the Dominoes, and the Drifters. You would find a few like Buddy Johnson and Count Basie. Most of these people in the early fifties were recording. The way you broke in was through a thing called 'Amateur Hour.' If you were the first-prize winner, you had a chance to sing the following week and then you would be discovered from there.

"You felt different singing professionally, even though you were singing gospel. We had gotten used to singing before an audience. We got a better response when our records were hits on all the international and national stations. Then when!you go out there, the people were dying to see the people who made these recordings. When you got out there singing, they started swarming all over you like an Elvis Presley thing.

"It made you feel like a star, even though we didn't get paid for it. During all that, we were being paid salary. That has been the way with the Drifters all through the years. You know, someone must have cashed in on it. That's why there are so many groups of Drifters today. If they had been treated right from the very beginning, the get-go, there wouldn't be seven or eight different groups of Drifters. I could give you so many names who have sung with the Drifters. I know there must have been thirty. I counted my original group and there must have been twenty. You can't say you had a steady group when one guy came in for two weeks and another guy was on the record but you never saw him make an appearance.

"When Clyde was in the service, we were introduced to a guy who came up with these contracts and we signed them. He said, 'We're going to put everybody on salary and have a corporation. We're going to take the money, the overflow, and going to buy stock, this and that, real estate.' All you can do is take a man's word. He probably laughed when the signature was down there. If he did buy these things, he did it for himself because we had no other contract stating that. Later I found out that the stuff we signed with him weren't really contracts but agreements which were typed up on a piece of paper and notarized before two witnesses. By the time we had signed it, it was too late.

"I'll tell you what happened—bad management. I don't have to explain. If you don't know what you're doing, when it comes to the place where he doesn't want you and wants to get rid of you, then boom. He has a name but he doesn't have the personnel. You have built the name for him. He can get anybody else and keep going. It's a shame a man comes in and sings a song and is fired the next day. If it hadn't been for the fifties, there wouldn't have been any Drifters in the sixties."

As a result of a complicated mediation by the musicians union, Bill Pinckney was awarded the name the Original Drifters. In the summer of 1958, the man with the "contracts" saw a group called the Five Crowns with Ben E. King on lead at the Apollo Theater and made them the Drifters. King only stayed with the group for a year recording "There Goes My Baby," a song he supposedly wrote but never got the credit for. In 1960, he went on his own recording "Spanish Harlem." Today, Ben E. King lives in North Carolina and occasionally performs. Johnny Moore returned to the group long enough to record "Under the Boardwalk" and quit. Today, he performs in England. Charlie Thomas, one of the original Five Crowns, and later lead vocalist for the third incarnation of the Drifters, was later fired and struck out on his own. Andrew Thrasher of the original Drifters is retired. Bill is the only original Drifter performing today. All the rest, except for Andrew, are dead.

Bill Pinckney and the Original Drifters, while prevented from recording for two decades, have continued playing the places where it all began, where the people still remember. "I toured with Bill Haley and the Comets when they first started out. We did many shows with Peggy Lee, Billy Epstein, Nat King Cole, Laverne Baker, Roy Hamilton, the Big Bopper, and Eddie Cochran, who got killed in England. We all played cards together.

"I remember once doing a concert in Pittsburgh, Pennsylvania. I flew from Washington to Pittsburgh that afternoon. My plane, a four-engine, caught fire, so we made an emergency landing and then were taken to Pittsburgh. I saw this kid (in jeans) at the Morris auditorium there. He was sixteen years old. This kid started asking me so many questions about show business. 'Is it exciting? Is it hard to do? When they announce your name, do you walk out or run out?' I said, 'You use your own judgment.' I'm glad I took so much time with him.

"After we got through this, he said, 'The reason why I'm asking so many questions is because I'm an added attraction on the show. My name is Paul Anka. I'll be on the show. I did a recording and I'm hoping it will come out all right. The man who is my manager is giving the show and he's putting me on it.'

"Since that tour, we toured together for over a month, I haven't been able to talk to Paul Anka. He did such a wonderful job. This was before 'Diana' was a big hit. He's from Canada and we played his hometown. His dad ran a restaurant and invited the whole show over. Everybody had steaks, Italian food, and everything. It was in 1956. If I saw Paul Anka today, I bet he would remember."

Exiled from the recording business, Bill Pinckney has kept his group going around the "chitlin" or gypsy circuit, where groups play club after club without records, entertaining the clientele they have built up over the years. Since 1960, Bill has traveled under the constant threat of warrants, subpoenas, and litigation initiated by those who want him to stop performing with the Drifters name. Today at fifty-three, he's a patriarch of the club circuit. When asked by younger performers how he can stay out on the road, he replies, "Well, it makes me feel good they have competition. It just makes me strong." They say, "Boy I just hope I'm the man you are, when I get to be fifty-three years old." "I tell them, 'Take care of yourself and try and let nothing bother you.'

"We go everywhere these days. I've been to Africa, Italy, Saudi Arabia, and Germany. I'd like to mention I'm more known as a Drifter today than I was back then. The age of the crowds ranges from twenty-five to seventy. I'm doing lead now and bass. I believe I'm a better singer now than I was back then. Now my voice is strong and I believe I sound as good as ever."

Gary Lewis

On July 31, 1945, Gary Lewis was born in New York's Beth Israel Hospital, the first son of Mr. and Mrs. Jerry Lewis. He likes to start an interview with, "And I was born of fairly poor parents...," followed immediately by tommy gun laughter somewhat more than reminiscent of his old man. But actually, there's some truth in what he says. Jerry Lewis was only eighteen at the time and waiting tables at an Atlantic City club when he met his wife who was singing with Jimmy Dorsey's band. "I was born almost exactly nine months after they were married, the first of five sons, and she supported him for about four years until he met up with Dean Martin and got going. When I was old enough to know what was going on, he'd already made a couple of pictures. But I didn't think that was anything special. I thought everybody's father was in movies. I was just a little kid and you know how little kids think."

Soon after Gary was born, the family moved out to California where he grew up. When he started school he found out that not everybody's father was in movies. "Guys would come up to me and say, 'Hey, I saw your old man's last movie and it wasn't so good. In fact, it stunk, he stinks, what do you think of that?' And I'd say 'Oh yeah?' then boom! I was always getting thrown out of class for fighting. But then as time went on I realized that everybody could have their own opinion and it didn't have to mean anything to me. So it was a little uncomfortable for awhile, but it really wasn't that bad."

At the age of five, he decided he wanted to be a drummer. "You know, a little kid sees one of his idols on TV and says, 'I got to play just like that.' The *Gene Krupa Story*, or anything on TV with drums. Whenever I saw somebody playing drums, I wanted to be a drummer."

They didn't exactly cart in some piker to teach this kid how to play. "I took lessons from Buddy Rich for about two years. Probably did it as a favor to my old man or something. But he was really tough on me, no fooling around, made me practice all the time. It was good, though; I got all the fundamentals down. On a couple of my dad's specials he and I would sit down to a set of drums and trade off. He knew I had some kind of music in me and he was giving me a chance to let it out, see what might happen. In 1957 I had my first real experience. I was about twelve. My father had a booking in a place called the Riviera Theater in Detroit and he asked my grandfather to be on the show with him. My grandfather was a performer in the early vaudeville/burlesque days. He'd sing and my grandma would play piano. He had a few remote hits, the sheet music was printed up and all that, but mainly he just did the vaudeville circuit, the Henny Youngman scene. He's my old man's father, Danny Levitch. My dad's real name is Joseph Levitch. I don't really know whether he changed it legally or now. All I know is my name's Lewis. Hmmm, I ought to find out about my roots. Where's Alex Haley?! Wouldn't that be a riot if my old man was adopted. That would open up a can of worms! Anyway, he and my father thought it would be neat to have the third generation on the show too, so I went along on a string of fourteen one-nighters. The first show I sat on my old man's lap and we sang that old Jolson tune, 'Sonny Boy,' together. Then I had my own spot. It was a heavy-duty thing to do at the time but I sang 'You Ain't Nothing but a Hound Dog.' I guess you could call that my first performance."

After that Gary took care of finishing high school. "Then when I was sixteen I started playing guitar, just for the heck of it, just felt like learning. So I bought all the chord books, all the sheets. My first guitar was a Fender Jaguar. At the time I thought it was great, I loved all the knobs and everything. But I wasn't really into music then and I probably would have been happy with a simple little Stratocaster that would be worth billions by now. Ah well,

Gary Lewis and the Playboys.

live and learn, right?"

Next stop, college. "I figured I liked theater, the arts, so I enrolled at the Pasadena Playhouse College, a regular four-year accredited college in theater arts. I was there for about eight months and all of a sudden the Beatles happened. So much for school. I said, 'Here we go, get the drums out of storage, get the guitars, I want to play, get all my clothes ripped off, just got to do it!' Everybody w's into the Beatle thing. It was in the air. Groups were springing up all over. I got some guys from the college and said, 'Hey, let's do it, get a group together!' And that's when I started the original Playboys. I never figured we'd have a hit or anything with all the competition. But we practiced for awhile and a few months later, in the summer of '64, we went out and auditioned for a thing at Disneyland. Nobody knew who I was. I wanted to get the gig on my own and I did. It was a blast. Played outdoors, out in the park by the water. We played there all summer. Then the last week, Snuff Garrett, our eventual producer, just happened to be out there with his family. He says, 'You guys are pretty good. I work at Liberty Records and I got a tune called "This Diamond Ring" that's been sitting on my desk for two years and Bobby Vee won't do it. Why don't you?'"

As the story goes, Al Kooper (Blues Project, Blood Sweat & Tears, Super Session) had submitted the song to Snuff at Liberty, but Bobby Vee, who Snuff produced, didn't like it and the president of Liberty didn't either, so it was just lying around. "We went into the studio and cut the record with Snuff producing, then went back to Disneyland to finish out the week. It jumped on the charts three weeks after we did it, and three weeks after that it was numer one, kicking the Beatles out of the top spot. I liked that. We held it for a week, then I guess it was the Temptations who kicked us out with 'My Girl.' But suddenly something was happening, that was for sure. Whenever I bump into Bobby Vee I say, 'So, you didn't like that song now did you? Eh? Eh?' "

Snuff Garrett then impressed upon Gary and the band the age old maxim that the most crucial point in an artist's career is the follow-up to the first hit. Bargain bins are strewn with flashes in the pan. "But if you hit with the second one, you're home free. And Snuff had a re-markable sense of timing and material. He had us do 'Count Me In' and it went right to the Top Five. We were rolling. I think everything else we did went Top Ten. It all happened really fast. I couldn't comprehend it right away. But then two years and about eight straight Top Ten records later, good old Uncle Sam nailed me. January 1967. I was stationed in Korea, not doing a damn thing. I had a lot of time to think and I said to myself, Hey, well goddamn, I really had something happening there. I didn't realize it until I didn't have it. So I made up my mind that when I got out, I'd really learn my trade, get out the guitar, and get serious, a musician with an instrument instead of just a prop."

But the Army decided he ought to stay in Korea until the end of 1968, so there was a delay. "Didn't play a thing over there. They put me in the supply room handing out the boots, the shirts, the insect spray and the soap. The other guys knew who I was, but I guess it's just lucky I am the way I am because they could have made it rough on me. That's all I'd have to do, come off like I was better than somebody else. I would have been killed. But the guys I was with were really out of sight and everything was fine. I hated having to go in but I'm glad I did. I can't really explain; it's just one of those things."

Meanwhile, back in the states, two songs Gary had put in the can before heading for Korea, covers of "Sealed With a Kiss" and "Listen to the Rhythm of the Falling Rain," had come out and were hits. On the strength of that, Gary and the Playboys toured for another year and a half after he was discharged. By the end of the sixties, Gary had toured the world—America, Europe, Asia, Australia. "Fun? Are you kidding? Man, it was a gas. Screaming girls, hair pulled out of heads, clothes ripped off at all times, bleeding, everything. One time we finished a gig up in Boston and it was snowing like hell. We hit the last downbeat of the last tune and I just threw down my guitar and tried to make it through the back door to the car before all the kids got loose. I threw open the door but I was too late. There were millions of them! It was great. I was totally declothed, and left lying in the snow. All the guys were sitting in the car with the heater on laughing. I guess I wasn't too happy about it at the time, but it's funny now. We could just about count on that happening regularly back then. One time the police even let German Shepards loose on the chicks. That was pretty weird. Things got a little crazy in those days.

"The Phillipines were the greatest, best place we ever played. There were thousands of people at the airport when we arrived, like one of those Beatle scenes. They went berserk. I couldn't believe what was going on. Like an earthquake had hit the airport. When we were driving to the colosseum, where we were playing, there were these giant billboards all along the road with giant pictures of me. They read, 'Gary Lewis and the Playboys, America's answer to the Beatles.' I just went 'Wow!' I couldn't figure it out. What had happened was Liberty Records sent all our albums over and the radio stations picked whatever songs they wanted for singles. They used so many I had forty-two hits down there, most of them other people's songs that I'd covered. 'Runaway' by Del Shannon, 'Love Potion Number 9,' 'Tossin' and Turnin',' they thought they were all mine. Snuff had me covering everything on the albums, a few hits of mine and the rest me doing other people's. An album with nothing but hits. They don't put them out like that anymore. It sure shook up the Phillipines.

"Japan was strange. They all came out to the airport but when we got off the plane, they just stared at us and held up signs. I figured they were waiting to see if we were good guys, so I went over to the fences and shook hands. They went crazy. But Japan gets too confusing for me."

When not in the studio or on the road, Gary found himself in front of a camera, doing a few cameos in some of his father's movies, and some beach movies. "You know, all the girls in bikinis start screaming, 'Hey, there's Gary Lewis and the Playboys in the water!', and there we'd be, out in the middle of the ocean playing on a floating platform."

On television, he did "Shindig," "Where the Action Is," Paul Revere's "Happening '68," the talk shows, and hosted a few "Hullabaloos" with his father. And of course, "Ed Sullivan." "Everytime we had a new tune we'd break it on his show. He was tremendous, what a market! I mean who did *not* watch 'Ed Sullivan.' I knew him pretty well too, but whenever I talked to him I had to go through his interpreter."

In 1971, Gary decided to take a break for awhile. "Now we get into the limbo years. There just wasn't a market for me anymore, what with Hendrix, Joplin, and all that. And I didn't want to change my style just for the sake of staying in. So I just laid back and stopped. I went down to Tulsa, Oklahoma, where my old pal Leon Russell was. He had arranged and coproduced everything we had done and I really admired him. I was down there for about three years, just paying some dues, sitting in with Leon and his people in clubs in the area, not making money but really

learning about my business, the music, like I had planned."

In 1974, Gary was in Phoenix doing a state fair gig and was approached by an agent who wanted to book him. "I was feeling pretty good about my music by then, writing it and so on. I learned a lot with Leon. So I felt it was time to start it up again. I got another band together and we were off."

Today, Gary lives in Reno, Nevada, with his wife of two years, at least when he's not on the road or heading back to the studio. "We've been playing all over the country exposing our new material to the people before we record, finding out what they like so we know what to add or pull. All our new stuff is very simplified, something like early Beatles rock 'n' roll, but with a taste of the thing that will make people say, 'Hey, that sounds like Gary Lewis.' We're a rock band, three guitars, bass, and drums. I love it. Got to get that name back up there, get a hit record. We've got a number of record companies who want to record us so it's just a matter of working it out. We should be cutting a record by the end of this year. I'm ready. I feel great."

Tom Giuliano

1966 was a curious year, don't you think, Virginia? The
largest-selling record in the country turned out to be an
iron-jawed rebuttal of the "Eve of Destruction" called
"The Ballad of the Green Berets" by S/Sgt. Barry Sadler.
Two guys who once called themselves Tom and Jerry
when one of them wasn't going by Tico and the Triumphs
sold a few million "Sounds of Silence." And Frank Sinatra
made his first appearance on the charts in eons with that
eternal anthem of blue collar shot-and-wash joints,
"Strangers in the Night," while daughter Nancy struck ter-
ror in the hearts of boys by threatening to stomp their
faces with her stiletto heels. Soon after they would get together and do "Something Stupid." Meanwhile, four guys
from North Jersey who had cut their teeth on the
Pocono/Catskill circuit changed their name from the Four
Graduates to the Happenings and came out with one of
the all-time great summer tunes, "See You in September,"
proving that America still had a place in its heart for top-
notch four-part harmonies and a slick stand-up act.

Tom Giuliano, original member, was born in Brooklyn
in 1943 into a "typical New York Italian family," and later
moved to Paterson, New Jersey, where he went to high
school and began brushing up his vocal chords. "I was
listening to music from the start. Tony Bennett, Johnnie
Ray, and Frank Sinatra. The Four Aces and the Moonglows. Frankie Lymon and the Teenagers, Dion and the
Belmonts, the Four Seasons, everybody."

One night in 1961 soon after Tom had graduated, he
went out to a local dance. "There were about thirty-five
guys all singing down in the men's room. I just happened
to end up with these three other guys down there and we

started singing together." So Tom, along with Ralph De-Vito, Bob Miranda, and Dave Libert became the Four Graduates and started playing local dances and clubs.

A few years later they experimented a bit with a few things in the recording studio. "I can't even remember the names of the songs. Nothing ever came of them. They just got canned. I do remember the first song, though. It was called 'Step into the Future.' It was years ahead of its time. People who heard it said 'What's that?!' Essentially it was acid rock. Later on we were into jazz rock before that started to happen. People looked at us like we were crazy. I remember packing this one club every night and we decided to put together and perform a whole jazz rock act. The club owner said if we didn't go back to our regular act he'd throw us out."

Experiments aside, they were also in the process of developing a finely tuned nightclub act on the mountain resort circuit of Pennsylvania and New York. "Four-part harmony standards, choreography, impersonations, the whole shtick. We always had an act. And that's why we're still around today. Because when you have an act it's easy to integrate any new musical trend right into it. We've always been basically a stand-up singing act."

By 1965, Bob and Dave of the Four Graduates were writing songs for various local groups, and while in New York met Jay Siegal, Hank Medress, and Phil Margo of the Tokens ("The Lion Sleeps Tonight"). "Eventually we were all getting together to work on some material, write some songs. We were rehearsing one day when Herb Bernstein, the Tokens' producer, overheard us. He needed some background vocals done, so we ran in and backed the Chad Mitchell Trio who included John Denver at that time. Herb then introduced us to Bob Crewe who was one of the heaviest producers in the business at the time, with the Four Seasons, Mitch Ryder and the Detroit Wheels, and others. We ended up doing the background vocals for all of them. Meanwhile, Herb Bernstein decided he would arrange and produce some songs for us."

One of those songs turned out to be "See You in September," a minor hit when originally recorded by the Tempos in 1959, but a giant for Tom and the boys who were now called the Happenings. By the time all the returns were in it was the number nine song for the year in the country according to *Cashbox*, and that doesn't account for what were enormous international sales. "It's what I always wanted to happen. But I'll tell you the truth: right before the thing took off I thought I was really doing great. I was going to beautician school full time. I was recording background vocals for Crewe and Bernstein four nights a week and making incredible money for someone barely twenty years old. It was an excellent setup. And of course we were rehearsing a lot and playing clubs on weekends. I didn't really want to have to go out on the road, but then it all fell into place, the whole formula. I wasn't really ready for it, but everything just came together."

So ready or not, it was time for the Happenings to hit the road and tour with their hit single. "We did one of Dick Clark's bus tours, all the big outdoor stuff, and we promised ourselves we'd never do another. You're on that bus for twelve hours, arrive in some place you've never heard of, your eyes are barely open from exhaustion, and they push you out in front of 30,000 people. We did that for thirty days and it really drained us. I was a chubby little kid when I started in this business but I think I lost forty pounds on that tour.

"Plus, you were only onstage for about fifteen minutes, just enough time for the people to recognize you, and then it was back on the bus. I hated that. It was really pimping off an act. And the groups got nothing compared to what the producer was getting. And you never even knew it until it was too late. That kind of thing happened with a lot of the black groups. Some of it was really disgusting. Some of those guys would have half a dozen million-selling records, but they wouldn't get paid. They'd be given cars and clothes which made them happy because they never had such things before. But if you got them to sign the piece of paper, you could really take advantage. It still

Tom Giuliano (second from the right) with the Happenings.

happens today, probably always will, so you really have to watch out for yourself."

On the bus tour, the boys met Gene Pitney. "And the story's true. He really did sleep in the luggage rack when we were traveling. He was a very quiet guy. We really had to pump him to get him to talk. Unbelievable! As a matter of fact, though, we were on his honeymoon with him. We toured with him later that year in Italy, did a few television specials, and were singing at the San Remo Song Festival when he got married there. It was a real trip. I think I've known him now for fifteen years and if he's spoken more than thirty words to me that would be a lot. He lived up in Connecticut for a real long time. He likes sitting on his porch in a rocking chair counting his money, but I don't know."

Then, of course, there was television. "Mike Douglas was great. Della Reese too when she had her show. And Steve Allen, Merv Griffin, the Smothers Brothers, 'Where the Action Is,' and Johnny Carson. We'd always do those when we had a new record out. But Carson has always had the same format for rock groups. Just get out there, sing, and that would be it. A really great experience was when we did a telethon in New York. That was a little later. As you know, the Happenings would always have hits with old standards, or at least old songs, that we would do our own version of. One was 'Go Away Little Girl,' which Steve Lawrence had done years before. He was on the telethon and we all did it together. He's great. We did quite a few shows with him.''

In 1967, the Happenings had their second big hit with "I Got Rhythm." "We went on tour with that down to South America, Rio and Sao Paulo. That was incredible. There is no middle class there so we did the country clubs, entertaining the so-called elite. We also did a couple television specials. Sergio Mendes was our guest. He was red hot at the time. In Sao Paulo we were met at the airport by 30,000 kids. We were biggies. The press was always with us and anything we did was news. Everywhere we went, popping flashbulbs. We were treated like royalty, two limos, interpreters for all of us. The people loved us because of the music; they're really into melody. And the press loved us because very few American groups ever went down there. The language barrier almost drove us crazy, even with the interpreters. We really didn't know what kinds of things were ending up in the papers, but it didn't matter. We didn't want to leave.''

But they managed to tear themselves away for a concert tour of American colleges and universities, the places where the group's sound had first started to get recognition a few years before. "Between Ohio and Massachusetts there are so many colleges, you could play them for the rest of your life and get old doing it. As a matter of fact, it was the college kids in Massachusetts who first went for 'See You in September.' The colleges always went for our sound. But then Kent State happened and a lot of the schools started having riots. Actually we were only about fifteen miles away in Sharon, Ohio, when it oc-

curred. We heard about it that night on the news and we were at the airport the next morning when all the kids were being led out of the state by the state police. We knew then it would hurt the college circuit and it did. So we went back to where we started, night clubs. When the colleges went out, the clubs started coming back in."

In the late sixties and early seventies, the Happenings continued to record, but musically the times were confusing. "The British thing was still going on and hard rock and acid rock were getting real big. We were in the middle of all that and went through a lot of changes. But we didn't know what to record anymore. I guess our last hit was 'Hare Krishna, Where Do I Go from Here?' in 1971."

That year Ralph and Dave left the group. Tom, along with Bob Miranda, have kept the Happenings alive ever since. "We've kept right on with the club thing. Two front men and four backup musicians, sometimes more depending on where we play. And we've made ourselves an East Coast band, Maine to Miami, because there is no money in it out West. We work all the time. For a few years we had a deal going with a record label but they were putting all their money into Travolta. I don't blame them. Right now we are in the process of looking for another deal, but we are being very careful about it. We really got ripped off when we first started. 1966 was when the bootleg record thing got underway. "I Got Rhythm" sold around two and a half million records, only 900,000 of which were accounted for. They couldn't even certify that it went gold. That's how heavy the bootlegging thing got. Nothing ever happened with all those subcommittees in Washington. They're still doing it. Luckily we were a performing act and got some of it back in that respect.

"At one time I thought, 'Okay, that's the price you pay to be in the business.' Not any more. I've paid my dues. I've been in the business almost twenty years, so I paid them long ago. So if we record again, and I hope we do, I'll be very careful in terms of contracts, agreements, royalties, and all that. It's really sad that people are still getting ripped off, but that's the industry. But I don't plan to have it happen to me again."

Today Tom lives in Fair Lawn, New Jersey, with his wife of twelve years and his two sons. "They know their father is an entertainer. It was fairly easy for them to get acclimated to it because they were born into it. Sometimes in the summer when we are booked at resorts I'll take them along with me. They love it. They love music. I get a lot from them about music today. They're right in the swing of things, disco, Kiss, the Bee Gees, Travolta. I really enjoy being with my sons.

"Despite the ripoffs and the hassles, being in the business has been fun, especially when we were in the Top Ten. The glamour was always there. A lot of interesting people wanted to meet you. You do television and endorsements and whatever else branches out from it. It was an experience. Thank God I lived through it. And I'm still living. I haven't lost my ear and who knows, there's always hope for another hit. You can never say you're dead or you can't do it again. If you dig your own hole and lay in it, yeah, then you're dead. But if you keep pumping, something can always happen. I love the music business, always have and always will. I don't regret a bit of it. I'll always be a part of it, if not performing and recording then in booking or promotion. And when disco dies I'll be waiting. The most exciting thing is performing in front of a lot of people; that's where the true artistry is. To make the people happy by letting them get involved in your music. That's what I do."

Sam "The Sham" Samudio

In 1965, the British invasion, led by the Beatles, the Stones, and Herman's Hermits, was in overdrive. The Temptations, the Supremes, and the Four Tops spearheaded the Motown sound. Phil Spector was beaming the Righteous Brothers into orbit. It was the year of "This Diamond Ring," "The In Crowd," "Hang on Sloopy," "I Got You Babe," and "The Eve of Destruction." So who was this cat in a turban and his band of Egyptian nobles singing about some Wooly Bully creature that made Sally go batty and sold more records than just about anybody?

Domingo Samudio was born in the sun-carved farmlands outside of Dallas, Texas, in 1937 to a Spanish-speaking family of Mexican descent. "My father, Santiago Samudio, was working construction for the Sherman Concrete Pipe Company. Everybody knew him as Jim. We lived in what they called shotgun shacks, just three rooms in a straight row. They called them shotgun shacks because they said you could fire a shotgun at the front door and it would go right through it and out the back door. The nearest well, the nearest drinking water, was about a mile and a half away. Of course that is all part of the megalopolis now. But it was a nice environment, a nice place for me to grow up. Ever since I can remember, someone was always singing around the house. My father played Mexican folk music. He was part of a trio, doing parties, weddings, not for money, more like family get-togethers."

When Sam was four, his mother died, leaving his father to raise Sam and his older brother and sister. "My father is an amazing individual. He raised his own brothers and sisters too. His mother died when he was fifteen and he supported the family. His father had seizures from time to time evidently caused by a blood clot. Because of ignorance that was considered a weakness at the time. But he was a very gentle soul and my father took the initiative and provided for everybody. Then when he got married and my mother died he did it all over again. He's still alive and to this day works construction. He's seventy-three. We taught him how to read and write English when we were in fourth grade. He worked at practically anything to support us, helped put my brother through college and get my sister and I through high school. Today my brother is a surgeon and my sister is a teacher."

A lot of black people lived in the shotgun shack community, and they turned out to be Sam's main musical influence. "I remember one man called 'Webfoot.' That's all I ever knew him by. He was always playing slide guitar and singing the blues."

And if things ever got a little hairy, people took care of each other. "There was a family, Dick Rose, his wife named Sister Rose, and their kids who were all about our age. She and my mother were real close when my mother was alive, and after my mother passed away, she took us under her wing, always staying on top of things while my father was away working on the railroad. They always had T-Bone Walker and all the blues singers on the radio. We had to stay with relatives for awhile and that was rough. Anytime something went wrong, we'd split to Sister's house and hide out there until things cooled off. Those were the people we learned to speak English from."

By the time Sam was ready for school, the family had moved to Dallas. "When I started grammar school, I was pretty basic. My first grade teacher just about hit the ceiling when I asked to go to the toilet, saying 'Please! Refer to it as the bathroom or the basement.' I couldn't see the difference, but you don't hassle those kind of things, you just adapt and keep going."

Meanwhile, Sam was singing. He made his debut when he won a contest to represent his school on a Saturday radio program. He sang a song called "I'm Always Chasing Rainbows." "That's when it started. I guess I've been chasing them ever since."

In his early teens, they moved back out to the country. "I was always romping around in the woods and down around the Trinity River bottoms. I did a lot of hunting and fishing, but only for food; I don't like to kill anything unless I have to. I was going to high school at the time and fiddling around with the guitar. We got a group together, didn't have a name or anything, just got it together. Trini Lopez was in that group. He sang with an accent. I sang the blues. I've always been primarily a blues singer."

He graduated high school at seventeen and went right into the Navy. "I'm bilingual. They rent me to Panama and I was stationed there for six years. First year I was in school and then I became an aerial photographer. It was all right. There's a saying that only a fool will allow himself to be uncomfortable. So I figured if I was going to be in the service I might as well play their game until I got out. I really got into the music down there, too, and sang with a number of groups. I picked up a lot of good ideas and was exposed to many different lines of thought."

It was just 1962 when Sam got out of the service and started working as a floorwalker at a club called Smitty's in Jacksonville Beach, Texas. "There are bouncers, and then there are floorwalkers. A sober person can go crazy if you tell them to shut up and sit down and you know a drunk will, so I used a quiet voice, addressed them as gentlemen, and never had any problems. But I noticed that when there was a problem, the band playing was never affected. No matter what went down nobody ever bothered the musicians and I thought to myself, 'I'm on the wrong end of the club.' I started as an emcee, and then I decided to go for it all the way."

Before long Sam was doing some serious singing with a group he had gotten together. "We had a nice cross section. One guy was into electronics, there were a couple guys I had known for awhile, and we had a sixteen-year-old drummer who was on probation for carrying a gun at

Sam the Sham (top) and the Pharoahs. *U.P.I. photo*

a public dance when we met him. Me and the older dudes in the band had to talk to his probation officer, saying we'd watch out for him, that whole trip."

That group became the first incarnation of the Pharoahs. "We were trying to find a name that was different. It was around the time the movie *The Ten Commandments* was out and we thought Rameses, the king of Egypt, looked pretty cool so we decided to be the Pharoahs. Now this is in Texas, mind you. So we started playing in every kind of place, 'gun and knife clubs' we called them. Like any other new band, you start out with the dregs. There was one place out in the boondocks called the Satyr Club, a place called the Manhatten, the Maverick in downtown Dallas, and some private clubs. Our deal with any club owner was that if we packed a place we'd get a raise. But club owners are a special breed, like musicians I guess, because we'd pack a place and they'd say wait awhile until we get the air conditioner fixed, or we got to do this or that. Finally I said 'I'm not going for it anymore.' "

He left the band and started working at a state fair. "I was a carny, working the midway, selling french fries and things like that. And this carny I worked for was really slick, taught me a lot about money and how to survive if you were willing to work. One time he and I were working all through this fair and come upon this organ exhibit, Hammonds, all makes. He knew I had played some in that first band when I could borrow one and asked me if I liked the one he was pointing at and I said sure. He said he was opening a club and would buy it and hire some musicians if I would play there."

So Sam started himself a blues band, called them the Pharoahs, and started playing some Little Junior Parker, Bobby "Blue" Bland, and John Lee Hooker at Jack Pyland's Blue Room, which featured the Branch Office Lounge. "Some of the dudes in that band were real good, went on to record later. I was surrounded by mature musicians but I was still pretty new to the organ and didn't know how to play that much. That's how I got my nickname, The Sham. That's what they called me, also because I was the guy out front jumping around and keeping everybody cranked up. That's called shamming. Everybody had a nickname back then. Omar Lopez from the first band was called 'Big Man' because he weighed about three hundred. Then there was a guy we had in the second band called 'White Snake.' Mine stuck."

The blues band didn't stay together too long and Sam set out to buy his own organ. There weren't many keyboard players around, especially ones with their own instrument. So Sam hocked everything he had and invested in one. "I had it three days when David Martin, this dude I'd gone to high school with, and who had backed up people like Muddy Waters, Chuck Berry, and Jimmy Reed, came up and said his band, the Night Riders, were losing their organ player and would I take his place and sing the blues with them down in Louisiana. I told them I'd only had it three days but I'd give it a shot if they wanted me to. So we went on down to this place on Highway 171 in Louisiana called the Congo Club, played there until we were tightened up, then headed up to Memphis. Booker T was hot up there, so was Willie Mitchell and Jerry Lee Lewis. We went up there cold and landed a job at another gun and knife club called the Diplomat playing ten at night to four in the morning."

The Night Riders broke up when two of the guys headed back to Texas. "They held on long enough for me and David Martin to replace them and we renamed the new group the Pharoahs. But everybody knew me as Sam the Sham so it was Sam the Sham and the Pharoahs. We got it tightened up again and pooled our money to do a recording of 'Betty and Dupree,' an old Chuck Willis number that few people had heard of. We just walked into a studio, paid the tax, produced it ourselves, and walked out with the master."

So they had their own recording. Unfortunately, the industry has a tendency to eat people alive when they try to do it on their own. In this case, Sun Records, for whatever reasons, came out simultaneously with a version of "Betty and Dupree" recorded by one of their contracted artists. "So it was us against the big company. We didn't know anybody in the industry at the time so it was really us against the world. We had a hearse we had bought to get around in and we had some records pressed from the master. Only five hundred at a time because we didn't have the money or the credit to get more. We'd drive from Memphis to Louisiana, straight on through, one driving and the rest sleeping. We tried to meet distributors, check out the radio stations, and drive back in time to play ten to four at the Diplomat. But we couldn't get anywhere. The other version was already too big. It was pretty discouraging, depressing.

"On one of those trips down to Louisiana in that old Packard antique, the side door blew open, and when I tried to close it I got sucked out. We were going about sixty miles an hour. Fractured my leg and got skinned up pretty bad. But we were too poor to die so I told the doctors to just give me a tetanus shot and a painkiller so I could be in Memphis that night for work. But they kept me five days anyway."

Then Memphis closed down the Diplomat. "They gave several reasons, but it was the jumpinest club in town and you know how politics are. So we played the High Hat and a few other places, doing blues, rock, anything. We could do three hundred songs without repeating."

Sam and the Pharoahs decided to record again, this time an old rhythm and blues thing by Johnny Williams called "Haunted House." They had some records pressed but no distributor was interested until they performed it on an afternoon radio dance show and the calls started coming in. One of the companies sent a guy named Gene Simmons (no relation to fire-eating Kiss bass player) to see if Sam wanted to make a distribution deal. "I told him I'd think it over. After he left I guess the devil got in his ear because he went back and said I'd said no, then recorded the song himself. I was definitely getting an education in how these things go down."

But they weren't ready to pack it in yet. In the summer of 1964, XL Records came along and asked them to record a song for them. "We recorded their song, but it was a jive thing and didn't do anything. So we said we had something they might dig, just a little rhythm thing. They heard it and asked if we had any lyrics to it. I said kick it off and I'll make some up. We did three takes on it, all of them different. They liked one so I said put a label on that thing and watch it go. That was 'Wooly Bully.' It went."

Obviously, the company was real happy about that. Unfortunately they got locked into the idea that Sam the Sham and the Pharoahs should be a novelty act. "Actually, 'Wooly Bully' wasn't a novelty thing, it was a dance song. I get people coming up to me today saying it was one of the original discotheque tunes. And from what I understand it was the first American record to sell a certified million during the onslaught of the British groups. We were serious about what we were doing. We told them to let us record what we wanted to do because we did that better."

Fat chance. The company had them cut "Ring Dang Doo" hoping for what they thought would be another novelty hit. But it didn't do much. Meanwhile, the band was touring with "Wooly Bully." "But we were getting real tired of it. One day in Denver the group was tired, frus-

trated, and disgusted, and said they wanted to try it on their own. I couldn't blame them and said good luck, gentlemen. I went to New York and met up with a group called Tony G and the Gypsies at the Metropole. They became the next Pharoahs when the record company came up with 'Little Red Riding Hood' and we went on tour again, all over the country, Europe, and the Far East. But it was getting to me. I was primarily a blues singer and they still wouldn't let us record what we wanted so I decided to hang it up for awhile. When you're not happy, you can't do it right."

He went back to New York and studied for awhile at the Herbert Berghof Drama Studio in Greenwich Village until he got an offer to go to England and play with a British blues-oriented group called the Clan. "While I was over there, one night I was hanging around a pub with John Lee Hooker and Freddy King. This man walks up and says,

'Hi, Sam. Ahmet Ertegun. How are you? What are you doing?' [Ahmet Ertegun, son of a Turkish diplomat, head of Atlantic Records, head of the New York Cosmos soccer team.] He asked me if I was signed with anyone and I said no because I had split with MGM. He said to give him a call when I got back to New York. I said yeah sure, because you know how those things are. But I did and he offered me a deal and we came to an agreement. So I went down to Miami some time around 1970 and recorded an album which I was very pleased with. It was called *Sam, Hard and Heavy*, which didn't necessarily mean I was, but that the people on it were serious. Duane Allman on guitar, the Dixie Flyers were the rhythm section, and the Memphis Horns were on it too. But the album never really got into the market because by the time it was finished, it was time to renegotiate the contract and we couldn't come to an agreement. As it turned out, though, I won a Grammy for the liner notes which I wrote. Signed them Sam Samudio. I don't know where you could find the record; it was rare to start with. But in the notes I just decided to thank everybody for everything, good and bad. We are the total sum of everything that's happened to us. So I was nominated as a writer, an annotator. Previously I'd been nominated for Song of the Year twice, and for Best New Group of the Year. After all that, I just decided to go out and spend some quiet years, but at the same time work on my writing and composing. I've been at it ever since."

Today, Sam lives with his wife in Memphis and is currently recording his own music, country and western, Cajun music, rock 'n' roll, and even some semiclassical things including a piece written for a ballet played by two guitars, two violins, a string bass, and a harp. He's also put together an unpublished book of poems and prose. "I'm a composer, not just a songwriter. That's part of the frustration. When I walk into the record company with a new piece of material they say 'No, no, no, you're too serious.' Well I am serious, man. The only sham about me is in the title."

Lou Christie

What's Lou Christie, ne Lugee Sacco, up to these days? Is he a distributor for Billy Beer? The owner of Land of a Thousand Dances parking lots? Werner Erhard's right-hand man? Nope. Maybe you didn't think "The King of the High Falsetto" was really a person but a sound created by studio hijinx, a group of black girls four-tracked until they got the "gypsy to cry." Well, Lou Christie is not in a state of remission.

Did you catch that boob-tube fluff called "People?" "Everybody will be famous for fifteen minutes," Andy Warhol used to exclaim. That's about as long as the show lasted. It had only one thing going for it—the theme song. Blasting out over the opening credits, the song was about a hundred notches above the Here's Johnnys and Thanks for the Memories pap. It had a driving disco beat and a singer who didn't play iron hands with the lyrics. That was Lou.

You might have caught a glimpse of him behind Liza Minnelli, and Halston on "People." They were entering Studio 54, the chic UFO of a disco in Manhattan. The strobe lights were flashing. Unemployed models in leopard skins danced on roller skates for attention and a possible meal ticket. The Pillsbury Doughboy of the literati set, Truman Capote, giggled at the scene. The man in the moon was snorting cocaine from a giant silver spoon that hung from the ceiling. Well, besides the camera crew, Lou was the only one working. He sang the crashing disco song while rotating columns of light made it appear as if a thousand bees were swarming his body.

Or did you catch the Country Music Awards on CBS in 1975? Johnny Cash stared into the camera with glazed eyes when Charlie "The Silver Fox" Rich made a torch of the card that announced John Denver as a winner. Johnny looked as if someone had handed him a note saying that the bus was leaving for Folsom prison and he would be on it. Charlie stomped off backstage where Minnie and Dolly were scrawling their names on a white autograph dress worn by Nashville's Rona Barrett, the bewigged Renee. Charlie took one glance at the telephone attached to Renee's shoulder and saw red. Renee was harmless enough, promoting her gossip show "Ring Renee," but Charlie thought otherwise. He stabbed her with a pen and proceeded to whack her around. The man behind the photographer snapping the whole affair was Lou, Renee's manager, producer, and business partner. He was incognito as Lou Christie of the New Christy Minstrels or so they thought. "Yes, they thought that's who I was. A lot of them thought I was 'Green Green.' "

The Nashville Banner carried the story front page for four days. Renee's bruises provided copy for *People, Rolling Stone,* and other mags. Lou didn't miss a beat. He proceeded to syndicate Renee's "Rhinestone Rambles" column and her talk show crammed with gossipy tidbits about the country crowd. "She said things about Dolly that Dolly didn't even know about." Then he wrote and produced RCA's *Backstage With Renee* record album. "It was another Lou Christie test-tube baby." The record was hailed by Dave Goodrich of *Pittsburgh Music Magazine* as a sign from heaven that "the important artist in the mid-sixties was preparing a comeback in the tradition of Neil Sedaka and Lesley Gore."

Today Lou camps out at the Great Southern Center in Bridgeville, Pennsylvania, where the thirty-five-year-old media master concocts new ways of dumping a 2001 Disco in your neighborhood. He must be doing something right. At least, *Billboard* thought so when they presented 2001 with their marketing award. As Lou explains, "I know where the middle of the road is, where the McDonald's hamburger lies. Oh, you can do anything in this business. You're talking about the world."

You folks around Pittsburgh might have seen our boy popping off a plane, getting pancaked in the dressing room while notable notables uttered the backstage ritual how-dos, mingling with the grand poobahs of chic before blasting off a new number on the local "Evening Magazine" television show. The kid is back home in the land of Andrew Carnegie, the Penguins, and the belch of industry. Lou lives with his wife Francesca, his son Christopher, and daughter Bianca Lucia right next door to the airport. "So I can leave town in a moment's notice."

How did Lugee leave town in the first place? Glen Willard was a stone's skip across the river from Beaver Falls. Broadway Joe Namath knew how to split. Toss the pigskin and take your talents down South before hobbling around Shea Stadium. Henry Mancini, who grew up nearby the desolate landscape off that monument to monotony, Route 80, hit the road to fame. Lou at first tried Joe's route out of town. But after he noticed that Bobby

Lane's puss was abnormally cleated, he knew that football wasn't what it was cracked up to be. No one told Lou that Bobby was the last to play football without a faceguard.

The same small farm in rural Pennsylvania was nice for Pops Sacco after a day at the steelmill where a buddy could get fried and poured into an ingot. The long shadows of a rural night could convey their own type of tranquillity. Come home and get the brood around you. There was Amy, Pete, Mary, Marsey, Shauna, and Lou. But they had to think up something other than watching "Jackie Gleason" and the "Cavalcade of Stars." How many CYO dances can you go to? How many times could you visit the parish priest without anything on your mind? Lou and the Sacco household first packed up and traveled down to a town fifty miles from Wheeling, West Virginia, where WWVA piped out its Jamboree of country tunes. Lou's parents would spend downtimes singing ethnic tunes. On the family's return to Pittsburgh Lou heard the black beat. The lightbulb lit. He formed the high school teen machine, the Classics, and started sneaking off to the studios as a background vocalist.

In 1960, Lou laid down a few tracks that didn't sound promising. His father was not amused. What happened to the football? Then Twyla Herbert and Lou teamed up on the ditty, "The Gypsy Cried." "I did the sound in my own basement. 'The Gypsy Cried' was one of the first things and I wrote it. My sister played background; Twyla's daughter also sang background. We rehearsed it right there and we walked into the studio twenty miles away and made the record. That was it."

Then Pops Sacco thought he'd help the kid along and be his escort service to the record hops. "Did I play record hops! I played every record hop. No, not on the bus tours. We didn't *just* play western Pennsylvania. We played the Pittsburgh area, West Virginia, and even parts of Ohio. All the Catholic gymnasiums. I would stand up there and lip-synch the record while it skipped and bounced at the end. My dad would drive me there. He had an old beat-up car. Sometimes, we'd run out of gas. When we drove up to the place where the hop was going on, we would have to park the car away from the others so no one saw us. I couldn't be embarrassed by dad's car. After all, I had the star thing to protect," he laughed.

After "The Gypsy Cried" stoked the furnaces of Steeltown, U.S.A. in the fall of 1962, Roulette Records hawked the saucer around the land until Lou had a hit on his hands. His high falsetto voice became a trademark and a brand on his head. Promoters thought Lou's voice was a banshee chorus manipulated by the wonders of technology or a black girl's larynx not yet attached to a group. "On my first tour, I was booked as a black girl. I showed up at a rehearsal in some auditorium in North Carolina and they said, 'Where is she?' 'She? What are you talking about?' I said, 'I'm Lou Christie.' The agency that booked me was a black agency that booked black musicians. Somehow they assumed that 'The Gypsy Cried' had been done by a black girl. But I played the South and had a ball."

With "Two Faces Have I" and "How Many Teardrops" Lou had his three songs to lip-synch at the hops and hoot and scream on Dick Clark's caravans. He hung a looie on the Pennsylvania Turnpike and headed toward the Liberty Bell and the walk-in heart at the Franklin Institute. "Oh, I traveled with all of Dick Clark's tours. I played every state in the union. Every auditorium which would hold over 2,500 up to 12,000. The book I should write is *The Stench of Dick's Bus*. We drove that bus everywhere. We did all his tours for practically nothing. Sometimes, we used to get the 'Do it for Dick' rap. But I've always had a good relationship with Dick.

"Yeah, Dick curled up and slept with everyone else. I mean like everyone else. Sorry about that. Let's see, I did the tours with Freddie Cannon, Gene Pitney, Johnny Tillotson, the Crystals, Dick and Dee Dee, the Orlons, the Dovells, and Brian [Hyland]. Brian and I were roommates. I'd have to get Brian up and make sure he got his laundry together. He was a really introspective guy even then." (Brian Hyland now resides on a commune in Oregon. His phone is in a deserted building. "Just keep ringing;

someone's bound to hear it.")

Lou eventually made his way out to Hollywood, the land of removeable sets, the airbrush, and hot tubs. Lou's songs became hot with sexual innuendo. In "Lightnin' Strikes," Lou tries to be faithful to his honey but can't help his roving eye which lights on a bundle of beauty. Then lightnin' strikes. The windshield wipers drive Lou into a frenzied passion and results in "Rhapsody in the Rain." "Sure, of course I went out there. What didn't you hear about it? I went out before 'Lightin'' became a hit. I did my 'Lightnin'' and 'Rhapsody in the Rain' days out there. It made the boy a little wiser. I had a ball. I don't want to talk about my film work. Our house got raided one time. But I don't want to talk about it."

While Lou thought he was standing "Outside the Gates of Heaven" and having a "Big Time," he would soon "Shake Hands and Walk Away Crying." In the late sixties, while he recorded "I'm Gonna Make You Mine" and "Are you Getting Any Sunshine," Lou formed a miniconglomerate with such diverse personalities as Al Kooper, Hank Medress, David Appel, the disc jockey Bobaloo, and the British band Badfinger. They did the Alka-Seltzer commercial where the animated head talks to the stomach. What's a poor boy to do but break out into other media fields when the British are breathing down the necks of the American artists.

"The teen idols were going down the tubes. If the British thing hadn't happened, it would have been something else. It wasn't a collapse. It was a time for change. Those people would've fallen by the wayside anyhow. If they couldn't get their act together, wake up and do something, then they obviously wouldn't get it on. A lot of people never grew. When you get comfortable with a certain sound, that's when you give up and quit creating. Ninety percent of the performers didn't even have an act. A lot of the Motown people like the Temptations and the Supremes were getting off. But it didn't bother me that much. I had some of my biggest records during that period. I enjoyed the British thing because my records were

hitting then in England.

"One of the reasons I left for London around 1970 was because everything had turned into a big business thing. It's all business and you really have to treat it like one when you get down to it. But there was no room for creativity. I had a manager who was a brilliant businessman. I listened to him so much that it wiped me out. There was no creativity left because he would always logically put it together. It all sounded right on paper but when it wouldn't work, I was left having to scrape up the ashes. Artistically it just messed it up. We all ended up just watching the dollar go round the room."

So were the Feds. Unknown to Lou, his manager had dealings with the mob and was soon indicted for a conspiracy involving the corruption of a judge in New York City. "At that point, my manager was on the front page of the *New York Times* and the *Daily News*. So I said, 'Time to move on.' Bits of it are still hanging around. It was dismal, to put it mildly. Royalties? Sewn up and locked up. Not just in this country but other countries. They took the English stuff. We had a company over there, too. Everything was looked over quite well.

"I was working over in London because I thought it time to get away from all this nonsense. Besides, I was becoming more popular in Europe than I was in America. I thought it a good time for a transition. I was concentrating more on recording in America. When I went to Europe, I was putting my energies into creating a very successful show. It was me having to show a personality or different aspect of my singing.

"I traveled with a guitar player and I thought I would never perform without this person because he knew exactly when to bring things in. I was performing with Linda Scott without Ronnie and the guys who backed me. I thought, 'My God, what am I going to do? I have to pull this off.' I was all by myself at that point. Linda went onstage. She had a personality which took everyone over. I sat back there and thought, 'How am I going to follow her?' That was the turning point. I said, 'Hey, forget about being self-conscious and get out there and do what you're doing.' That evening was the first night when I let it all go. At that point I realized that you had to forget about yourself and just go on and do it. Just project as much honesty as you can. I tried to steer myself as far away from Sammy Davis, Jr. as possible. When I find myself getting into that type of thing, I have to break the mold. There is the danger of becoming that Las Vegas person. That turns me off. You just have to remember that most people go out for an evening to dance and boogie, drink and have fun.

"I went around England about three times. I played the top clubs and kept going back and said, 'Is that all there is?' I did a couple of command performances for mum, Princess Margaret, and Lord Snowden. I had a jolly good time. I played a couple times with David Bowie before he freaked out and started singing about spaceships. It was before the 'Hunky Dory' stage. Then I played Germany and Spain in 1973. I did Spanish television shows. Terrible stuff. I was traveling at that time with a girl who was the new Brigitte Bardot. That was really interesting with the press around. She stopped traffic in Spain."

Lou and his wife returned to the States in 1973. "Changing countries took me a few years to settle down again. It was such a totally different thing over there. I came back here with the kids and tried to get the personal end of things straightened out." Plopping down in Pittsburgh again, Lou launched the *Beyond The Blue Horizon* album. You can hear him on "Riding in My Van," "You're Gonna Make Love to Me," "Spanish Wine," and the recent disco hit, "I Wake Up Screaming in the Middle of the Night." He produces numerous groups like Free Beer, who had the country hit "Queen of the Purple Sage." Groups today? "Well, you have to deal with a certain intelligence. They are so much more aware. I mean there are not so many turkeys out there who are so dumb. The innocence of everything, the whole culture, is gone. No one is as innocent as we were in the old days. People are much more aware and sophisticated in a lot of areas." Recording plans? "I'm working with a Pittsburgh group, Sweet Breeze, and they're hot. My act is hot. You think about hot and that's it. I'm making it as hot as I can make it. Something should soon be released . . . pink, hot vinyl."

Peter Noone

"When I was fifteen, I first experienced girls screaming through my act. I thought it was natural and that I would always get it. I never provoked it. I just got up there and did what I had always done—played Peter Noone. When I was onstage, I would be embarrassed if I couldn't be treated like a normal person. I was a member of the evening, someone who was there to make girls scream. But the best gigs were in places like Salt Lake City because people didn't scream there."

In the spring of 1964, after Beatlemania swept the country, another group from Liverpool called Herman's Hermits led the second wave of the British invasion. The group's organizer and lead singer, Peter Noone, known to his fans as Herman, captured girls' hearts with his impish, little boy looks and his obvious sense of fun. At the height of the group's popularity, Hermits concerts were seething scenes of giggling, shrieking prepubescents drowning out Peter on "Mrs. Brown, You Have a Lovely Daughter" and "I'm Henry VIII, I Am." "The most favorite places on the tour were obviously the Ohio State Fair where 100,000 people screamed all through the show and Pasedena's Rose Bowl where 38,000 did the same. It's an amazing feeling." Although the Hermits had more hit singles in England, they had their biggest following in America, where the pleasant, gentle, well-produced sounds of "No Milk Today" and "There's a Kind of Hush" combined with the natural stage presence of the bright, blue-eyed sixteen year old made the Hermits immediately lovable.

America at the time was still an uncharted land for British groups and the Hermits' tours initiated the great rock bands, The Who, the Animals, and the Hollies into the

American music scene and the joys of touring. During one forty-five-day tour with The Who, Peter taught the late Keith Moon the finer aspects of show business. "Moon as well as other people on the tour learned that even Herman's Hermits with their very Bible-belt type of image really had a good time. After playing Asbury Park's Convention Hall, Moon and I jumped off the end of the pier into the ocean. I taught him a lot. We introduced him to cherry bombs. Nobody had seen them before so it was good fun blowing up toilets. Touring had to be fun because you had to fill up the time somehow."

From 1964 through 1968, Peter's life consisted of working 365 days a year in a whirligig of studio sessions, press conferences, television shows, and global tours. The Hermits played all the variety shows like "Danny Kaye," "Dean Martin," and Dick Clark's "Where the Action Is." They became favorites of Ed Sullivan who always cringed when other rock stars appeared on his show. "We got along with Ed Sullivan great because he really liked the band, almost as much as the Dave Clark Five. After singing my song, he would say, 'Come over here a minute, Peter.' That was the only time we spoke to him. Then he would introduce the Samoans, 'Next on our show from Samoa are the Samoans,' and we'd leave the stage." The Hermits even managed between concert dates to appear with Connie Francis in a beach party movie called *When the Boys Meet the Girls*, a sequel to *Where the Boys Are*. The band lasted almost ten years and finally broke up in 1972 after it battled the chronic show business disease, protracted litigation over back royalties.

Today, Peter Noone is thirty and lives with his wife of ten years, Mireille, in the mountains outside of West Hollywood. After a few years in France as a solo artist, Peter moved two years ago to the West Coast for "the warmth and to get back into rock and roll." He likens the California scene to the early Liverpool days when Herman's Hermits were hustling for their big break. "Now if you want a band, everybody's over here. I keep bumping into people from Liverpool out here. Unfortunately, I'm falling back in with all the English guys because they're my neighbors. I get the guys over to my house where I have a pool house in the back with all the gear and we just rock and roll. It's nice and free. We've all learned the lesson by being over here and working all the time." While Peter hasn't needed to work professionally for five years, he keeps writing and playing music because he says, "What I really want to do is be a hungry rock and roll singer again because that's when you do things right."

The Hermits' sound and Peter's preference for living here are the results of his early exposure to American music. "I always thought that America was the place where all music came from. I've got an American soul. It comes from day one of music, when I listened to the American Armed Forces Network which used to play rock and roll and a lot of country western music like Skeeter Davis. I became a fan of Elvis Presley, Chuck Berry, Buddy Holly, and Ben E. King. I grew up in Liverpool but my father, who was a musician, sent me to the Manchester School of Music to read music better than he did. When I was attending classes in music theory, I used to hear people in the next room playing songs like 'Roll over Beethovan' and 'Reeling and A-Rocking.' So I thought 'That's the music for me and got up and joined them. The guys went on to become doctors and accountants."

His first group, the Cyclones, later the nucleus of Herman's Hermits, was formed in 1961. "We only had one amplifier between the three of us and could only practice over at a friend's house when his mother was out getting her hair done. At that time, everyone just played an instrument, because it was cooler to play Ventures hits and the Shadows than sing Lonnie Donegan's hits like 'Does Your Chewing Gum Lose Its Flavor.' One guy finally quit because he had to take his O levels in physics. I really got the bug and went out to get other guys. We didn't have a singer but we wanted to do Buddy Holly and Chuck Berry songs. Well, if there was going to be a singer, it was going to be me because I didn't want to stand in the back. That's when I became a singer. I bought a second-hand silver

Peter Noone (second from left) and Herman's Hermits in 1965.
Wide World photo

lamé suit from a guy, Deke Rivers, who was built like a
truck driver. I was thirteen and had no shoulders, so a
friend of my mother took it all in. Now that we had a
singer, we needed to have a real flash name. So we became Peter Novak and the Heartbeats.

"We started to get gigs at football [soccer] clubs. We
played a lot of workingman's clubs. They are the places
where the coalminers, the breadmakers, etc., go after
work to drink themselves silly until seven o'clock when
they can go home and have dinner. We used to play three
two-hour gigs a night. We had a van to carry three
amplifiers, a set of drums, and a PA system. We'd unpack
it, play from 5:30 on, and then drive off to another town to
do the ten o'clock to midnight show. In 1962, we got four
pounds a night [about $7.50].

"To buy the van, I used to sell programs at the
Manchester United Football Grounds where I made sixty
pounds [$112.50] on a Saturday. After the game, I would
sell newspapers with the halftime results of the other
teams to all the local pubs. So I managed to get high pur-
chase, which in England is credit. I signed my father's
name on the slip, put down a big deposit, and got the van.
The band would pay me back after each gig.

"We started to become popular locally and had a fan

club. Like all the bands from that era we got so good because we made all the mistakes. Then you didn't ruin your career by going onstage and dying. We learned by dying one night in particular. We were playing a workingman's club called the Domino Club in Manchester. The twist had just come out in England so the manager of the club billed me as the Crown Prince of Twist. It was supposed to be someone else. He had made a mistake so I had to twist through every number. We really died that night.

"Then, Gerry and the Pacemakers and Freddy and the Dreamers had just started in Liverpool. Everybody was dropping the second name so we felt that Peter Novak and the Heartbeats just couldn't go. One night at a club we sat around and made a list of names. I said, 'Why don't we call ourselves Sherman and the Supermen.' Finally, we came up with Hermits but we couldn't find another name to go with it. Finally, we came up with Sherman's Hermits and that became Herman's Hermits. I think it goes together well.

"We then began to do one audition a week for a recording contract. But everybody was turning us down because they said we were too American. We could hear all the American performers on the American Armed Forces Network and learn them before anyone else did. They didn't like us because we did Chuck Berry, Bobby Rydell, and Ernie K-Doe. So we tried to get an independent producer to sign us. One of them was Mickey Most [later the producer of Lulu and Donovan] who we flew from London to Manchester. In those days, London was the end of the world for us. We prepaid his hotel and meals and tipped off all our friends and the audience that a big-time producer was traveling up to hear us. So we got all the girls to scream, really fake screams. Mickey liked what I was doing onstage and said he could make me into a pop singer. But he said that the band wasn't any good and that's why we were failing the auditions. So for the first time in my life, I became a businessman and fired two people. This was our big change-around. I got Derek Lackenby and Barry Whitman from a local band called the

Whalers and with Keith Hopwood and Karl Green all the Hermits were together for the first time.

"For a month we rehearsed and rehearsed an Earl Gene song I had heard on the radio. We then went down to London for an audition and cut the record, 'I'm Into Something Good' which became number one. We had more hits in England but nobody wanted to release us in America. Eventually MGM released a single and we started to do different songs for England and America."

The popularity of the Hermits from 1964 until their breakup was the result of the band's extreme willingness to travel anywhere to perform, often without getting paid. The Hermits could be called the inventors of the world-wide tour, even though none of them had previously traveled. From the ages of fifteen through twenty, Peter and the group criss-crossed the globe playing such exotic places as Tahiti, Fiji, Hong Kong, Japan, and Cambodia.

"It was incredible to go anywhere beyond Europe. We were just English guys who had never been anywhere. We'd go anywhere they wanted us. We didn't have a reason not to be on the road. We didn't have days off because we felt that the gigs were vacations. None of us had families so the touring was like having adventures. In those days, people didn't work hard so by going anywhere we were always so well received. When we arrived in a place like Australia, whatever record we had out would be number one, because we would be there."

In 1965, Herman's Hermits became one of the first Western rock groups to play Japan. While on tour in America that year, Peter became good friends with an American priest who ran the Good Shepherd Movement, an evangelical movement in Japan. The priest proposed that he promote the Hermits for his organization and in return he would pick up all the expenses. Peter seized on the chance to travel to Japan and as a consequence the so-called Mr. Clean of Rock became embroiled in a national scandal.

At that time the most popular Japanese rock group was the Spiders. a gang of hoody-looking, long-haired

Japanese teenagers, who played tinny versions of American rock and roll songs. Unfortunately, the day Peter and the band landed in Tokyo, one of the Spiders was busted for possession of drugs. As a result, The Hermits were seen as a barbarian invasion trying to convert Japanese youth to the rock cult of drug addiction. Throughout their stay, they were hounded by packs of Japanese journalists constantly pushing microphones and cameras in their faces and demanding to know what right the British band had trying to influence Japanese youth.

As Peter remembers, "It was the weirdest trip ever. The newspapers said that 'Long hair and guitars spelled drugs, so keep your children out of rock and roll.' It was just a pathetic thing. I said, 'Just because you like rock and roll doesn't mean that you're going to light up a joint in the auditorium.' Not every band was saying, 'OK, everybody, light up.' It was difficult to explain to the Japanese, 'Look, we're here. We're not getting paid. We're not here to tell your children what to do.' We got fantastic press after that. Everybody stopped in the streets and took photographs of us. I think we were the first blue-eyed boys who ever got all that treatment."

In the Philippines, Peter agreed to entertain an American air base in Cebu, thinking it only a small drive away. "They drove a truck onto an American beachlanding craft and drove us across a 300-mile sea to an island. It was 150 degrees and 900 degrees of humidity, when we landed on the beach. It was so hot that people were sleeping alongside the road in the jungle. After a few hours in the jungle, we came to Americaland, an air-conditioned hotel with Coca-Cola and American servicemen with their feet on the bar. We were back in civilization. We did a gig for the Americans who were out at this dreadful place for R&R. Then the American promoter, the owner of the only speedboat on the island, put us out on the stern of the boat in the water, tied it to the back of a station wagon, and towed us around the island. We were to wave to all the Philippino people who ran out of their villages to see us. They all had transistor radios which announced,

'Herman's Hermits are now at the junction of jungle and village X.' They came out and waved. But they didn't even know who we were.''

Always criticized in their native England as too American, the Hermits finally made it big back home in 1968 with "Just One Girl," "No Milk Today," and "There's a Kind of Hush." Suddenly in 1969, "The American thing fell apart and our record company wouldn't release our number one record in the States and they wouldn't give us the money. I finally said, 'Forget it. Let's do the rest of the world, do another go-around, and let the lawyers get it sorted out." The lawyers finally sorted it out two years later. By that time, Herman's Hermits were no more. Peter guessed that the rest of the band is in England but he hasn't spoken to them recently. However, he isn't bitter about the breakup. He still thinks, "it's fantastic when a cab driver remembers old Herman."

During the last years of the group's existence, Peter started buying interests in businesses as a lark. His most notable venture was a boutique in New York called the Zoo. It featured vinyl trousers, jackets, and see-through pants arranged in their own cages. He also owned a pub in

England. "All my businesses cost me money. There is only one business which I take seriously and that's the one I live every day—rock and roll."

In 1972, Peter landed a television series in England called the "Mike Yarwood Show." Yarwood was the British Rich Little impersonating England's politicians and celebrities. Peter did the music and occasionally a bit of light comedy on the show. "It was the first thing I ever did as Peter Noone and I got famous all over again in England."

After the TV series, Peter did more acting and slowly drifted away from the music scene. Finally, after a number of bad business deals, he made his first record since leaving the group. It was titled, "Oh, You Pretty Things" and featured another young British rocker who was on public relief and had used the advance to pay his back rent. The new star was David Bowie, who later rocketed to fame with a record called "Hunky Dory." "'Pretty Things' was a bit of a heartbreaker because it didn't make it in America. I think it was a state secret." Peter soon left for France, where he cut a number of hit singles.

Financially comfortable, Peter Noone lives with his multilingual wife who, when they are abroad, makes him feel like an idiot, around the corner from Dave Clark, who refuses to play drums for him, and a stone's throw away from his electronically rigged pool house where members from groups like the Beach Boys sneak in for some good-time jamming. He and his wife have no children because Peter says he has to grow up first and become a patriarchal figure. But Peter is ready "to start again completely and get back on the road to let people see what I do now." He hopes to make an album soon with a band composed of his neighbors. Dean Murray from Elton John's early group will play bass, Terry Shaddick of Tranquillity guitar, Steve Kittman from Tin Tin on drums, and Peter Noone, because he doesn't like to stand in the back, will probably sing. As Peter says, "This time it's going to be a family affair."

Bobby Lewis

Bobby ("Tossin' and Turnin' ") Lewis was Indianapolis born and bred. In grade school plays he was always chosen for the singing roles. Even though, he insists, "I don't have that good a voice. I have a strong voice. If you can't be good, be loud." He's quick to add, "But I carry a tune fairly well." While a kid, he did radio concerts as a member of the glee club in grammar school. He remembers singing "Now the Day Is Over" as one of the three tunes. He also soloed in church.

One day a Cadillac pulled up at the corner of his neighborhood and out jumped an Indian with long braids who claimed to be the chief of his people. Not knowing whether the Indian was a salesman or a medicine man, Bobby volunteered to work for him in exchange for movie money. Expecting to help set up the man's sign and stand filled with bottles and jugs, Bobby found himself wearing what looked like a large Halloween mask over his head and shoulders. To get the crowd cozy and in a buying mood, the chief recited the history and accomplishments of the Indian peoples. He gestured at Bobby's mask, remarking on its "special big medicine" in curing diseases and fighting enemies. Naturally the people bought the snake oil, the Indian never returned to that part of the city, and Bobby was left without a job.

The first decent-paying work Bobby had was delivering twenty-five- or fifty-pound blocks of ice to people's homes. He carried them up the stairs, sometimes three flights, placed them in the iceboxes, and emptied the water pans beneath the ancient boxes. In the winter, he hauled baskets of coal. Once a friend of his secured him a job riding shotgun on a coal truck. Asked to drive, he jumped at the chance and promptly wrecked the truck since no one had ever told him that you had to slow down around curves.

Another friend, later a minister for the Apostolic Church in Indianapolis, helped the fifteen-year-old Bobby out by recommending him as a combination bellhop, porter, and desk clerk to a small neighborhood hotel across from the Greyhound Bus depot. He mopped floors, carried bags, got wires crossed on the old-fashioned switchboards with those snakes with plugs on the end. Finally, the management trusted Bobby enough to walk the evening take in a canvas bag to the bank. Bobby quit after four weeks because, as he remembers, "It was all work, no money." The twelve bucks for a week's work didn't feed his face, so Bobby sauntered over to the shoestore. At first he carried large boxes of shoes up from the basement. Then he was moved from the back to the front as a salesman of ladies footwear. The clientele didn't appreciate his appearance and he soon lacked a paycheck.

He was still only sixteen and couldn't get any decent job with a living wage. Outside his house were plastered posters advertising the various entertainers passing through the local dance hall and theater. He was taken by the notion of making money by singing on a show. It was 1948. "Walking the streets ain't doing nothing. So that's when I started going on the main drag."

Indianapolis had two downtowns—one white, one black. The blacks' center city was adjacent to the white section. Eight blocks of little radio repair shops, theaters, cafes, soda fountains, restaurants, pawn shops, and the clothing stores with the latest zoot suits. They called this stretch of town "The Avenue." One day Bobby took to cruising it. He discovered a sign for the Bimbo Show, a local affair for neighborhood performers.

At the theater, he slipped past the ticket-taker and found a seat in the dark. From this vantage point, he watched as an old woman blues singer, two skimpily clad dancing girls, and a comic in black face entertained. The emcee, a man named Bimbo, got up onstage with his well-

pressed suit, derby hat, a long cigar, and a diamond ring.
He looked the slick shark. Bobby thought he'd apply for a
job loading equipment, taking out the trash, and sweep-
ing up after showtime. He expected twenty-five cents a
show, the going rate. Bimbo himself interviewed the
young man. In a staccato bark, the emcee-producer asked
whether Bobby could sing, dance, and play an instrument.
The kid bluffed his way past the first two queries and
frankly admitted he couldn't play an instrument. "I
couldn't get away with that." Bimbo said, "Come back
tomorrow afternoon and we'll see if we can use you."

Bobby cloud-nined it back home. The next morning,
anxious for his shot at the big time, he waited for hours a
block away from the theater. Afternoon finally arrived and
he found all the troupe draped about the theater asleep.
Bimbo woke up and asked Bobby to sing—anything. Bobby sang "China, China, Chinatown. Where the Lights are
Low . . ."

He got the job, went home, washed and ironed his

pants and tie, and returned to play the last three days of
the Bimbo Show. No one offered him any money and
Bobby didn't bother to ask. Instead, after the show every
night, Bimbo would take his troupe to his headquarters, a
little teaky, filthy restaurant which he owned. The entertainers crowded into a booth and wolfed down chili, hamburgers, hot dogs, and soup, the entire menu of the joint.
No money exchanged hands and Bobby didn't offer to
pay for the food. That Sunday night, the same routine was
repeated. The show had finished around midnight. The
chatter was broken up by Bimbo saying, "All right, I'll see
you all tomorrow." Bobby found out then he was heading
out to another town in Indiana.

He had never been outside the city before. The farthest
he had gotten was the city limits when he and a white kid
once tried to hitchhike out to another town. The white
boy slowed a car down and hopped in, leaving Bobby
standing by the side of the road waving good-bye. With
the Bimbo Show Bobby finally got his chance to hit the
road, traveling to Evanston, Terre Haute, and beyond into
Kentucky and the southern part of Ohio. It lasted six
months and Bobby returned home.

Now he was accepted by the other black entertainers
and soon began playing shows for ten bucks a weekend. A
magician named Prince something or other wore a turban
and played simple card and sleight of hand tricks with a
bucket of money as a prop and the source of his revenue.
A blues singer named Sue provided the music, another
girl the dancing sights, and Bobby did a sand dance. He
threw a handful of sand down on the floor and scraped his
feet along in time with the music. He did this until Sue
threatened to fire Bobby if he didn't use salt instead because the sand got into her skin, legs, and up the
elsewhere. Bobby switched and the crowds just got qui-
eter so they could hear those shoes scraping across the
floor.

Shortly after that, Bobby joined the JJ Page Carnival
singing and helping acts along with his guitar. For a dollar
or two, he would put up the Ferris Wheel, tear down the

rides, clean the equipment, carry the water, and put up the tents. Business had been bad and the circus people believed in luck, mostly bad. Bobby was trying to learn how to play guitar. The Performers singled out the good-looking, bad-sounding guitar as the source of their crowd problems. Bobby felt so bad about it that he took the instrument behind the tent and broke it into pieces over a rock.

It seems that wasn't his only source of discomfort. The shill for the Alligator Man loudly registered a strong dislike for Bobby's complexion and hair. Bobby's friend, nicknamed Smiling Jack because of his riding boots and pants, waited until nightfall to cold cock the shill. Bobby heard the screaming from his cot in the carnival tent. He went out as the bloody man crawled back to his Alligator booth. Bobby left the carnival a week later, observing the adage, "Don't be where you're not wanted."

Back in Indianapolis, Bobby always managed to raise enough coin to keep his wardrobe up to snuff, even if his shoes were marked-downs. He was walking the Avenue one day when he spotted another sign, this time for a Ferguson's Theatrical Agency. He turned in the door and spun out with a job for a Mr. Leo Hines, a cousin of Earl Fatha Hines.

"The biggest band up 'til then had five pieces. I thought it would be something like that. I walked there. It was a park six or seven miles on the other side of town. I carried my suit and an extra suit and a little bag, a cardboard suitcase. I got there and to my surprise there was a fourteen-piece orchestra setting up. My face was sweaty, greasy, and shiny. I had to get my hair combed again, straighten myself up, and get my tie. I said, 'Is Leo around?' He was standing over there. I nervously went over there and said, 'Mr. Ferguson told me to be here.' 'Oh yeah, you're Bobby, right?' 'Right, here's the note he gave me.' 'It's fine. What songs are you going to sing?' I told him. It was the first band I ever worked with. It was a beautiful show that night. I sang ballads at the time. I sang two tunes the whole night. In those days, the singer would sit alongside the band and wait for his turn to do his song. It wasn't like today when a singer comes out and does an hour and a half. Then, if you had two tunes, you were lucky. I did two tunes; some nights I'd only do one."

He joined Leo Hines for a tour on his raggedy bus, a wreck which collapsed every five or six miles. "Once when we went to Corpus Christi, the bus broke down. It couldn't make the hills. We would all have to get out and push it up a hill."

In Corpus Christi, the band members fanned out across the black section of town to private homes which would rent to entertainers and visiting black civic and religious leaders. The hotels were reserved for whites. One time, ignorant of the town curfew for blacks, the band was stopped by a policeman on their way back to their rooms. "Whatchaya niggers doing around here?" The officer shoved a flashlight in Bobby's face. "We just finished doing our show at the club," said Bobby. "Oh, yeah, yeah, you pretty good but keep straight on," the cop replied. And Bobby recalls, "We went straight on, too."

That lasted for four months before the bookings got bad. There were no crowds where Hines's band was booked and finally the group got stranded in Arkadelphia, Arkansas. After a week of waiting for the agent in Indianapolis to wire money to the destitute band members, Bobby struck out on his own. At first he worked a Little Rock club but soon ended up on the street corner dancing and singing to another's guitar accompaniment. After entertaining at a party thrown by an airline pilot at a local motel, Bobby hightailed it back to Indianapolis.

Back home again, he found Ferguson's closed, but refrained from hunting for him. Gigs were sporadic: clubs would open, last a few months, then close while another would pop up. "There was always one, but they didn't last long," states Bobby. He soon hooked up with guitar great Wes Montgomery and his brother Monk who played bass. A woman named Lucy Johnson sang ballads, while Bobby was called on to provide the pep. "That's when I started singing boogie blues and the crowd came alive."

He continued playing weekends until the crowds thinned out and the club owner's brother, Tony Lance, offered to find him work in Detroit, an idea he found less than appealing because the Motor City had been racked with rioting. Finally, he agreed to venture away once again from his hometown. Bobby remembers the moment fondly: "I saw my picture in the local black newspaper with a headline saying, 'Bobby Lewis Managed By Tony Lance Going To Detroit, Michigan. Good Luck To Him.' They thought I was going to make a big splash because I was a local kid seeking his fortune."

He arrived in Detroit by bus and immediately embarked (for California) in Tony Lance's new Chrysler Imperial with fins. It was his first time behind the wheel since the coal truck days. He fared no better this time, fiddling with the new invention called automatic transmission. The car kept skidding over the slick ice from one side of the road to the other. His manager finally had to take the wheel and drive all night to St. Louis. From there they went to Texas.

"I remember going up those long roads which were straight as a stick. But there were hills. It was Texas hill country. We'd go up one hill and down another, up another hill and down another for mile after mile on end on end on end. You just wished one of those roads would turn. He had that Imperial up to ninety to one hundred miles per hour. The next thing I knew we were crossing the border into Texas. I remember the desert sand being red, dark reddish brown clay, and a sand storm was blowing up. We stopped at the border where the cars were inspected for fruits and vegetables."

When he reached California, he saw the familiar face of Lucy Johnson and the elegant figure of Duke Ellington at the Oasis Club in Los Angeles. "For the first time I saw the Great Duke. My eyes were as big as saucers. I said to Lucy, 'Wow, you singing with the Duke.' She said, 'You knew that.' 'I crossed the continent and I didn't know that. As a matter of fact, I didn't know we were coming to see you.'"

For the next month, Bobby bummed his room and

meals by hanging around with the Ellington band. Bobby wistfully remembers: "I was eating steaks. It was the first time I'd ever seen tables so small. There would be eight chairs around a little bitty one with people sitting sideways, enough room to get your arm in there. Here I am with a big steak and one table. I thought that was big stuff."

One night Duke let Bobby sing with his orchestra. "Duke was sitting at the piano. The place was jammed and he looked over to me and said, 'Come on up.' I said, 'Huh.' He said, 'Come on up.' I said, 'Aiiie.' I ran up those stairs onstage. He hadn't said he was going to bring me up on the show to sing with the orchestra. Duke said, 'What are you going to do? What key do you sing in?' 'C.' 'Then we'll have blues in the key of C. The "Shuffle Blues." ' I sang a few tunes that night. It was one of the highlights of my life."

When he returned to Detroit, he gigged around all the small clubs on Hastings Street, until one day, he checked into his agent's office and found that he had been booked on the "Soupy Sales Show." At that time Soup had a night show for adults starting at 11:30 PM after the news and a kiddie show at noon. The band members on the show got such a kick out of Bobby that he kept getting invited back. In 1956, he cut "Mumbles Blues" on Spotlight Records and soon became a regular on a daytime television show emceed by Detroit's head DJ, Ed MacKenzie.

Bobby Lewis then met Jackie Wilson, who helped him get spots on shows with such luminaries as Pat Boone and his white bucks. In New York, every three months, Bobby played the Baby Grand and the Apollo with Nipsey Russell. But he remained in Detroit with his wife and three kids doing shows at the Coliseum with Soupy Sales and cutting another record in 1958 on Mercury called "Oh, Mr. Somebody." Finally, Jackie Wilson asked Bobby to join him in New York.

"These were the real highlights. They didn't pay no money but the money wasn't important to me. I knew I was moving up and I never considered myself a good vocalist. I considered myself a good entertainer. I thought it was just as important to be a good entertainer as a good singer. I met a lot of singers who can't entertain. It's miserable when you get on the floor and can't put yourself over. You got the voice. I compensated for my voice with that fact. I said that I didn't have any money when Jackie invited me to New York. The next thing I knew he and Nat Tarnapol sent me train fare to come to New York. I talked with my wife about it. She agreed I should go because I had done all I could, it seems, in Detroit. I said, 'I guess I'll go give it a try.' I went to New York and met Jackie."

For two years, Bobby played shows around the New York area, became the master of ceremonies at the Apollo, the Howard Theater in Washington, and the Royal in Baltimore. He soon made the circuit with Little Willie John, Brook Benton, Hank Ballard, James Brown, and Jackie Wilson on one bill. But his career was going nowhere.

Jesse Belvin of the Bluenotes, the cowriter of the Penguins hit "Earth Angel" and the tunesmith of "Goodnight My Love," the closing theme of Alan Freed's popular WINS radio show in New York, had promised Bobby that he would help him get something going once the Wilson tour ended. But on February 6, 1960, Jesse Belvin was killed in a car accident.

"The night we'd done the show, there was a lot of disturbance around the dance hall. Arthur Prysock had been on the show and someone had sliced the tires of his Lincoln Mark II. Someone else's car had been banged up. I didn't know why that had happened. A guy named Beans, a big saxophone player out of Detroit, was in the band. I was riding in his Ambassador with another guy. We were coming along the road going toward Dallas from Little Rock.

"When we got on the road, we saw smoke going up into the air, blue smoke, black smoke, purple smoke. On my right I could see the railroad track with smoke billowing up in the air. From my experience of having worked on railroad dressing ties and rails, I thought someone must have been burning ties. I didn't think anything about it until we got right up to it. I saw that a car was on fire. It was Jesse Belvin's car. His Cadillac was smashed in half.

"We stopped our car and tried to get them out before the car exploded, before it blew. We had to get a chain to pull open the door and had to tie it to a truck. I took the chain and wrapped it around the car doors to get them open. We pulled Jesse out and his wife with him and his guitar player in the back and his driver. We got them all out of their car. The other people, God bless their souls, had landed head-on with Jesse's car. They didn't get out of their car and were burnt. I thought, 'Well, that's the end of that. It's bad enough the boy gets killed but he could have helped me.'"

But, in 1961, Bobby Lewis made it to the top of the pops with his recording, "Tossin and Turnin'," a song penned by Richie Adams, the former lead singer of the Fireflies. "That was numero uno. It stayed number one longer than any record fifteen years prior to that. It was unbelievable. It was like the country getting behind the record. I guess the record just told what everyone wanted to hear. I received fan mail from parents saying that the record sent their daughter home and straightened out their son who was in the service but was mischievous. It was a great experience and I won't forget it."

That same year he followed with "One Track Mind," and "What a Walk." In July 1962, he released "I'm Tossin' and Turnin' Again." Since then Bobby has been doing nightclub and theater work as both an entertainer and a black Dick Clark reuniting old acts and introducing new ones. He's living on New York's West Side and recently performed at the New York Technological Institute and the Knights of Columbus. He hopes to record a new single soon.

"In God's way and through His loving mercy, we have all endured. Life never stops. It hasn't been easy. It's been an experience. I can't say it was dull. It's very humbling. You realize that there's more to life than having ham and eggs in the morning."

Jackie Wilson

The teeming throng jammed to the rafters busts its collective gut in anticipation as the house lights dim in the Fox Theater in Brooklyn. And then, with casual but fine-tuned elegance, he appears, slowly walking toward the microphone at the center of the stage, a freshly lit cigarette in his hand. The crowd goes crazy. The women in the front rows press into the lip of the stage. And Jackie Wilson calmly goes about finishing his cigarette. Then with one last puff, he grinds it out with his foot, grabs the mike, and wails into "That's Why." Just when you thought the frenzy had reached its peak, the theater erupts. It has become a runaway nuclear reactor and Jackie Wilson is the plutonium core, splitting, spinning, leaping, burning, Mr. Excitement blistering another audience.

Over ten years later it is September 29, 1975, a Monday night and Dick Clark's Rock and Roll Revue has come to the Latin Casino in Cherry Hill, New Jersey. Jackie Wilson headlines a show that also features Dion as well as Cornell Gunther and the Coasters. Two shows are planned. There will only be one. The crowd is in ecstasy as Jackie works out on "Lonely Teardrops" near the end of the first show, his virtuoso vocal gymnastics in perfect counterpart to the heated contortions of a visionary stage act. He begins to go into one of his patented back bends, face aimed toward the sky, when suddenly he collapses, his head banging off the stage. He is not breathing. Cornell Gunther rushes out to Jackie's side and begins to give mouth-to-mouth. A paramedic unit is dispatched from the Cherry Hill Medical Center. Cornell keeps working on Jackie literally keeping him alive until the ambulance arrives.

By the time they got him to the hospital he was comatose. The doctors did all they could and miraculously Jackie hung on. Days went by without any change. Then one morning a nurse found him still in bed but with a broken nose and two black eyes. A wooden arm broken off from a wheelchair was found beneath the bed. No one has ever figured out what had happen. He was transferred immediately to a private hospital in Philadelphia.

In the next four months he was shuttled to eight different hospitals. Eventually the court moved in when the medical bills weren't getting paid and had him placed in the Medford Leas Convalescent Center in Medford, New Jersey, where he is today.

Although it has been very slow, he is starting to make progress. He has conscious periods, but is virtually paralyzed and can only communicate with his eyes. During the eight months after his collapse he was given no physical therapy whatsoever. He just lay in bed, accumulating bed sores all over his body while his muscles atrophied. As recently as two years ago, doctors believed he would be a vegetable for the rest of his life, but now with special treatments every day seven days a week, he is showing improvement, and they believe if Jackie has the will and the fight he can effect at least a partial recovery. It remains doubtful whether he will ever perform again. One thing is sure. He can't do it alone.

Soon after the tragedy struck, The Friends of Jackie Wilson was founded by Paul Wolfe, East Coast promoter and longtime friend of Jackie's who was at the Latin Casino that night in Cherry Hill, Bobby Lewis, Cornell Gunther and the Coasters, and Johnny Moore of the Drifters. Pat and Debbie Boone are now also on the board of directors. It is an organization whose purpose is to let Jackie know that his friends are behind him, and to help raise money to pay Jackie's sky-rocketing medical bills.

We spoke to Paul Wolfe. "First let me make it absolutely clear that every cent we raise goes directly to Jack. The members pay for all expenses incurred by by the organization. Now, what we are trying to do is get a representative cross section of the music industry behind Jack, not just

Paul Wolfe photo

artists but those who have known him, worked with him, or who are just fans. When I found out that Pat Boone had worked with Jack and that Debbie admired his music, I asked them to join the board and they accepted. It's growing. We've been able to raise some money at a few benefits we ran and have more planned. A little bit here, a little bit there. Presently, his medical bills total nearly $200,000. Dick Clark had an insurance policy on Jack and the company was paying some bills for awhile but that has run out."

Jackie Wilson was born in Detroit, June 9, 1934. When barely a teenager he learned how to fight on the streets. He said at one time, "If you don't know how to fight, you don't survive." At the age of sixteen he won the Golden Gloves but never considered going pro. As he once told Paul Wolfe, "I didn't for two reasons. If you get hit on the head too many times it will damage your brain, plus I figured I'd be safer onstage than in the ring."

That decision made, Jackie put all his energies into singing. One group he particularly admired was the Dominoes whose lead singer at that time was Clyde McPhatter. They came into Detroit in 1953 and Jackie dropped by one of their rehearsals. He heard that Clyde was leaving the group to form a new group called the Drifters. Jackie auditioned and was heartily welcomed as the new lead voice of the Dominoes.

Then in 1957 Jackie left the group to go solo. In September of that year he launched his career with a song called "Reet Petite" written by Berry Gordy Jr. who would later head the Motown empire. In 1958 he struck gold with another Gordy ballad, "To Be Loved." And then in 1960 he recorded his biggest seller, the double-sided "Doggin' Around" and "Night."

By that time Jackie was one of the giants in the industry, headlining in Vegas, at the Copa, the Hollywood Bowl, and just about any theater, arena, or civic center you want to name. He also had Europe reeling with power visits to the London Palladium and comparable joints on the continent. There was no limit to his energy. When he was on tour he'd always be rambling around town with the roadies. Once when he was on the West Coast he finished a gig that would totally exhaust any normal man and proceeded to head for Disneyland at four in the morning and have the run of the place until ten.

Good sport at the time was comparing Jackie with James Brown. Many of Jack's fans say that James took a lot of his act from Jackie, which causes quite a flap among James Brown fans. The two of them used to kid each other about it. James would walk into a room, see Jackie, and say, "Well, look at this, Mr. Soul meets Mr. Excitement," and then the two of them would crack up.

Elvis had tremendous admiration for Jackie. There was a time in Las Vegas when they were both playing but at different places. Elvis made his way to the club Jackie was working, went into his dressing room, and said to him, "I thought it was about time the white Elvis Presley met the black Elvis Presley."

But then in 1961 a bullet almost found Jackie Wilson's heart. According to Paul Wolfe, "Jack was backstage with a group of other artists at a local club in Atlanta. And you know how women are, always going backstage to talk with the stars. He was talking to some fans and autographing some pictures when a woman came up to him to wish him luck. Another woman who felt that Jack and herself were the newest couple in town thought he was two-timing her. Of course this wasn't true.. But when you're an artist, the public are the people who make or break you. In this case the public had a pistol and shot him. He was hospitalized for four weeks and to this day still carries the bullet in his body just next to his heart."

Soon after the shooting, and for a number of reasons only Jackie knows, he started using drugs and was eventually dipping into the many varieties, ups, downs, heroin, and even LSD. As always, dope in the music industry was as common as aspirin. Many people near him felt he started in order to get that extra boost, to make his performance that much better, and to make sure the audience wouldn't get shortchanged just because, like any artist, he would be doing the endless strings of one-nighters. He wanted to give the public his best every time out, but as with others, it caught up with him. It didn't affect Jackie Wilson the entertainer. Its ravages were visited upon Jackie Wilson the private man. People around him saw it happening, but knew that no matter what, he'd be out on that stage. If hell freezed over, Jackie would have been out there on skates.

Finally, in 1968, with the exception of "Higher and Higher," his recording career was sagging, his private life was in pieces, and Jackie admitted himself to a drug rehabilitation center. He was in an outpatient program for a little over two years. He pulled himself together and was on the rise again. He toured Europe and Australia, and sold out practically every country in Africa. And in what had to have been one of the most spectacular events in music history and one of the few moments of national unity in that strife-torn country, he did a show in Zaire with James Brown and Wilson Pickett.

Through the first half of the seventies Jackie was steaming toward a monumental comeback and even getting back into the recording studio. In 1974 Dick Clark produced the first all rock 'n' roll show in Las Vegas. The hotel owners felt that rock was the music of the fifties and that people wouldn't come out for it in Vegas with the exception of Elvis because Elvis was Elvis. But Clark put it together and it was boffo box. Freddie Cannon was part of that show. "The show was myself, the Coasters, Dick Clark of course, and Jackie Wilson. We proved the owners wrong. We broke all attendance records at the Hilton. The lines were all through the hotel and out into the streets. We were supposed to get a two-week trial and ended up playing almost two months. It was probably one of the best-packaged rock shows ever. I guess I was one of the last artists to spend so much time with Jackie. We did another hotel in Vegas right after, so that comes to about three months in the dressing room together. Myself, my wife, my whole family, we all became friends of his. I knew what he had been through and I had heard all kinds of things, but he was beautiful, and the show he put on, I've never seen anything like it. Total showmanship. The performance, the stage presence, and the voice, a voice that could never be imitated. Jackie had it all. Every time out nothing less than a standing ovation, sometimes two and three a show, the people going up and down. That was basically the same show Dick Clark was presenting in New Jersey when Jackie went down."

So today Jackie is fighting once again for another comeback against almost-impossible odds. Potential recovery calls for time, heart, support, and money. Unfortunately, the fulfillment of these requirements is being undermined by a giant tangle of legal, familial, and financial complications that go back years.

Since 1957, Jackie has been under contract to Brunswick Records. Since 1959 he has been personally managed by Nat Tarnopol who is currently president of Brunswick. Jackie was a one-man million-dollar industry. According to Paul Wolfe what happened to the money is in question. "After his collapse, the IRS put in a claim for nearly $300,000 in back taxes which Jackie does not have. The IRS wondered why with such a career he didn't, and got a court-appointed investigative team to check the books at Brunswick. First they found that Brunswick had sold masters of Jackie's recordings to other record companies and received three to four million dollars in the process, none of which went to Jackie. They also discovered that there seemed to be more than one set of books and that it was virtually impossible to account for monies that Jack entrusted to Brunswick to hold on to for him down through the years. People close to him say that he never took much more than expenses even though millions must have been coming in from touring and record sales.

"The IRS took the information to the courts and since that time the courts have been attempting to look at the books again, but it's turned into a cat-and-mouse game with all kinds of legal snarls. At this point it is unresolved. The IRS has said they will wait on the claim until it is, so right now the main concern of The Friends of Jackie Wilson are his always-mounting medical bills which have to be paid if his progress is to continue."

The situation is further complicated by the fact that since Jackie has been incapable of handling his own affairs, his next of kin have been responsible. His mother had always been the one at his side when things got rough, in Atlanta when he was recovering from the gunshot wound, when Jackie was beating drugs. She came to his side from Detroit right after the collapse figuring to pull him through once again. But she died a week later and to this day Jackie is unaware of her passing away.

Who would then be responsible became a very curious question. Jackie was seventeen when he first got married and soon after thought he was effecting a divorce by ripping up the papers, but he ripped up the wrong ones. Then in the sixties he married his second wife, Harlean. They were separated in the late sixties and later on he married Lynn but without divorcing Harlean. Essentially he was married to three women simultaneously. Instead of trying to straighten that situation out, and because the medical bills weren't being paid, the court appointed a lawyer from New Jersey as legal guardian and had Jackie moved to Medford Leas. But about a month after, the lawyer was asked to be removed from his duties after he had taken a number of associates to a Disneyland hotel and returned to the court with receipts in the thousands of dollars to be reimbursed by the court for business relating to Jackie's affairs. The next lawyer to be appointed stepped down after nine months, unable to handle it. Another was appointed and lasted until the spring of 1978 when Harlean, Jackie's second wife, sought custody. Since she was a New York resident, she brought in a New Jersey lawyer, John Mulkarin, and the court appointed them co-legal guardians.

Meanwhile, Jackie's been getting ripped off by the octopus arms of the bootleg record industry, a situation that Paul Wolfe is working to remedy. "Someone called me in the fall of 1978 and said Jackie Wilson records were being bootlegged down in Atlanta. I called Brunswick and they claimed they knew nothing about it. So I went down there to talk to the authorities and the D.A. I told them what I knew and an investigation was started that resulted in the confiscation of almost a million dollars worth of Jackie Wilson records. The whole situation is still being investigated. In the meantime, they had all the illegally pressed albums melted down and the covers destroyed."

Along with keeping up with the medical bills, the most important thing is letting Jackie know that his friends and fans care. The list of people who juggle their schedules in order to visit him is endless. When they do you can see his eyes light up. He knows. Diana Ross recently had a two-day layover in New York on her way to Europe and came down to spend a morning with him. Tony Orlando visits regularly and calls practically every day to sing to him when he's on the East Coast. Others include Redd Foxx, the Drifters, the Coasters, the Platters, the Chiffons, Chuck Berry, Bo Diddley, Chubby Checker, Bobby Rydell, and more. Cornell Gunther of the Coasters, the man who saved his life, will call up and say, "Get off that bed, nigger, and get back to work." Jackie lights right up.

Paul Wolfe points out, however, that some people who are indebted to Jackie aren't doing all that they might. "Jackie is the type of guy to take the shirt off his back for you. There are some people in the industry today who are a bit afraid that Jackie might actually some day get up off that bed after having received nothing from them, not even a card to find out how he's doing. These are people Jackie has loaned money to, paid bills for, and stood behind when their careers were in bad shape. Jack never turned his back on anyone. Where are these people now? These are big people in the industry now; you'd recognize their names right away. It's shocking."

Recently, Jackie received some long overdue recognition. With the help of Paul Wolfe, who obtained the sheet music from some guys in Jackie's old backup band, Rita Coolidge was able to record her own version of Jackie's 1967 hit, "(Your Love Keeps Lifting Me) Higher and Higher," and had a national hit with it herself. She is sending the gold record to Jackie care of The Friends of Jackie Wilson for safe keeping.

Meanwhile, at the end of 1978, Ben Vereen appeared with Harlean Wilson to announce that he and four other men including John Mulkarin, co-legal guardian with Harlean, were starting a medical trust fund to raise money through concerts and other fund raisers. Mulkarin assures the fund's legitimacy because he must answer to the court that appointed him legal guardian. The returns aren't in yet.

We recently talked to Tony Williams of the Platters and his wife Helen. Helen said, "People were always out to use Jackie, rip him off. He never had anybody in his corner." Obviously that's not entirely true anymore and there appears to be room for optimism in Jackie Wilson's future.

Billy Joe Royal

"I didn't know I would have any kind of success. I just wanted to sing, even if it was at the back end of a Holiday Inn. I thought I could do a little better than the next guy. I didn't have any education and I didn't want to work in a factory. Singing was what I wanted to do with my life."

A small-town boy from southern Georgia, Billy Joe Royal was born in 1945 and lived with his brother and two sisters in a housing project. "It was a happy family but we were as close as you could get to poor. We had plenty to eat and clothes but not a lot of material things." As a kid of eleven, Billy sang on the radio with his uncle's band. When the family moved to Marietta, Georgia, north of Atlanta, Billy formed his own band, the Corvettes, in high school. The Corvettes played around the Atlanta area with other local groups such as Mac Davis and the Zots, Joe South and his Believers, and the Jerry Reed and Ray Stevens bands. In the later part of 1959, Billy Joe Royal quit his job at the local car wash, dropped out of school, and packed off with Joe South to Savannah.

The big band shows were broadcast out of Montgomery and Birmingham; the Grand Ole Opry played country; and the Cincinnati Barn Dance and the Louisiana Hayride broadcast the rockabilly of Elvis, Roy Orbison, and Jerry Lee. But Billy became engrossed with black music as he and Joe South made the rounds of Savannah clubs, cutting a few discs. While playing the Bamboo Ranch, a local hangout for country and black stars touring through the Savannah area, Billy met Sam Cooke, his idol.

"When I first started, I worked the Bamboo Ranch. When Sam played there, I used to marvel at him. He could do more with his voice than a monkey could with a peanut. I was just learning how to sing and here's my idol complimenting me. He had a knack of making you feel good. I've got a picture of Sam Cooke and myself. To this day, I treasure it.

"At the time I was making $150 a week. I felt I should have been sweeping the bus stop. I thought I was doing absolutely zero for the loot. When you're that young, it's hard to adjust."

During this time, Billy played the "Big Ape Show" out of Jacksonville, a showcase for young talent heard across the South on the Bennett Network. With a record called "Perhaps," Billy scooted down to Louisiana in 1963. " 'Perhaps' was a hit there and nowhere else. We were booked down there at a place called Bolger City which has miles of clubs. I thought I'd see nobody down there but, my God, all the Boogie Kings like John and Edgar Winter were there. There were some deadly groups back there and a kid called something Jackson, who was unbelievable. He was a white Otis Redding. There was nothing but miles of soul groups down there. They were killers. And I expected to see absolutely no one."

Finally, Billy with his guitarist Joe South caught the train back to Atlanta and for eight hundred smackeroos cut "Down in the Boondocks" and "I Needed You When" on the same session. The label soon faded out of business. But a local DJ named Bill Lowrey connected with Billy and interested Columbia in the cuts. In 1965, "Down in the Boondocks" soared to the top of the charts and was followed by "I Knew You When," "The Greatest Love," "Hush," and others.

"I was in a state of shock. I took all my friends to Mexico and Hawaii. We had a good blowout, doing the crazy things you do when you're young. You blow money like it's going to rain money forever. Luckily Bill Lowrey invested it all in land north of Atlanta. We had about five years of good things happening.

"They had big plans. I did the Greek Theater and 'Ed Sullivan.' They really thought the kid was on his way. That was hard to take because you'd sit home and think, 'This is it. I'm over at the Greek Theater tonight.' You'd see the searchlight go over and light up your name. 'It's just like the movies, only it's happening to the kid here.' And it didn't happen. Since that day on, I believe in things after they happen."

Billy Joe Royal regularly did Dick Clark's Cavalcade of Stars for four and five tours a year. He hopped about the bus tour when it started in Omaha, Nebraska, and scrunched into a springless seat for a madcap criss cross of the nation. Later, he did "Where the Action Is" at night, only to discover he was being filmed the next day on the road at some state fair. After Paul Revere and the Raiders concluded their star-making tenure with Dick Clark, he joined them on their own tours.

His success was unusual because it came at the peak of the British invasion. "I wasn't blown out by the British invasion because I had a long nose, long hair, and people thought I was British with a name like Royal. In fact, I went to England a couple of times. It was cold. The weather was nasty and the food was lousy. I didn't like it much. The people were nice but didn't know me from Adam. I went over with Roy Orbison who was the King then. We got off the plane and it was like the Beatles had landed. A lot of press was there. I had a record over here and was trying to get exposure over there. It wasn't like coming off a hit record, believe me. It wasn't a highlight of my life." His song "Hush" became a monster in the United Kingdom but the American audience didn't recognize it until the British group Deep Purple came over to the States with their version years later.

Life on the road got harder. "If you stay in a room all day, you'll drive yourself nuts. I used to worry about the show all day. The main thing is trying to fill the void during the day. I went through the whole shooting match. As a kid you go crazy. Every night's Saturday night. Thank God, I lived through it. I think I'm a better person for it. I was never into the heavy, crazy stuff or got hospitalized or anything like that. Many people did. But everybody who's been in this business five or six years sometime along the

way does it. When you work every night, some nights you just can't get up there. You have to have help from the old friend. I used quite a bit to get to the next day.

"I did ninety days one time, every night until three or four in the morning. Then you travel on the bus the next day. You got to have booze or some kind of chemical to keep you going. I found out that you didn't have to. I'm into this health kick now. I go into a town, find the local spa, and work out three times a week and run the other two. It would be great if I could get up in the morning and go to work and get it over with. You have to keep yourself busy because those soap operas are the worst. I'm happier now than I've ever been."

Billy soon acquired a fear of flying in 1968 after he was in a serious plane crash. "I thought it was all over and I think about it ever since. It scared me to death." With contracts to play the Flamingo Hotel, the Sahara in Vegas and Tahoe, Billy moved from his native Atlanta to California in an attempt to avoid air travel. "It was easier to go there from California so we packed up our bags and moved. I bought a bunch of horses and started to play Hollywood." But with the acid-rock craze engulfing the music scene and his record company MGM staggering around like a punch-drunk fighter with its perennial activity of playing musical presidents, Billy soon found himself boxed out of the action.

One day he went over to MGM only to discover that his publicity still had been torn down off the wall. Then, "When MGM was bought out by Polydor, I was out on my keister." For Scepter he cut an album, *Trying To Get The Feeling*, but its release was held up because the company didn't have the rights to the songs. With that smart move, they issued the album and it promptly died with the company following soon after. Billy cut two more discs for the Private Stock but the company treated them like well-kept secrets. Unfortunately, the company didn't live long enough to tell, because it too soon went down the tubes.

Then in 1973, the economy crunch hit Vegas and Lake Tahoe. The main room of the Flamingo was closed; the Sahara's great lounge was torn down and made into a keno parlor. "I moved back to Atlanta from California because there wasn't any loot in Vegas and I was up to my earlobes in horses. They eat better than I do. It made sense to move back East because the work was here. I sold them suckers when I moved back to Atlanta. They're fun but it's an expensive hobby. I showed my first two but I had to keep them with a special trainer. It was an ordeal. It just made more sense to come back East where all the work was."

His horseback riding got him a film part as a cavalry trooper in *Johnson County Invasion* with Bill Bixby. "I think I had but two lines. One was 'Put the weapons in the wagon.' We had this shootout. Twenty million people were killing each other and the cavalry rides in and everyone drops their guns."

Billy next appeared with Robert Culp in *Name for Evil* which, according to Billy, was shot in a men's room at a Shell Station somewhere in Canada. "It was the pits. This rich kid wanted to make a movie and star in it. He was so bad, they started shooting around him in order to cut his part out. They had to glue the thing back together. They called me in and it made no sense whatsoever. It looked like they had run out of film. There was no end. The kid had a lot of loot and wanted to make a film. He only forgot one thing—talent."

While his music career wasn't exactly being trumpeted over the globe, Billy did latch onto a national Coca-Cola commercial. "They were looking for Gene Pitney, so they could change from 'Things go better with Coke' to something, anything. When they do that, you, me, anybody in the world can send in a jingle. This guy, he was 112 or 115, was looking for Pitney but he was in Europe. He thought I sounded like him. He flew me to New York. His commercial was 'It's the real thing.' We went into this old hall and he sang [Billy imitates a wizened old voice] 'Itttt's the Realll Thing.' I thought, 'Oh, my God, Coke isn't going to go for this. I don't even go for this. It's the worst.' "

Both the Fortunes and Billy recorded the jingle. A year later, Coke called Billy to film the commercial in the Grand Canyon. "We got up at five o'clock in the morning and rode this mule down the side. I had to shimmy down this rock. What I thought was so dumb was putting this microphone on this rock in the middle of the canyon like I have a PA system out there. I got to sing and put the bottle down which looks like it's real frosty and irresistible. It was an experience." Billy recently appeared in the Coke commercial where the kids on the steps are looking up at a man on a roof, who is enraptured with the thought of an ice-cold Coke. He's the one singing.

Since he moved back to Atlanta in 1977 with his wife Georgia, he's cut a revamped version of the classic "Under the Boardwalk" and tours with his new band for six weeks at a clip around Indiana, Kentucky, and the South. He regularly plays the Myrtle Beach scene, started up at the Beach Club ten years ago, and the Asheville area of western North Carolina. His act consists of his hits, some Waylon Jennings and Kenny Rogers songs, and his new material which he arranges at his house.

As for the Southern rock scene which exploded back into the forefront in the seventies after a decade of incubation, Billy reflects: "I think the South is a trendsetter for music and always has been. I understand Southern music and Southern people better than I do California folk. We sit around and exchange ideas. Here you really participate. A guy may come up with an idea which is bad but it may give you a good idea. It's a sounding board and really is laid back and comfortable. In California, you go in and they put a sheet of music in front of you and you play what's on the sheet and go home. I think you get better records this way.

"I want to start recording again just for the hell of it. I'd love to get one more hit while I'm young enough to enjoy it and people will stop coming up to me asking where have I gone. Well, I was hit by a train, whatever happened to you?"

NOW YOU CAN ORDER
TEMPO BOOKS BY MAIL!

Whatever your game,
Tempo's unbeatable line-up
of sports books
will make you cheer!

17346-8	**Baseball's Hall of Fame (Revised)** Smith $1.95	
14741-6	**Beckenbauer, Rote, Banks, Best** Wohl and Goldstein $1.50	
14661-4	**Benchwarmer's Sports Trivia** Alexander 95¢	
16241-5	**The Complete All-Time Pro Football Register** Neft, Deutsch, Cohen $1.95	
14016-0	**Daredevils of the Speedway** Olney $1.50	
14621-5	**Fitness Guide for the Weekend Athlete** Rosenthal $1.50	
14624-X	**Great College Football Rivalries** Rappoport $1.95	
12615-X	**Great Moments in Pro Basketball** Goldaper $1.25	
14476-X	**Heaven Is a Playground** Telander $1.95	
14663-0	**Kicks! Learning Soccer the Easy Way** Wernersbach $1.95	
14623-1	**The Missing Links: Golf and the Mind** Morley $1.95	
16253-9	**Monday Morning Quarterback** Neft, Johnson, Cohen, Deutsch $1.95	
14955-9	**Payton, Jones, Haden, Dorsett** Gutman $1.50	
14654-1	**Showdown! Baseball's Ultimate Confrontations** Fischler $1.50	
14134-5	**Sports Stumpers** Fischler $1.50	
05735-2	**Weekend Tennis: The Hacker's Handbook** Long $1.25	
14595-2	**Whatever Happened to Gorgeous George?** Jares $1.95	

TEMPO BOOKS Book Mailing Service
P.O. Box 690, Rockville Centre, N.Y. 11571

Please send me the titles checked above.

I enclose $_____. Add 50¢ handling fee per book.

Name_____

Address_____

City_____ State_____ Zip_____

T-13

NOW YOU CAN ORDER
TEMPO BOOKS BY MAIL!

The passionate puzzler will be busy for hours with these puzzles and crosswords from Tempo.

CHAMPIONSHIP WORD FIND PUZZLE BOOKS

05703-4	#1 Art 95¢
05707-7	#2 Art 95¢
05736-0	#3 Art 95¢

THE DAILY CROSSWORD BOOKS

07421-4	#2 Robert Gillespie, ed. 95¢
07422-2	#3 Robert Gillespie, ed. 95¢
07448-6	#7 Robert Gillespie, ed. 95¢
07449-4	#8 Robert Gillespie, ed. 95¢
12778-4	#9 Ettenson, ed. 95¢
14147-7	#10 Ettenson, ed. 95¢

TEMPO BOOKS Book Mailing Service
P.O. Box 690, Rockville Centre, N.Y. 11571

Please send me the titles checked above.

I enclose $_____ Add 50¢ handling fee per book.

Name_____

Address_____

City_____ State_____ Zip_____

T-14